P9-BZB-226

949.5072 CLA

Clark, Bruce, 1958-

Twice a stranger

**Please check all items for damages
before leaving the Library.
Thereafter you will be held
responsible for all injuries
to items beyond reasonable wear.**

Helen M. Plum Memorial Library

Lombard, Illinois

A daily fine will be charged for
overdue materials.

APR   2007

TWICE A STRANGER

TWICE A STRANGER

The Mass Expulsions that Forged
Modern Greece and Turkey

BRUCE CLARK

Harvard University Press
Cambridge, Massachusetts
2006

HELEN M. PLUM MEMORIAL LIBRARY
LOMBARD, ILLINOIS

949.5072
CLA

Copyright © 2006 Bruce Clark

All rights reserved

Printed in the United States of America

First published in Great Britain by Granta Books 2006

Turkish photographs by Iskender Özsoy.
Greek photographs from the collection of Mrs. Anna Theofylaktou.
Maps by Peter Winfield and Justin Jacyno.

The moral right of the author has been asserted.

Library of Congress Cataloging-in-Publication Data

Clark, Bruce, 1958–
Twice a stranger : the mass expulsions that forged modern
Greece and Turkey / Bruce Clark.
374 p. cm.
Includes bibliographical references and index.

ISBN-13: 978-0-674-02368-0 (alk. paper)
ISBN-10: 0-674-02368-4 (alk. paper)

1. Greco-Turkish War, 1921–1922—Refugees. 2. Population
transfers—Greeks—History—20th century.
3. Population transfers—Turks—History—20th century. I. Title.

DF845.52.C53 2006
949.507'2—dc22
2006043516

3 1502 00635 7717

This book is dedicated, with love, to my parents
Wallace and June, who first brought me
to the Aegean

This book was made possible by the kindness, forbearance and moral support of many people, some of whom have no connection with Turkey or Greece. Special thanks go to Renee Hirschon, for insights into social anthropology and much else; to Ayca Duffrene, a deservedly acclaimed radio journalist; and to Marianna Koromila, a popular historian in the best senses of both words.

Iki kere yabancı
Twice a Stranger

Geç kaldık anıları kaydetmeye
        o ilk malzeme yitti gitti
ilk mübadiller götürdüler anılarını
oysa onlar hemen kaydedilmeliydi
üzerinden 80 yıl geçtikten sonra
        anı savaşları
        her türlü manipülasyona açık
Mübadeleyle ilgili her metnin özü aynı:
'Yerinde dogup yabanda kocamak'
iki yerde de yabancı olmak.

It's late for us to be preserving our recollections;
The essence of them, the first essence, has vanished
already.
Those first migrants took away their memories;
the memories that ought to have been
recorded without delay.
Eighty years have passed,
and the memories are warring with another,
ripe for distortion.
But the core of every migrant's statement
remains the same.
Birth in one place,
growing old in another place.
And feeling a stranger in the two places.

Professor Ayşe Lahur Kırtunç, whose
family came to Turkey from Crete

Contents

Out of Ayvalik, into Ayvalik

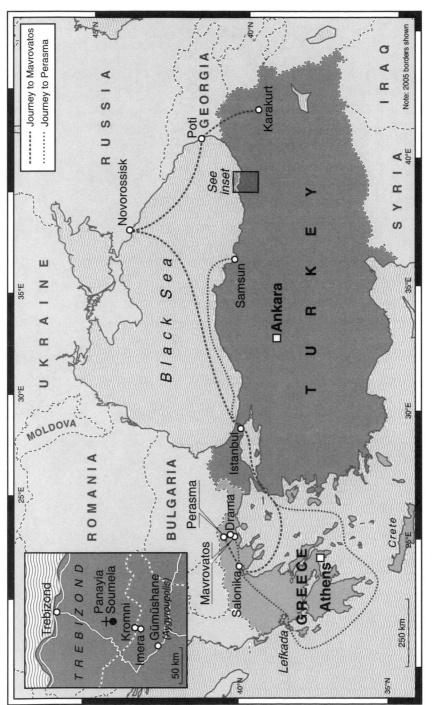

Destination Drama

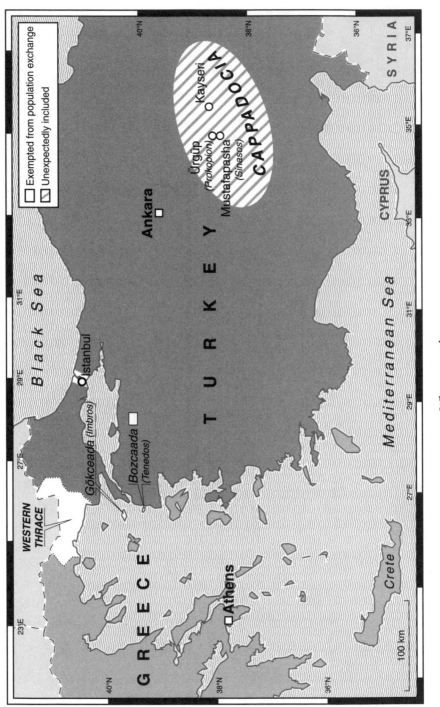

Who goes, who stays

Lausanne's children

Whether we like it or not, those of us who live in Europe or in places influenced by European ideas remain the children of Lausanne; that is to say, of the convention signed on a Swiss lakeside after the First World War which decreed a massive, forced population movement between Turkey and Greece. As a working journalist with a special interest in southeastern Europe, I am continually reminded of the treaty's baleful legacy.

Lausanne's abiding importance was reaffirmed one more time in spring 2004, when efforts to bring peace to the war zones of the Balkans were shaken by two days of rioting in Kosovo. Under the noses of police and soldiers from some of the world's leading military powers, thousands of people, mostly Serbs, were driven from their homes. Several villages inhabited by newly returned Serb refugees were burned down, a dozen historic churches were destroyed and twenty people were killed. The stated goal of western policy – to enable all the region's peoples to live decently and amicably without fear of persecution on ethnic or religious grounds – had been dreadfully mocked. In response to these events, a statement was issued by a think-tank known as the European Stability Initiative (ESI). Its authors, young Europeans with experience of political or humanitarian work in the Balkans, made an appeal: whatever governments now did, they must not succumb to the old temptation of using the 'Lausanne principle'. In other words, they should not take the easy way out and solve an intractable dispute over territory by splitting up the disputed area and forcing everybody on the 'wrong side' of the newly drawn line to move, until boundaries and ethnic groups coincided perfectly. That was what the governments of Turkey and Greece, with the encouragement of the 'international community' had done in Lausanne in 1923. As a result, about 400,000 Muslims were forced to move from Greece to Turkey, while at least 1.2 million Greek Orthodox Christians were either shifted from Turkey to Greece or, if they had moved already, told they could never return to their old homes.

As was pointed out in that idealistic document, written eighty-one years after the Swiss conference, there are still many people inside and outside the Balkans who would like to see the 'Lausanne principle' reapplied; for example, by allowing Bosnia to break up into one or more states, or by dividing up Kosovo. Yet to yield to this sort of pressure, the document asserted, would betray the values which have underpinned all western policy in Europe's most volatile region, at least since 1996 when Bosnia was placed under international tulelage. Whatever its failings, the agreed aim in the Balkans had been to give a 'principled and effective answer to the vicious logic of ethnic separation'. Especially since the massacre of 7000 Muslims near the Bosnian town of Srebrenica in July 1995, the basis of this policy has been an 'anti-Lausanne consensus' – or so the ESI think-tank argued.

Whether their conclusion was right or wrong, the ESI paper's authors were correct when they pointed out that the Lausanne convention, providing for a population transfer between Greece and Turkey, has haunted the region, and in some ways the world, ever since it was concluded. Indeed, its long-term effects have not been confined to the Balkans or to Europe. For the remainder of the century, the memory of the giant Greek–Turkish exchange was a powerful influence on policy makers all over the world. It was taken as proof that it was possible, both practically and morally, to undertake huge exercises in ethnic engineering, and proclaim them a success. Massive population exchanges, agreed by governments over the heads of the ordinary people, became a conceivable and often attractive option for world leaders. As the history of the 20th century shows, the temptation to use such methods is especially strong in certain types of political or geopolitical situation. For example, it can arise where one form of imperial authority (from Soviet communism to British colonial rule) is collapsing; or when a new nationalist power wants to consolidate its authority; or when a new strategic order is being created in the aftermath of war.

Thus Nazi Germany negotiated several population exchanges, both with its Italian allies and, during their 1939–41 partnership, with Soviet

Russia. All these agreements were intended to 'tidy up' the ethnic map of Europe and consolidate German populations in strategically useful ways. In 1937, as Britain was considering the future of Palestine after the eventual expiry of its mandate, a government commission, headed by a bureaucrat with experience of settling refugees in Greece, strongly advocated a Lausanne-style exchange between Arabs and Jews. It urged the leaders on both sides to demonstrate the 'statesmanlike' flexibility which Greek and Turkish leaders had shown in 1923.

After the Second World War, up to 12 million German civilians were deported from their homes in eastern Europe to the shrunken territory of Allied-occupied Germany. This was a process which Winston Churchill and Franklin Roosevelt consciously modelled on the removal of Orthodox Christians from Anatolia in 1923. Soon afterwards, the end of British rule in India and Palestine led to *de facto* population exchanges across newly established borders, on an unprecedented scale.

Those upheavals were not decreed by any international agreement. But the Greek–Turkish example loomed large in later discussions of how to respond, and of how far mass population movements were an inevitable consequence of old empires collapsing. Even now, in Israel's political debates, the view is sometimes heard that the 'population exchange' brought about by the fighting in 1948 should have been completed, or that it should be completed now. In other words, all Palestinians, whether living in Israel or the West Bank, should be obliged to move to Jordan or some other Arab country. In Israel that is deemed an extreme opinion, but not so extreme as to be beyond discussion; and there are some American politicians who strongly advocate that option.

It is sobering to admit that we are still haunted, at the start of the 21st century, by the legacy of a treaty that was concluded early in the 20th, when colonial empires were still intact and the right of powerful nations to dictate the destiny of small and powerless ones was broadly accepted. In Europe, in particular, politicians would much prefer us to believe that we are not the children of Lausanne, but of Helsinki. It was the Helsinki agreements, signed by thirty-five European governments (plus America and Canada) in 1975, that combined two old principles in a new way, with the aim of freeing Europe from war and from the hatred and oppression that can fuel war. On the one hand, it was agreed, countries must respect the human and cultural rights of their citizens, including minorities; and at the same time, states must respect each other's borders, or at least avoid imposing boundary changes by force.

For an optimistic moment, the fall of the communist system offered hope that the Helsinki accords would prevail in practice as well as theory. Where countries did break up (as happened to the Soviet Union and Czechoslovakia) they would do so peacefully and by consent, without posing any deadly threat to the fate of people left in the 'wrong' place. The spirit of Helsinki promised to break one of the vicious circles of European history: national or ethnic grievances, real or imaginary, leading to territorial claims and hence to persecution, mass dislocation and war. Similarly outlawed by Helsinki was the practice of creating 'facts on ground' by driving out one ethnic or religious group – and then demanding border changes to ratify those facts.

The outbreak of wars in former Yugoslavia, and in the Caucasus, have dealt a terrible, though perhaps not fatal blow to Helsinki's message. As Croatia, Bosnia and Kosovo descended into violence, the supposedly civilized world reacted with bewilderment as well as dismay to the news that in places only a few hundred miles from Europe's prosperous and stable heart, tens of thousands of people were being killed, and millions driven from their homes. This was done with the express intention of 'cleansing' certain areas of inhabitants who had been deemed undesirable because they belonged to the wrong ethnic or religious group. Especially chilling was the fact these mass deportations were not the result of spontaneous or impulsive actions in the heat of battle; they were planned at the highest level by state authorities.

For the international agencies which have overseen Balkan troublespots in the aftermath of war, reversing these practices has seemed an overwhelming moral imperative – hence the talk of an 'anti-Lausanne' consensus. Both in Bosnia, with a degree of success, and in Kosovo, with rather less success, peace makers have insisted that everybody who was violently uprooted must be allowed to return. Great pressure has been applied to governments which have expelled minorities, either in cold blood or in the heat of battle, to allow them to reoccupy their homes.

But it would be hypocritical to claim that the spirit of Lausanne has been finally exorcized, from the Balkans or anywhere else. For the Balkans' international overlords, restoring a degree of multi-ethnic harmony has often felt like pushing a stone uphill. Billions of dollars' worth of aid and expertise, and tens of thousands of soldiers have been required to strengthen moderates, isolate extremists and make it possible for some refugees to venture back to homes and farms from which they were thrown out at gunpoint. It still looks all too possible that any slackening of that huge international effort would simply restore to power the very nationalist politicians and warlords who thrive on ethnic hatred and conflict. If that is true, then it proves that Lausanne's phantom is devilishly hard to dispel.

To the modern sensibility, there is something especially repugnant about the Lausanne accord's explicit use of religion as a criterion for a mass population transfer. The liberal westerner draws back in horror at the memory of an international authority telling people that they must leave their ancestral homes because they were of the wrong faith. Freedom to choose any religion or none, without fear of discrimination or persecution, has come to be viewed as one of the most basic human rights, and above all as a 'private' matter.

Yet even on this issue, it has to be admitted, the modern world is far from being honest or consistent. In Northern Ireland, one of the last places in the western world where conflict rages in the name of religion, it would certainly be considered beyond the limits of civilized discussion to propose that the Lausanne model be followed; in other words, to suggest sending all Protestants north and all Catholics south of a certain line. Yet in practice, there are many districts in Northern Ireland where the authorities either cannot, or consciously choose not to protect the lives or property of people of the 'wrong' faith. When that happens, local population exchanges occur with no government prompting. Thanks to a mixture of physical threats, social pressure and general discomfort, Protestants find it impossible to go on living in mainly Catholic places, and vice-versa. At least in the short term, the staking out and cleansing of territory is gathering pace in Northern Ireland rather than receding. Only a very strong government could reverse that trend, and Ulster's British administrators have chosen not to show that kind of strength. So there too, the Lausanne demons have yet to be exorcized; and they are as obviously present in Europe's cool north as they are in the volatile south.

But there is a certain, very literal sense in which the legacy of Lausanne, as a fateful landmark in European and world history, will soon be gone.

The generation of Orthodox Christians and Muslims, now living in Greece and Turkey respectively, who can still remember the mass population transfer will not be with us for much longer. Anybody who has a clear memory of the exchange, and has managed to survive into the 21st century, must be aged at least ninety; and even the generation whose parents were affected by the exchange is now elderly.

Before the memory of this forced migration fades entirely, it seemed a good idea to undertake a journey through both Turkey and Greece, to investigate the Lausanne agreement and its legacy: the effect of the treaty on the politics, economic life and culture of each country. As a journalist who comes from Northern Ireland but has reported for many years from the Balkans, I bring to bear an unusual mixture of concerns and passions to such an enquiry. Others will judge the use I have made of this unusual toolbox.

This journey has required travel through time as well as space, through remote villages as well as libraries in Geneva and London. In every area affected by the exchange there are layers of contradictory evidence, both in the physical environment, and in the consciousness of ordinary people. In all the Greek and Turkish places where some new people were taken in, and others thrown out, local people have been left with a swirling mixture of memories and feelings; some reflecting what they have been told to believe, some reflecting their real, lived experiences. To have any hope of understanding Lausanne, it is necessary to disentangle these memories, as well as consulting newspaper archives and diplomatic records. Dusty records and politicians' memoirs can give a sense of why the Greek–Turkish population exchange seemed imperative at the time. The memories of humbler people can provide an important counterweight to the claims of officialdom to be acting in everyone's best interest.

The journey has been both moving and illuminating. Quite apart from its wider implications for 20th century history, there is much about the contemporary state of Turkey and Greece which cannot be understood except in reference to Lausanne and the population exchange. Why do the two nations exchange insults in political speeches and school textbooks, yet express a profound yearning in their songs, novels and movies, to reconnect? Why is this love–hate paradox especially sharp in certain regions and certain individuals? How was it possible for Greece and Turkey, within the space of a few weeks in autumn 1999, to veer from a climate of hostility, close to open war, to one of intense mutual affection and compassion, prompted by deadly earthquakes which had struck both countries?

The answers to all these questions are not merely of interest to specialists on the Aegean region. They speak of an ambivalence that underlies all relationships and all conflicts between peoples or individuals whose destinies are intertwined, so that they cannot entirely be separated, however hard anyone tries. In all such cases, it is perhaps inevitable both that separation will be attempted; and also that it will never entirely succeed. If I have thrown some light on that paradox, and on the meaning of Lausanne for the European past and the European future, this book has been worth writing.

INTRODUCTION

A world torn asunder

Sevket! Don't you recognize me, my friend? For years we reaped laughter and tears together. Ah Sevket, we have turned into monsters . . . So much suffering, so much tragedy. If only it could all be a lie, if only we could go back to our land, to our gardens, to our forests with their songbirds, sparrows and tiny owls, to our orchards with their tangerine trees and flowering cherries, to our beautiful festivals. Guerilla fighter of Kor Mehmet, give my regards to the earth that gave us birth! Selam Söyle Anadolu'ya, Farewell Anatolia! Hold it not against us that we drenched you with blood. Kahr olsun sebep olanlar! A curse on the guilty ones!

Manolis Axiotis, narrator of the Greek novel
Farewell Anatolia by Dido Sotiriou

All over Turkey and Greece, you can see the physical remnants of a world whose component parts seem to have been broken apart, suddenly and with great violence. On remote hilltops in the heart of Anatolia, there are gutted shells of stone whose original, sacred purpose is revealed only by a few streaks of ochre paint on an inside wall; the last remains of a Christian fresco. In a nearby village, amid the wandering livestock and muddy tracks, you can often find a sturdy building of two or three storeys, now used as a hayshed or stable but clearly designed for some nobler purpose. On enquiry this turns out to be the remains of a school where Turkish-speaking Orthodox Christians were taught to be a little more Greek by teachers dispatched from Istanbul or Athens. And in the stark, featureless towns of northern Greece, the evidence from buildings is equally startling and puzzling. For those who know where to look, the neon-lit monotony is often relieved by structures which are clearly much older and of greater architectural interest: mosques, religious schools, bath houses or inns, erected before the time when the whole Aegean region fell in love with concrete. According to conservationists, there are at least 2300 Ottoman monuments in Greece which, on aesthetic or historical grounds, ought to be preserved. Yet most of them are neglected, ignored and used for unsuitable purposes.

In Greek guidebooks, these Ottoman landmarks are little mentioned, just as Turkish handbooks, informed by official ideology, often deal in a perfunctory way with the Greek and Christian heritage of the places they describe. In both countries, there are curious silences. Where buildings have not been pulled down, and are too well constructed to decay naturally, people half pretend they do not exist. In Athens, for example, there was a vigorous public debate during the run-up to the 2004 Olympic Games about whether and where to build a place of worship for visiting Muslim athletes. In the end, a temporary arrangement was made for the Olympic village, while the Muslims, mostly migrant workers, who live in downtown Athens continued to use more than thirty informal, unlicensed places of worship. Few participants in this debate ever mentioned the fact that in the city's central Monastiraki district, there was a 500-year-old mosque, of great historical significance, waiting to be restored. It was standing shuttered and abandoned, with its garden overgrown and frequented only by feral cats.

Indeed, if you were trying to work out the history of Europe's southeastern edge from architectural evidence alone, you might well conclude that some terrible catastrophe, either natural or manmade, had struck both sides of the Aegean many centuries ago, and that the region had not fully recovered. In fact, the cataclysm was relatively recent. It is just over eighty years since the newly established republics of Greece and Turkey, with the blessing of the leading world powers, agreed on an almost complete and final division of the geographical and cultural space in which their peoples, languages and religions had previously co-existed. It is true, of course, that a gradual separation, both in a psychological sense and a more literal one, was already well advanced when a final, nearly total rupture between Greek society and Turkish society was undertaken, in 1923. This was the process known as the population exchange. It was supposed to be the cornerstone of a long-term settlement that would leave both states stable and satisfied. But the separation was more than just an endorsement of something which had happened already; it was a cause of pain as well as a response to pain.

What makes the landscape of Turkey and Greece even more poignant, and thought provoking, is the fact that in the early 21st century there are people still living who can remember what it was like when some of the half-ruined buildings, now stranded in the 'wrong' place, still functioned properly. There are nonagenarians in Turkey who can describe the time when the Muslim almshouse of Kavala and the minarets of Yannina were still in use; they have not forgotten that Salonika was a city of Muslim dervishes as well as priests and rabbis. People of the same age on the other side of the Aegean can recall the time when the Turkish Black Sea port of Trabzon was, among many other things, a flourishing outpost of Greek finance, education and culture; when the Christian traditions of Cappadocia, going back 1700 years, were still unbroken; and when the greatest centres of Hellenic enterprise and commerce were known by their Greek inhabitants as Constantinople and Smyrna. On both sides of the Aegean, this generation knows the pain of separation from ancestral homes, whether this happened in the heat of war or under the supervision of international bureaucrats. Like so many migrants, they also remember the difficulty they faced when they were taken across the sea and obliged to adapt to an unfamiliar social and physical environment. In some cases, the difficulty was at times exacerbated by the fact that their new place of residence was, in theory at least, their national motherland. They were supposed to have a sense of 'coming home' but the appropriate feeling did not always come.

Like any distant memory, the recollections of people who lived through the population exchange can easily slip into sentimentality, but more often they provide a healthy antidote to sentimentality. Not everything about the vanished world was good, and the circumstances in which it vanished were often so appalling that almost anything which followed came as a relief. To a condescending visitor from a peaceful and prosperous part of the western world, the ruined chapels of central Turkey, or the remains of a *tekke* or Muslim shrine on the Greek–Albanian border can indeed evoke a charming lost world, far more appealing, on aesthetic grounds at least, than anything which has been constructed since. What these feelings ignore is the poverty and brutality of the peasant culture in which these buildings may have provided the only solace; and the atmosphere of terror, persisting over several decades, which may have preceded their abandonment. To people who are fleeing persecution, a new country, however unfamiliar, is not simply an alien or hostile place, it is also a life-saving refuge. That too is worth remembering. The Greek playwright Euripides expressed one part – but only one part – of a profound truth when he wrote that: 'There is no greater sorrow on earth than the loss of one's native land.' At least two studies of the events of the 1920s by liberal-minded Turkish scholars have quoted that line. But beautiful as it is, the statement is not the whole truth; moving to a new place is on balance a lesser sorrow than being killed in one's native country.

Was it *necessary*, then, to separate the Christians and Muslims, the Greeks and Turks and assign them to different places? There are two different ways to examine that question: from the viewpoint of the decision makers, and from the perspective of those who were affected by the decision. The Christian–Muslim population transfer, decreed in 1923, can only be understood by looking from both ends of the telescope.

That understanding may in turn throw some light on the real meaning of the abandoned chapels and disused Muslim shrines of Turkey and Greece. At one level they speak to us of the passage from traditional life to modernity, with all the pain, trauma – and liberation – that accompanies such a transition. They also remind us of something else, which is difficult for liberal-minded westerners to grasp, but central to the understanding of conflict in many corners of the earth. In the Ottoman world, as in many places where religions and ethnic groups were obliged to live together under an authoritarian roof, the advent of modernity, and of freedom in the contemporary sense, has led to ethnic division, not to integration. Religions, languages and national traditions that used to co-exist now live separately, because no new terms of co-existence could be found. For better or worse, the Sultans provided a sort of shelter under which Muslim sheikhs could receive the faithful in Salonika, and Christian mystics could work their miracles in the villages of Cappadocia. When that authoritarian roof collapsed, people on both sides of the religious divide had to flee for their lives.

The sad fact is that multinational empires have given way not to multinational democracies but to sharply defined nation-states; and the process of redefinition has often been a violent one. Even if it does not lead to outright war, it often traumatizes the people involved by sharpening divisions which may once have been blurred. It draws lines and forces people to step to one side or the other. The elderly folk of Greece and Turkey who went through the population exchange understand all that very well, as do the people of Bosnia and the Caucasus. The children of the population exchange grew up in a world where cultural identities were rich, complex and ambivalent. They were forced to adapt to one where national affiliation was simpler and more strictly enforced, and there was a high price for questioning this simplicity.

At one level, the great separation between Greeks and Turks can be understood as a practical way of handling an immediate political and humanitarian crisis. As a result of the war which had just been won by Turkey, hundreds of thousands of people were homeless, destitute, ill and despairing. A mutually agreed mass population transfer offered a way of containing this crisis, at a high but manageable cost, and many people thought there was no other way. At the same time, the population transfer was the culmination of a much longer historical process which had been unfolding for more than a century. In many different ways, the old Ottoman model of co-existence between communities and faiths was doomed by the advent of the modern age. In its classic form, this Ottoman system depended on a careful and ruthlessly enforced division of labour between the subjects of the Sultan. Very broadly, the empire's formidable armies were commanded and manned by Muslims; recruits to its elite forces were gathered up as children from Christian families, but they were automatically converted to Islam. Nobody bore arms for the world's greatest Muslim ruler unless he himself was Muslim. Meanwhile the empire's non-Muslim subjects, the Christians and Jews, were exempted from military service but obliged to pay extra taxes instead. As long as they remained loyal to their sovereign and his local representatives, and respected the privileges of the Muslims, the minorities were more or less free to go about their business as merchants, craftsmen or peasants. A handful of Christians enjoyed enormous influence as local seigneurs or diplomats.

As a way of governing a vast and diverse realm that stretched from North Africa to the Caspian, and of harnessing the energies of religious minorities and co-opting their elites, the system had been moderately effective. But from the early 19th century, it started to unravel. This was partly because of recurring wars with Russia, another traditional empire wrestling with modernity, and partly because of the economic and ideological changes that were gathering pace in western Europe. The empire's Christian communities, such as the Greeks, Armenians and Slavs, were particularly susceptible to subversive liberal ideas coming from France and Germany, even if such ideas were received with alarm by their bishops. Among the new ideas was belief in universal secular education and in making knowledge in the form of printed books available to all. Also travelling westwards was a modern conception of liberty and democracy (albeit not always very well understood, as it entered the Ottoman lands) and a new belief in the abiding importance in history of nations and nation-states.

The Ottoman minorities were also susceptible to external influence of another kind. As the world industrialized, and the empire was connected to the outside world by steamships and railways, it was the Christians and Jews who were best placed to act as mediators between the Sultan's realm and its eager foreign partners. From the end of the 18th century onwards, the Ottoman Greek minority in particular enjoyed a surge in prosperity, and some of its leading members made fortunes as bankers to the Sultan. The Victorian version of globalization had turned the Ottoman empire into a more dynamic place, but also a more unstable one. As the empire's masters tried to devise ways of avoiding complete disintegration, the 'Greek factor' was a wild card in their calculations. On one side of the Aegean there was a new Hellenic kingdom, poverty stricken but ambitious, created by a mixture of rural discontent and the romantic dreams of a new classical age, or else of a new Byzantine empire, which had fired up some members of the Greek elite and their western friends. On the other side of the Aegean, Greek Orthodox subjects of the Sultan were flourishing as traders, entrepreneurs and financiers, and fostering the Greek language and culture among Ottoman Christians who had almost forgotten it. It did not take a geopolitical genius to see that this made for an intensely volatile situation. A definitive struggle for control of the Aegean, and hence for the role of dominant power in the east Mediterranean, was an ever present possibility.

The Sultans' retreat from Europe had been set in motion by the Serbian uprising of 1804, and the proclamation in 1829 of a new Greek kingdom which was self consciously and exclusively Christian. Any Muslims who had lived on its territory were killed, evicted or converted to Christianity. By 1878, the Ottoman empire was obliged to recognize the full independence of the new, mainly Christian states of Serbia, Romania and Bulgaria, all of which had aspirations, as Greece did, to further territorial expansion. Meanwhile, part of the empire's Muslim elite, especially the westernized bureaucracy, was growing more discontented; it was demanding its own share of the fruits of modernization, both material and cultural. At the same time, the Muslim share of the population in the Ottoman heartland was growing. After every round of conflict with the Russian empire, and every extension of the Russian territory, hundreds of thousands of Muslims fled into Anatolia rather than live under the Tsar, and Christians migrated in the opposite direction. As the Balkans grew more Christian, Anatolia was becoming more Islamic.

Yet by 1900, this trend was far from complete, nor was it certain that it would ever be completed. Neither did it seem absolutely inevitable that some final clash between Greece and the Ottoman empire would take place. At least in the short term, the interests of Greeks and Turks seemed potentially compatible. Wealthy Ottoman Greeks were enjoying much greater commercial opportunities than the struggling Hellenic kingdom could offer them, and they were in no hurry whatever to join the new kingdom. Many subjects of that struggling kingdom migrated to the Ottoman empire in search of relief from the new state's grinding poverty. Ottoman Macedonia, meanwhile, had become the object of a ruthless competition between three Christian powers, Greece, Bulgaria and Serbia. These Christian states assumed that an Ottoman pullout from Europe was only a matter of time. In the early years of the 20th century, many Greeks saw the Ottoman empire as a tactical ally against the Bulgarians. Some thought the Greek interest lay not in snatching territory from the Ottomans, but in Hellenizing the Ottoman world from within, a project with which some Muslim Turks might be willing to co-operate. It was even believed that a sort of Greco–Turkish condominium might be the best chance of asserting a degree of local control over the region's assets and preventing outsiders from enjoying an entirely free rein. In 1908, when a group of radical young officers rebelled against the Sultan, proclaiming a spirit of fraternity between the empire's Muslim and non-Muslim peoples, many Greeks welcomed and actively supported this, at least in the very early days.

From 1909 onwards, though, it became clear that a brief upsurge of multinational idealism was over. The Young Turks, the empire's new masters, hardened their position in the face of challenges that ranged from

religious conservatism at home to territorial disputes with Austria and
Russia. In the Balkans, even the empire's Muslim subjects, in Albania and
Kosovo, were straining to break free. Hopes of an historic reconciliation
between the Greeks and the Turks suffered a devastating blow in 1912,
when Greece joined a pan-Christian alliance with the Serbs and
Bulgarians to drive the Ottoman armies out of the Balkans. This conflict
brought enormous territorial gains for Greece, including the city of
Salonika, which the Greek army entered with only a few hours to spare
before the Bulgarians marched in.

These territorial advances also meant that for the first time, the Greek
state found itself governing a large number of Muslims. In many parts of
its newly won territory, where Christians were divided by language and
ethnic affiliation, Muslims were the biggest single population group.
There was a widespread Greek belief that a large and 'docile' population
of Muslim peasants could serve as a helpful buffer against Bulgarian
expansionism.

Even at this late stage in the disintegration of the Ottoman world, conflict in the Balkans could never quite be reduced to a straightforward
'civilizational' contest between Orthodox Christians and Muslims.
Alliances could shift with bewildering speed, and no side felt any shame
in stitching together treaties that cut across religious lines. Months after
the 1912 conflict, which did involve a shortlived pan-Christian coalition,
the Balkan states were at war once more. This time Ottoman Turkey, with
discreet help from the Greeks and Serbs, managed to claw back some territory from what they deemed to be an over-mighty Bulgaria. In the
longer term, however, the 1912–13 wars played a significant part in poi-
soning the atmosphere in Anatolia and making it harder for Christians
and Muslims to co-exist. Hundreds of thousands of Balkan Muslim
refugees, mostly fleeing from Serbia and Bulgaria, poured into Istanbul,
taking shelter in every mosque or public building they could find. In part
spontaneously, and in part at the authorities' behest, these refugees displaced Greek Orthodox Christians from their homes in western and
northern Anatolia.

During the First World War, much of Anatolia became a charnel house.
Hundreds of thousands of Turkish soldiers were killed in battles with the
Russians and the British. In one of the most ghastly chapters of modern
history, the entire Armenian population in most parts of Anatolia was

deported southwards and at least 600,000 died as a result. To this day, bitter arguments rage between the Turkish government, its defenders and critics over the cause of these deaths. Were they the result of a deliberate policy of mass killing or, so to speak, negligence? A few courageous Turkish historians have argued for the absurdity of the latter position.

On the central part of the Black Sea coast and in its hinterland, many Greek Orthodox Christians were deported from their homes by Turkish authorities who claimed that Christian armed bands were collaborating, or preparing to collaborate, with the Tsarist forces who had already occupied northeastern Anatolia. After 1917, when Greece joined the anti-Ottoman Entente, it was the turn of Orthodox Christians on the west coast to be deported.

But even before these tragedies unfolded there was one fateful development that accelerated the disintegration of relations between Orthodox Christians and Muslims in Anatolia from 1908 onwards. This was the fact that for the first time, a serious effort was made to force Christians to serve in the Ottoman army, mostly in a menial capacity. The old division of labour between Muslim soldiers, and Christians who paid a disproportionate share of tax, was no longer considered acceptable by the would-be builders of a more unitary Ottoman state.

Christians were not usually trusted to bear arms, so they were often assigned to backbreaking work in forced-labour gangs. Many Christian peasants left home rather than join up. Some emigrated to Russia; others joined the gangs of armed outlaws which roamed the Anatolian countryside. Higher up the social scale, many of the Ottoman Greek politicians who had remained loyal to the empire changed their minds and concluded there was no future for their people under the Sultans' rule.

Whatever remained of the old Ottoman equilibrium received a death blow, almost everywhere, as a result of the conflict which engulfed Anatolia from May 1919. That was the month when, with the blessing of the western powers, a Greek expeditionary force took control of Smyrna, the Aegean's greatest port; and it was also the time when Mustafa Kemal, a charismatic Ottoman army officer who had emerged creditably from the national fiasco of the First World War, began his campaign to set up a new sort of state in which Muslims Turks would be masters in their own house. As Kemal's military and political movement gathered momentum – in opposition not only to the Greeks but to the old Ottoman authorities in Istanbul, which he saw as beholden to the western powers, it became clear that a great military showdown was looming between Greeks and Turks, both combatant and civilian.

The contest for Anatolia was particularly cruel from mid-1921 onwards. The Greek army killed or put to flight Turkish civilians in the area south of Istanbul before embarking on a fresh march eastwards. Meanwhile in the Black Sea region, hundreds of thousands of Orthodox Christians – seen as actual or potential collaborators with the Greeks – were forced to leave their homes and trek over the mountains in conditions which only the hardiest and luckiest survived. The last few weeks before Turkey's final victory over Greece in September 1922 had horrific consequences for the people of western Anatolia. The Greek army, fleeing from central Turkey towards the sea, burned several medium-sized towns, leaving the survivors homeless and hungry. The Turkish victors slaked their thirst for revenge on local Greek Orthodox civilians with no regard for age or gender.

Yet despite all the pain they had inflicted on one another, the subtle web of relationships between Greeks and Turks, Orthodox Christians and Muslims, that supported the late Ottoman world had not entirely broken up, even in 1922. Whatever agonies they had suffered during the final years of their co-existence, people on both sides of the Aegean did not react to them simply by regarding one another with hatred, or by giving thanks for the day when the two nations had been physically separated. Those sentiments did exist, of course. Yet mingled with the memories of terror and betrayal, feelings and recollections persisted which somehow transcended the Greek–Turkish divide; personal friendships, commercial partnerships, a sense of common participation in a single world, constituted by landscape, language, music, food and all the trivia of everyday life.

That helps to explain the psychological trauma of a separation which brought pain and relief at the same time. It also illuminates the weirdly mixed feelings which can surface even now in transactions between Turks and Greeks, whether collective or individual. Because diplomatic and military relations have so often been strained, it is above all in the world of culture – novels, films and songs – that the two peoples have felt free to express the depth of their commonality, and to question the official ideology which relegates them to separate, unconnected worlds. To this day,

there is a huge emotional response to any book or movie or musical per-
formance which gives expression to the passion, and the sense of
common destiny, which Greeks and Turks can still feel for one another –
despite the giant divorce settlement that was devised, and harshly
enforced, more than eighty years ago.

The agreement to make a formal separation between the populations
of Greece and Turkey, through a two-way process of deportation, sent a
convulsion through the region and the world when it was announced,
tentatively in December 1922 and definitively the following month. There
was undeniably a certain cold, deadly logic about it. New borders were
being drawn, economic assets were being reallocated, and as a natural
consequence, people were being divided up as well. Henceforth, it was
determined, Greece would be an almost entirely Orthodox Christian
country, while in Turkey, the overwhelming majority of citizens would be
Muslim. Anybody who lived in the 'wrong' place, from the viewpoint of
religion, would be deported across the Aegean to start a new life in the
'right' country. It was a natural move, in the sense that the atrocities and
humanitarian disasters of the past few months, the war of the past three
years, and the economic and social changes of the past century, all seemed
to point in that direction; and at the same time, it was profoundly unnat-
ural.

The terms of the divorce were laid down in the grim words of a convention signed on 30 January 1923 at the conference in Lausanne, where
a triumphant Turkey, an exhausted Greece and the leading world powers
had gathered to map out the future of a volatile region then known as the
Near East. The conference, which did not conclude for another six
months, was intended to put an end to a decade of continuous warfare
and, from Turkey's point of view, to consolidate in the diplomatic arena
the hard-won gains of the battlefield.

Article One of the Lausanne convention reads as follows:

. . . There shall take place a compulsory exchange of Turkish nationals
of the Greek Orthodox religion established in Turkish territory, and of
Greek nationals of the Muslim religion established in Greek territory.
These persons shall not return to live in Turkey or Greece without the
authorization of the Turkish government or of the Greek government
respectively.

While the principle and the desired end result seemed perfectly simple, the immediate practical consequences of this decision were not simple at all. The convention meant different things to different categories of people, affected in varying degrees by the conflict that was now being settled. For roughly 1 million Greek Orthodox people from Turkey and 100,000 Muslims from Greece who had recently fled, or been chased from one country to the other, the convention simply implied that they must give up all hope of returning to their birthplaces. For families whose menfolk were prisoners of war or engaged in forced labour, the decision offered a glimmer of hope their loved ones might return alive. For people who had already been displaced from their homes but had not yet left their respective countries, especially Orthodox Christians of the Black Sea region, the decision improved the prospects for getting away safely.

Finally, for about 450,000 people who had not been directly affected by war (roughly 400,000 Muslims in Greece, whose mother tongues included Greek, Albanian, and Bulgarian as well as Turkish, and at least 50,000 Turkish-speaking Christians who lived in the Anatolian interior, far from any war zone) the convention came as a harsh, gratuitous blow. It implied that they must abandon forever the towns or villages where they had grown up, and where they had reasonable hope of continuing to live.

These deportees were given no choice in the matter. Nobody asked them whether they would have preferred to stay put, with all the attendant risks of being a small minority in a state where the majority was bent on affirming its domination. Nobody asked them how they felt, or to which nation or community they felt most attached. The personal feelings of the people involved were the last thing considered by the politicians who decreed the population exchange. What they wanted – and this was not an ignoble desire – was an arrangement that would be durable and minimize the risk of further war, either in the immediate future or in a subsequent generation.

People are easier to shift than buildings or civilizations; and once moved they can be reprogrammed, so to speak, in all manner of ways. That, at least in part, was the thinking behind the population exchange. But remoulding large numbers of people, encouraging them to think about themselves and their identity in a new way, is never a gentle process. Above all, it means forcing people to suppress certain feelings, the feelings which still connect them to the places where they or their forebears used to live. At the same time, it means encouraging migrants to deny any difference between themselves and their new compatriots.

For hundreds of thousands of people on both sides of the Aegean, the trauma of departure – of being deported, often in dire conditions, from a home village to which they were deeply attached – was compounded by the difficulty of adapting to their new country and deliberately forgetting most things that connected them to the old country. So if, when contemplating the physical environment of Turkey or Greece, we sense that we are in a place which has suffered a terrible shock or trauma whose effects are still being felt, that intuition is perfectly well founded.

It has been estimated that about 20 per cent of the population of Anatolia died violently during the last ten years of the Ottoman empire's existence: some 2.5 million Muslims, up to 800,000 Armenians and 300,000 Greeks. To put it another way, a third of the Christian population and one eighth of the Muslim population had been killed, making the Ottoman empire a far more rural, and Islamic place: its population was now at least 96 per cent Muslim, up from 80 per cent before the decade of mutual slaughter began. The population exchange marked a final, cold-blooded conclusion of the process whereby Anatolia became Muslim and the southern Balkans became mostly Christian.

It was not just the migrants themselves who were affected by this extraordinary episode in European history. It is hardly an exaggeration to say that the modern societies of Turkey and Greece were constituted by the population exchange; not only because of the newcomers that each country was obliged to absorb, but also (especially in the Turkish case) because of the population each state forfeited. For certain parts of Turkey, the departure of the Christians meant the loss of virtually all traders and entrepreneurs, as well as most professional people and skilled craftsmen. In those parts of central Anatolia where commercial life was once heavily dominated by Christians, there is still a sense that the local economy has never recovered.

Greece was affected more by an influx than by an exodus. In many of its northern regions, and in certain districts of Athens, the population is still overwhelmingly of 'Asia Minor' stock. In other words, a clear majority of people in Greek Macedonia or the refugee quarters of the Greek capital can trace family roots to Turkish Anatolia or Thrace. It is hardly

possible to analyse the recent politics, culture or even the religious practices of any part of northern Greece without first asking the question:
which part of present-day Turkey did the people involved come from? On
the Turkish side, there are only a few places where Muslim migrants from
Greece have played such an important role, but Turkey's economy and
society have developed in a way that can scarcely be explained unless the
removal of its nascent bourgeoisie, which happened to be Christian, is
taken into account.

Were the mass deportations of the 1923 convention an exchange
between Greeks and Turks, or between Christians and Muslims? By the
letter of the treaty, it was clearly the latter. But even at the time, people
were ambivalent about this. Sometimes they used the words 'Greek' and
'Christian' or 'Turk' and 'Muslim' as though the terms were quite inter-
changeable, sometimes not. In fact, the entire region was halfway through
an enormous change in the way human society was imagined and cate-
gorized. That transition – from a religiously defined world to a nationally
defined one – was never fully completed, and it may in recent years have
gone into reverse. But in the 1920s, that shift of consciousness was at a
much earlier phase. Indeed, to anyone who understood the world in the
old Ottoman way, the choice of religion as a criterion for determining the
fate of large numbers of people would not have seemed strange at all.

In the Ottoman system, spiritual affiliation had served as by far the
most significant distinction between the subjects of the Sultan. It made
a huge difference to your life whether you were an Ottoman Muslim, an
Ottoman Orthodox Christian or an Ottoman Jew. This determined how
much tax you would pay, what role you would play in public life and by
what law you would be judged. Because the empire was organized as a
Muslim theocracy, it expected its non-Muslim subjects to behave, as it
were, theocratically; in other words, to organize themselves into religious groups where the spiritual leader also doubled as head of the
community, and could answer to the Sultan for the behaviour of his
flock. In stressing the primacy of religion, the Ottoman authorities were
to some extent following the precedent set by the Byzantine theocracy,
as well as Islam's own theocratic tradition. In any case, at least in its classic form, the Ottoman system did not distinguish between its subjects
by virtue of their speech or customs or beliefs about their own 'national'
origins. An Ottoman Muslim might speak Serbian, Arabic, Albanian or

Turkish; it made no difference to that person's status in the eyes of his rulers.

By the end of the Ottoman era that was changing; religion was giving way to 'nation' as the main source of identity and affiliation. When the Ottoman theocracy was at its height, the Greek-dominated Patriarchate of Constantinople, which was an important agency of the imperial regime, enjoyed huge influence over all the Orthodox Christians of the empire; but in the 19th century, as the intensity of ethnic consciousness increased, new religious authorities were created or revived by the Slavs and Arabs in particular, which were identical to the Greek Patriarchate in doctrine but gave expression to a different national identity. Formally speaking, the bitter conflict which raged in Ottoman Macedonia at the end of the 19th century was between the bishops of the Greek and Bulgarian hierarchs of the Orthodox church; but this was not so much a religious war as a war over national identity in religious disguise.

In most parts of the Ottoman empire, as in most other places that were either in Europe or influenced by European ideas, the elite had been infiltrated by a new doctrine, that of modern nationalism. This was a theory which aspired to supplant religion as the main category by which people defined themselves, and was itself something akin to a religion in its claim to explain and guide human behaviour, and to deal in eternally valid truths.

In the west European nations like France and Germany, the victory of nationalism over sectarianism seemed almost complete: people felt a loyalty to the French or German state which in the early 20th century at least, transcended (without, of course, abolishing) the distinction between Catholic, freethinker, Protestant or Jew. It helped that belief in the tenets of those religions was fading. But in the traditional societies of the Ottoman realm, religious affiliation went too deep for it simply to be superseded. It was not so much that all Ottoman subjects were deeply religious; but in such a world, it was difficult to imagine an authority without religious underpinning. So when nationalism – the belief in ethnically defined 'nations' as the stuff of human destiny – descended on that region, it overlaid and intersected with the older religious divisions, but in no way abolished them.

To some extent, this persistence of sectarianism reflected a clever rearguard action by religious elites who knew, consciously or unconsciously, that by partially accepting the new nationalist dogma, and co-opting it, they could retain their own authority. The Orthodox Christian bishops of the Ottoman world redefined themselves as 'Greek Orthodox' or 'Serbian Orthodox' or 'Albanian Orthodox' and hence proclaimed themselves not only participants, but protagonists, in the new *nation*-building project. As a kind of payoff for this tactical surrender, they were usually able to insist that religion be retained as one of the criteria by which newly proclaimed nations defined themselves. They were able to specify, for example, that to be Greek, it was a necessary (though certainly not sufficient) condition to be an Orthodox Christian.

The new dogma of nationalism affected the periphery of the Ottoman world before it reached the empire's heartland. In the depths of Anatolia there were plenty of people who defined themselves as Muslims – people under the spiritual authority of the Caliphate – rather than as members of an ethnic or linguistic group. Even in the Balkans, moreover, the shift from one form of consciousness to another was far from complete at the time of the Lausanne treaty. Only twenty years earlier, as conflict intensified over the future of Macedonia, most Christian peasants there were certain of only one thing, their religion. If asked what nationality they were – in other words, were they Greeks, Serbs or Bulgarians? – they would not have understood the question; or else they would have given an answer designed to please the questioner. Likewise, many of the Christians in the heart of Anatolia – whether they spoke Turkish, Greek or both – would have described themselves, if pressed, as Orthodox people, living in a certain town or region, who were subjects of the empire. In the jargon of political scientists, they had a 'pre-ethnic' understanding of their identity. If they knew Greek, they might have described themselves as *Romios* – a folksy, evocative word for Ottoman Christians who trace their roots to the Byzantine, or east-Roman empire; but they would not have called themselves *Ellines* (people identified with the newly founded kingdom of Ellas) unless some schoolteacher, filled with nationalist ideas by the University of Athens, taught them to do so.

It would be going too far to say that words like 'Greek' or 'Turkish' had no meaning at all before the age of nationalism. In some contexts, Turk meant a simple Anatolian peasant, as opposed to a refined Ottoman Muslim. For many centuries before it was revived in a spirit of nationalism, the Greek word *Ellin* or Hellene had slightly pejorative overtones; it meant a pagan who still worshipped the old deities of classical Greece. But in any case, Greekness and Turkishness were fluid, imprecise concepts, with no specific legal or political implications, which were applied to a fluid and imprecise reality. Among the Christians of Anatolia, for example, there were those who identified strongly with the independent Greek state because they had emigrated to places in western Anatolia in the recent past; and others, hundreds of miles to the east, who spoke not a word of any language but Turkish and only had the vaguest notion of the Greek state's existence. And between those two extremes – Anatolian Christians who felt entirely Greek and those who hardly felt Greek at all – there were an infinite number of points on a spectrum. That is how things really are in human affairs. But the treaty of Lausanne, like the war that preceded it, was inspired by a new way of looking at human society: one that dealt in hard, hermetically sealed categories, and insisted that every individual and family must belong to one nation or the other and live within its borders. Despite the decline of Ottoman theocracy, the one category that everyone understood was that of religion. Even as religion itself declined, its importance as a badge of affiliation remained intact.

That, at bottom, was the logic behind the Lausanne convention of 1923, under which the 'problem' of religious diversity was solved at a stroke. Its architects had understood a paradoxical truth. It would be much easier to create a new, politically and ethnically defined community – a community of Greek citizens, say, or of Turkish citizens – if the 'raw material' for each national project was all of the same religion. In other words, to create a state in which religion was rather less important as an organizing principle, it was first of all necessary to gather in people who followed the same religion – and expel those who did not.

There were, of course, more practical reasons for a compulsory exchange, which all the politicians involved would have cited. For the founders of the Turkish republic, their Greek Orthodox Christian neighbours had lost the moral right to live in the newly established state by collaborating with the Greek army which had occupied much of western Anatolia for the past three years. The Rums, or Ottoman Greeks, were tarnished with collective guilt and their removal – whether by expulsion or worse – was a non-negotiable demand of the Turkish victors. For the battered Greek state, a country of 5 million people faced with an influx of more than 1 million refugees, the expulsion of the Muslim population (so as to 'make room' for the newcomers) was not so much a question of principle as a desperately needed expedient. But it was only the new ideology of nation-state building – the principle that every state exists solely or mainly 'for' a particular nation – which made the idea of massive, mutual exchange conceivable and indeed desirable for both sides.

In the schools, lecture rooms and army barracks of both countries, young Greeks and Turks are still taught to see this compulsory separation as a heroic story with a happy ending. In Turkey's official history, the removal of the Orthodox Christian minority, which had disgraced itself by acting as a pawn for foreign interests, is seen as a milestone in the country's liberation and emergence into modernity. For Orthodox Greeks, the expulsion of their co-religionists by Turkey, and their absorption into the Greek motherland, is a tragic and noble story with a happy ending. It is cited to prove the wickedness of the Turk, the incompatibility of Greeks and Turks, and the essential unity of the Greek nation, which closed ranks within the security of its own borders.

These ideas would not have gained such wide acceptance unless they contained a seed of credibility. The Turks' feeling of betrayal by their Christian neighbours, who abetted the Greek invasion of their country, was real; it did not have to be induced. And the nation-building efforts which both countries launched after the exchange were partially successful in their own terms – newcomers to each country really were persuaded to consider themselves 'Greeks' or 'Turks' – or at any rate, their children were. Once this ruthless exercise in national and ethnic engineering had been carried out, the two states more or less succeeded, over a generation, in absorbing their new arrivals and reshaping their consciousness. Whatever they may have felt about being deported to another country, the Christians of Anatolia and the Muslims of Greece were – at least superficially – remoulded as Greeks and Turks respectively.

Moreover, the official doctrine that presents separation as 'liberation' is not completely alien to the lived experience of people in both countries. Regardless of state ideologies, many ordinary people did experience the end of the Ottoman era as a liberation: for the Greeks, liberation from the arbitrary political power of the Ottoman authorities; and for ordinary Turks, liberation from the economic power of the Christians who dominated commerce and industry. And it was not entirely wrong to speak of a liberation from fear. After the sickening atrocities that Greeks and Turks had inflicted on one another during the final years of the Ottoman era, it was not meaningless to say that for many people, physical separation from the other community seemed, and in some cases actually was, the best guarantee of survival.

But that is only one half of the truth. It is the half which people have been allowed and indeed obliged to believe. The other half is that when the Aegean peoples were prised apart, each lost a part of its own identity, and hence lost the ability to understand itself. This paradox has found poignant expression in the arts – novels, songs and films – which hark back to a world in which Greeks and Turks, Anatolian Christians and Anatolian Muslims recognized each other as human beings rather than enemies. Thus far, it is only in the cultural world that Greeks and Turks have begun to glimpse the depth of one another's pain. But even as Turkey prepares to join the European Union, there is remarkably little room for such sentiments in the political discourse of Athens and Ankara.

As they stamp around the parade ground, Greek and Turkish army recruits are still taught to chant scatological slogans of loathing for one another. In a perverse way, that may be slightly encouraging. If the process of inculcating hatred has to be deliberate and self-conscious, that is because the spiritual partition of the Byzantine-Ottoman world was never entirely completed, even when the age of nationalism was at its height. That is what the half-ruined monuments in both countries remind us. It may conceivably be possible to repair broken identities and relationships, as well as broken buildings.

That is one of the reasons why the Greek–Turkish population transfer, as an exercise in diplomatic expediency, as a grim cultural and geopolitical landmark, and as a human drama that affected millions of people, is still worth studying. The following chapters will examine how the exchange was negotiated; how the politicians decided who to include and who to exclude from this vast and ruthless exercise in nation-building from above. It will look at how the exchange was experienced by ordinary people in various parts of Greece and Turkey, and see how the effect of the exchange is still palpable in the environment, the daily life and self-understanding of those places. It will look in microcosm at a historical process that began in the 19th century and is still in progress, nearly 200 years later.

CHAPTER 1

Ayvalik and its ghosts

Believers in a traditional Hellenophobia–Turkophobia would have stared at the sight of the Mytilene Greeks spreading farewell meals for their departing neighbours, and later accompanying them to the quay, where Christians and Mohammedans, who for a lifetime had been plowing adjacently and even sharing occasional backgammon games at village cafes, embraced and parted with tears. Then, seated on their heaped up baggage, with their flocks around them – the women weeping, the children hugging their pets, the gray-bearded babas all dignity, as is their wont – the Mytilene Muslims set forth for unknown Turkey.

National Geographic magazine, November 1922

At the beginning of October 1922, a young Turkish officer called Kemaleddin went down to the harbour of a deserted Aegean port and bade an emotional goodbye to a distraught Greek woman. As he did so, he murmured the name of one of his three sisters who had been killed recently by the Greek army in his home town of Bursa. He also promised the Greek woman, Agape, that he would do whatever he could to ensure the safety of her eighteen-year-old brother, Ilias, who was one of the 3000 Greek men and boys from the town who had been taken prisoner, supposedly to engage in forced labour. This encounter between Kemaleddin and Agape, recounted by her many years later, was the culmination of a poignant human story which unfolded against the background of the momentous, and for many people, unspeakably painful events which took place that autumn on the western edge of Anatolia.

Kemaleddin's parting message to Agape was delivered as she prepared to board the last ship leaving the town of Ayvalik. The vessel was carrying what was left of the port's civilian population, which until a month earlier had numbered around 30,000 and was almost exclusively Greek. In mid-September, the Turkish army occupied the town, consolidating the phenomenal success which began in August with the rout of the Greek army from an inland fastness where it had camped for a miserable year after narrowly failing to capture Ankara, the Turkish nationalists' headquarters, in the early autumn of 1921. By mid-September, a Greek force of more than 200,000 had been driven out of Anatolia. Some retreated northwards to the sea of Marmara, more or less intact, but the majority fled in disarray, torching Turkish towns as they went.

To this day, Turks are taught to look upon this period as sacred history, in which the name of every battlefield, every commander is memorized and treasured. Every Turkish child learns how Mustafa Kemal, later known as Ataturk or 'father of the Turks', kept his nerve during the darkest days of the campaign, when Ankara was a small, straggling, vulnerable town where there was hardly room to treat the wounded soldiers who kept arriving from the nearby front. They learn of his inspiring orders – 'Your line of defence is the whole country!' – and of the firmness with which he rejected easy compromises, bolstered the faint hearted and artfully neutralized treachery within his own camp. Teachers recount the skill with which Kemal faced down the British who were still in effective charge of Istanbul, and deeply in cahoots with a decadent Ottoman administration that was still clinging to a figment of authority over a fading empire. Almost everything in this story is true as far it goes, but it is only part of the truth.

On 9 September 1922, Kemal's cavalry marched into the foremost Aegean port and gave it back the Turkish name of Izmir. For the previous three years it had been the headquarters of the Greek army and bureaucracy, who called it by the ancient New Testament name of *Smyrni*. Even in late August, as the Greek forces were being ejected from their Anatolian stronghold, the port was still pulsating with cosmopolitan life; cafes, opera houses and merchants' offices were going about their business. Within four days of the new occupiers' arrival, three-quarters of the city had been burned to the ground and tens of thousands of people had been incinerated or drowned as they tried, in most cases vainly, to find succour on the British, French or American ships which were anchored nearby and did relatively little to alleviate the catastrophe.

The question of how the fire started – in the city's Armenian quarter, from where it spread rapidly – is still controversial. Minnie Mills, the dean of an American college in the city, gave a graphic account afterwards of seeing Turkish soldiers dousing Armenian houses with petrol and then watching them ignite. This is dismissed in most Turkish or pro-Turkish accounts, which insist that since the Greek army undoubtedly committed arson in many other places, it must presumably have done so in the great Aegean port as well. This contention, using what Islamic scholars would call 'argument from analogy', is a weak one. Ismet Inönü, the commander of the Turkish campaign, had something more enigmatic to say in his memoirs. Referring both to the fires started by the Greeks further inland, and to the blaze at Izmir, he writes: 'Subordinates say that they carried out these orders; senior figures that there was a breakdown in discipline.' At that very time, 'when joy struggled with pity in our feelings' he could 'remember Ataturk . . . saying that one day we might find ourselves making an alliance with the Greeks'. But that did not mean, according to Ismet, that his leader felt any regret over the Izmir fire: his response was simply to say, 'Let it burn, let it crash down.'

What is not in doubt, in any case, is that in very large measure, Greek life on the coast of Anatolia, which in one form or another had flourished for 3000 years, came to an end during the first half of September 1922. Izmir at the time was overflowing with Greeks: 200,000 who lived in or near the town, perhaps another 150,000 desperate refugees who had poured into the city from further east. Among those who survived the fire, males of working age were taken captive by the Turks, on the grounds that they must be set to work repairing the damage wrought by the Greek army. The women, children and old folk were given two weeks to leave. Many of those who were taken away owe their lives to Asa Jennings, a shy Methodist minister from America who, acting only on impulse and with no real authority to do so, sent a series of messages to the Greek government demanding that they send ships and threatening to expose their weakness of will if they failed to do so.

Because communications had broken down in the general chaos, the gravity of these events was realized far too slowly by the Greek people of Ayvalik. This was a community which, although much smaller in number than the Smyrna Greeks, liked to see itself as an almost equally important outpost of Hellenic learning and enterprise. They called their town Ayvali,* or in more formal Greek, Kydonies; both meaning 'quince orchard', a reminder of the town's fertile and pleasant hinterland. On 1 September, the Greek governor of western Anatolia, Aristides Sterghiades, sent a secret cable to his subordinates in the whole region, including the Ayvali administration, instructing them to close down the entire Hellenic police force and bureaucracy in view of the terrible military disaster which had just occurred. The secret of the impending flight, and the reasons for it, seem to have been kept quite successfully from ordinary Greek people, for a crucial few days. In early September, after watching with increasing dismay as the civil servants and units of the defeated Greek army sailed away, the town council held a meeting under the chairmanship of the local bishop, Gregorios Orologas, and made a fatefully naive decision. The local population should stay put and await the victorious Turkish army. As a token of good faith, all the local boats would be docked, and people would be actively prevented from sailing away. The council's hope was to try and restore the good relations with the Turkish authorities which the community had enjoyed, certain dramatic intervals excepted, since 1775, when it was granted handsome privileges by the Ottoman authorities, including the right to remain exclusively Greek and Christian. But as soon became obvious, the age of skilfully managed symbiosis between Turkish overlords and Greek burghers was over.

The Turkish army entered the port on 19 September. They were welcomed at the outskirts by Bishop Gregorios and other prominent townspeople. Local people dutifully cried, '*Yasasin!*' (Turkish for 'Long live!') as the Turkish cavalry marched through their streets. The townsfolk even helped to organize a reception, with music and dancing, for the officers in Kemal's army. But within a few days, an icier wind was blowing through the town. The cavalry were replaced by foot soldiers, and the decree went out that in this place, like everywhere else in western Anatolia, able-bodied Greek males would be gathered up and sent to labour units, while the remainder of the population would be deported to Greece.

This is what led to the dramatic encounter between Lieutenant

---

*The Greek community continued to remember the place by that name, even after their exodus; for the past eighty years, the port has been known by its new residents, and hence to the world, by its Turkish name of Ayvalik.

Kemaleddin and the Greek woman Agape. At the age of just eighteen, her brother Ilias was just old enough to be included in the roundup, but she became fanatically determined to get him back. During the final days of September, as most of the population was being evacuated by sea, Agape refused to leave with the rest of her family. For several days she wandered the streets in despair, looking for a Turkish officer who might listen to her pleadings for the release of her brother. Despairing and almost delirious with fever she ran into Kemaleddin, who looked after her, and eventually her father, for several days and was able to bring her as far as the building where her brother was detained, and where she could hear his cries. But efforts to secure his release were unsuccessful. After describing his own life story, and his own despair over the loss of his three sisters, Kemaleddin begged Agape and her father to save their own lives at least and take the last boat leaving the town.

The other events which took place in Ayvalik around that time are mostly grim, and lack even a saving trace of romance. On one ship that was about to transport Greek civilians away from the port, a Greek man who had somehow managed to join the women and children was crazy enough to destroy his fez, a form of headgear which Greeks only wore when trying to ingratiate their overlords, in full view of some Turkish guards standing on the quay. He was hauled off the ship and shot dead. As a result, the checks on departing passengers became much stricter. Many boys who tried disguising themselves or simply hiding amid the crowds were apprehended and taken into captivity. Ilias, the brother of Agape, did survive his ordeal, and went on to become one of the best-known Greek writers of the 20th century, under the pen name of Ilias Venezis. But in all only twenty-three of the 3000 men from Ayvali came back alive. Gregorios and all the other clergy of the town were taken to a lonely spot outside the town and killed; the bishop is said to have died of a heart attack shortly before an attempt to bury him alive. Ironically some of those who died were choristers and vergers who donned clerical clothes in the belief that they would be treated with greater respect.

On the nearby islet which is known in Greek as Moschonisi and in Turkish as Cunda, several hundred civilians of all ages were taken away and killed; only some of the children were spared and sent to orphanages. This was apparently an act of revenge for the killing several years earlier of a local Muslim judge by some Greek irregulars who came from the islet.

More than eighty years later, Ayvalik and Cunda, now linked by a causeway and both popular tourist destinations, are still haunted by ghosts from that era and many others. The evacuation of Greek Ayvali in 1922 is only one of the stories of exile and deportation which have shaped this place. Most of the town's current residents descend from Muslim families who were deported from various parts of Greece in 1923–4. Today's community consists, of course, of loyal Turkish citizens, and in local politics there is quite a strong flavour of Turkish national-ism. But if there is a place where the Ottoman Greek world of a century ago, at its most bustling and energetic, can still be imagined vividly, it is the centre of Ayvalik. You can see horse-drawn carts trotting down cob-bled alleys, houses built of volcanic stone with high ceilings and cool gardens, and a raucous street market where coppersmiths, watch makers and olive salesmen ply their wares. And in the traditional cafes of Cunda, the language spoken by retired fishermen as they play backgammon and sip coffee, is a colourful, old-fashioned form of Greek, the dialect of Crete. As the old men look out to sea, the horizon is half filled by a large island whose low mountains, vast olive plantations and pine forests are almost a mirror image of Ayvalik's hinterland. That island is Mytilene, where quite a few locals were born; but for much of the past century, pol-itics has turned this narrow channel into an almost impassable dividing line.

Look closely at Ayvalik and you will see a curious disconnection between the urban environment and its current occupants, just as there is in many parts of Greece. The two biggest mosques in the old town centre clearly began life as grand, colonnaded churches, a statement of bourgeois 19th century prosperity as well as devotion to God. Sunshine trickles down through rows of ingeniously placed fanlights, but these buildings lack the perfect match between light and space that character-izes Islamic architecture. On Cunda islet, the biggest physical structure is the shell of a giant cathedral, still known by its Greek name of Taxiarchis, or commander. Like many places of worship in this part of the world, it is dedicated to Michael, chief of the angels. The walls have been cracked by an earthquake, and the frescoes largely effaced. Its haunted emptiness recalls the Russian churches stripped by the Bolsheviks. But the local Muslim lady who acts as informal guardian of the church is a cheerful soul, capable of regaling the visitor with a stream of proverbs, poetry and songs for up to an hour without drawing breath, and all of them in her own Cretan dialect of Greek, learned from her parents.

Behind Ayvalik's beguiling facade, there are many half-hidden stories. One is that of the town's current inhabitants, a majority of whom have family roots in Greece. In other words, they descend from Muslim communities forcibly deported to Turkey under the Lausanne convention. The first batch came from the neighbouring island, Mytilene; a second, larger wave arrived early the following year from Crete. Their main, or usually sole, language was the Cretan version of Greek. Later in 1924, there was a final wave of arrivals from places like Drama and Serres in northern Greece.

Ayvalik's current residents are encouraged by officialdom to remember and recount the suffering which their families endured at the hands of their Christian neighbours during their final years in Greece. Their lives in that country had become so precarious that there was no chance of continuing to live there; therefore the population exchange was a narrow escape from the lethal consequences of continued exposure to Hellenic nationalist fury. That is the official story, and it is not entirely without foundation. But another layer of truth, which people in Ayvalik acknowledge rather more reticently, is provided by much warmer recollections of life in Greece and among Greeks. People in this town carry their Turkish passports with pride, but some also have a sense that for better or worse, the Greek world helped to shape them, to make them what they are.

The story of Avyalik's final days as a Greek Christian town had already been brought to an end well before the Muslim families now living in the port began arriving. But there are at least a few people in the town who feel the Greekness of the place, and of their own family histories, strongly enough to argue that the physical remains of that era should be preserved rather than neglected or deliberately destroyed. As these people realize, nowhere in this region can be fully understood or appreciated except in the context of a perpetually shifting symbiosis between Greeks and Turks.

Ayvali is about ten nautical miles at the nearest point from the island of Mytilene. For most of the region's history, the port and the island have formed a single cultural and economic entity. Over the last couple of centuries, both the port and the island have been significant international exporters of olives and their products, from oil to soap. From either place, the houses and farms of the 'other side' seem to beckon enticingly across a short stretch of sea. But from 1770 onwards, there was one difference: Mytilene, as an erstwhile headquarters for the Ottoman navy, had a substantial Turkish and Muslim population, while Ayvali was exclusively Christian and Greek. Ayvali's existence was interrupted for a decade or so in 1821 after some of the empire's Greek subjects revolted; and the entire community was deported to another part of Anatolia in retaliation. But from 1830, the port was allowed to flourish once more a bastion of Greek prosperity, education and high culture. At the turn of the century, as the Ottoman world was drawn deeper into the international economy, the people of Ayvali (like so many of the empire's Christian subjects) were profiting handsomely as exporters, importers and entrepreneurs. At the beginning of the 20th century, the prosperous Ottoman Greeks of both Ayvali and Mytilene were doing well under the Sultan's rule, and they had no great wish to join the independent kingdom of Greece, which had been soundly defeated by the Ottoman army in 1897. But from 1912 onwards, the region was convulsed by the broader crisis in Christian–Muslim relations. During the Balkan wars of 1912–13, Mytilene was taken by the Greeks, and the adjacent part of the mainland was crowded with Balkan Muslim refugees, who evicted tens of thousands of Christians from Ayvali's hinterland. In the town itself, the Greek residents were rounded up and driven out of their homes in 1917 – as a consequence of the Ottoman empire's war against an Anglo–Franco–Russian Entente which Greece had been induced to join with the bait of 'territorial concessions' in that part of the world. Then in 1919, after Greek troops received their mandate to occupy western Anatolia, the buzz of Hellenic enterprise returned to Ayvali once more; for three years, the town's Greek churches, schools, fishing fleets and agricultural markets enjoyed one last burst of life before their extinction.

In today's Ayvalik, there are not many people with detailed knowledge of that period. If a local person wants to talk history, it is more likely to be the history of Crete, and of what it was like to be a Muslim there. Among Cretan Muslims, the memories they cultivate most strongly are almost a mirror image of those cherished by the Orthodox Greeks. The moments which official Greek history celebrates, they lament – and vice versa. In their collective memory, the advance of Greek nationalism is an unfolding tragedy.

How does this correspond to what really happened on Crete? On one hand, the 19th century did see some horrific bloodshed between Cretan Muslims and their Christian neighbours, even by the standards of the Ottoman Balkans. The proposition that 'life had become intolerable' is an easy one to defend, especially with respect to rural areas where Muslim-owned farms and homes were burned systematically as Greek Christians gained the upper hand. Sectarian quarrels aside, the culture of the Cretan mountains had always been one of intense antagonism between heavily armed, extended families, perpetually stealing one another's livestock and exacting revenge for ancient wrongs. The quarrel between Christians and Muslims became the bloodiest local feud of all though it was not the only one.

On the other hand, Cretan Muslims continued to resemble their Christian neighbours (and often kinsmen) – in their speech, customs and attachment to the landscape – in a way that was unusual among Ottoman Muslim communities from the present day territory of Greece.

How had the Muslims of Crete come into existence? That question is an ideologically loaded one, and entirely different answers would be offered by the Greek-nationalist and Turkish-nationalist versions of history. It is clear, however, that almost immediately after the Ottoman conquest of the previously Venetian island in 1669, tens of thousands of islanders – sometimes individuals, but most often entire villages – converted from Christianity to Islam. An obvious motive was the avoidance of the heavy taxation which the Sultan's Christian subjects were required to pay. With every fresh conversion, Christian–Muslim tension increased: the Ottoman authorities expected to levy a given amount of revenue from the island, and as the pool of tax payers diminished, so the burden imposed on each remaining Christian grew. But while Christians remained the majority in most rural areas, such urban life as existed on the island was soon dominated by Muslims. This created a situation not dissimilar to Bosnia before the recent conflict.

But even as the economic interests of the two communities diverged, their manners and culture did not. In 1821, when the Greek uprising against the Ottoman empire began, the provisional leadership of Greece sent a revealing message to the Muslims of Crete, urging them to put their 'Greekness' before their religion.

For your houses are beside ours, and you wear the same clothes as us, and you have the same boldness, and the same gait, and the same language . . . For we ask you again to join our cause, for deep down you are not Orientals, or Arabs, you are rather true Cretans and you have Greek blood and you must abide by this . . .

In fact it was only Orthodox Christians of Crete (and initially just a few of them) who joined the revolutionary cause; but the remainder of the decade, and indeed the remainder of the 19th century was drenched in blood, as uprising triggered reprisal – and the island, in part thanks to international diplomacy, was given a progressively greater degree of autonomy.

Throughout all this strife, the bonds between Christian and Muslim were never entirely severed. Robert Pashley, an Englishman who wrote an account of Crete in 1834, reported that, before the uprising at least, it had been common for Muslims to act as godparents to the children of Christian friends. Such relationships were facilitated, Pashley reports, by the fact that despite the strictures of Islam, 'a Cretan Mohammedan drinks his wine as unscrupulously as any Christian'. As late as the 1880s, when Crete had won a large measure of self rule within the Ottoman empire, the island's political factions transcended sectarian divisions in a curious way. One camp grouped powerful Christians with lesser Muslim notables; another grouped the Muslim elite with Christians of modest but rising status.

Still, as critics of Greek nationalism always point out, it cannot be denied that the Muslim share of the island's population fell precipitously as the Christians' political status improved. On the eve of the 1821 uprising, the population was divided between two religions, at around 100,000 each. By 1880, there were 206,000 Christians and 72,000 Muslims; in 1900 the Christian population had risen sharply to 270,000 while the number of Muslims had declined to 33,500. Thousands of Muslims emigrated to Istanbul or Anatolia in the two years after 1898 when Greece's Prince George was proclaimed governor, and in practice asserted Christian control over the island's affairs, even though it remained notionally under the Sultan's sovereignty. The prince's assurances that Muslims had nothing to fear did not seem to reassure anybody. In the euphemistic words of a leading Greek historian of Crete: 'Most of [those] who decided to leave were those who dwelt in rural areas. The Cretan villages were thus relieved of a Turkish presence, and the villagers found that their land had been increased.' In other words, in a world of almost continual competition for land and livestock, the Christian farmers took advantage of the changing political conditions to drive their Muslim neighbours off the land and appropriate the spoils.

In the growing towns of Crete, the Muslims held their own better. They lost their dominant role in urban life, but those who enjoyed some success as merchants or professional people continued to live prosperously. By 1922, after a decade of Greek–Turkish warfare in other places, relations between the Christians and Muslims of Crete remained tense but in most places there was no open violence. Those Muslims who had stayed on included those who were most deeply attached to Crete, and who continued to believe that despite everything it might be possible to go on co-existing with their Christian neighbours. Even after the Turkish capture of Izmir and the arrival at the Cretan port of Iraklion of 13,000 Greek refugees from Anatolia, it was by no means obvious that the town's Muslims would have to be forced out to 'make room' for the newcomers.

Pandelis Prevelakis, a Cretan novelist who witnessed the Muslim exodus at the age of fourteen, said news of the population exchange came as a terrible shock to both the island's communities. They were 'like a couple whose divorce is pronounced at the very moment when they have buried the hatchet'. At least 1000 Cretan Muslims asked if they could make last-minute reconversions to Christianity, but the Archbishop of Athens refused this request. In the novelist's vivid words:

> From one end of the island to the other, groans of the Turks preparing to leave were heard, mingling with those of the refugees who had just been uprooted; and one asked oneself what profit there could be in such distress for the monsters who held human grief at nothing.

During their final hours and days on their island, the outgoing Muslims began ripping down doors and shutters from their houses. There were scuffles between them and the Christian refugees from Anatolia who expected to move in. As the steamers carrying the Muslims finally sailed away, they let out a great cry of pain which was 'wild and full of entreaty, bitter and menacing, carried by the wind in great surges to the shore'.

Compared with the appalling conditions in which many Anatolian Christians had sailed away from their homeland, the voyages to Ayvalik were not unbearably uncomfortable. The newcomers were greeted on arrival by the booming sound of the traditional drums or *daouli*; the Turkish villages near the port were hailing the arrival of co-religionists who like them, had suffered at the hands of Greek Christians. That was their formal welcome; but as the Cretans settled down in the solid homes of the town's former Christian residents, they were increasingly conscious of the things which divided them from their fellow Turkish citizens.

In Greece, the destitute Greek Orthodox Christians who arrived from Anatolia after 1922 were taunted as *Tourkosporoi* (seeds of Turks) in many places where they threw themselves on the mercy of local people. In Turkey, the equivalent insult for Greek Muslims newly arrived in the country was '*Yari gavur*' (half infidel). The mere fact that they had lived in the Greek state made their loyalty to Islam suspect. So too was the fact that they had not shared in the sufferings of the Greek–Turkish war in Anatolia. In some parts of Turkey, 'exchanged' Muslims arriving from Greece found themselves living in prefabricated cabins.

In Ayvalik, things were somewhat better. At least there was no shortage of accommodation; the old Greek homes were spacious, well built and plentiful. But for many new arrivals, especially those who had not managed to bring money with them, the early years in Turkey were a time of grinding poverty, with little employment and scant opportunity to sell whatever they could grow or make. For long periods, relations with their natural economic partners, the Christian Greeks who lived across the sea, were too tense to allow for much legal commerce; people smuggled instead. Only after 1960 did some families in Ayvalik begin to grow prosperous from fishing and selling their catch illegally to Greeks and Italians.

When Ayvalik's current inhabitants, or their immediate forebears, began arriving in autumn 1923, they found a ghost town. The stone mansions filled with dark, heavy furniture were dusty but intact, and in some cases there remained traces of half-eaten meals. It was exactly a year since the town's Christian population had been expelled, and tokens of the prosperous and refined life once enjoyed there were still ubiquitous. But that did not make it any easier for the newcomers to settle down.

This, then, is the background to Ayvalik's present, paradoxical status. It is a place where people live in Greek-built houses, and where (for entirely different reasons) some still speak Greek, or Turkish with a Greek accent. But they would not call themselves Greek. However they express themselves, they are Turkish citizens, and wave the Turkish flag more enthusiastically than many others. Ask almost any of them about their family history, and the first thing you will be told is that they were lucky to escape from Greek violence in the nick of time. There was simply no hope, they insist, for Muslims in Greece, whatever language they spoke and whatever their own wishes may have been. Exchange, painful as it was at the time, was a necessary evil. They must be grateful to Mustafa Kemal Ataturk, the founder of their republic, for calling them to the safety of the Turkish homeland.

That is what they have been encouraged to believe, and it reflects at least one part of their real feelings. But press them a little harder, and it becomes clear that for the Muslims of Ayvali – and especially for the Cretans – Greece and Greekness are not merely a deadly danger from which they narrowly escaped. The Greek language, in its expressive Cretan variant, the dress, cuisine and customs which they shared with their Christian Cretan neighbours; all these things are an indelible part of their story. They are not supposed to feel nostalgia for their homeland, or for its Christian inhabitants, yet they do.

Language apart, the Cretan community still has characteristics which unite them to their erstwhile fellow islanders and distinguish them from other citizens of Turkey. Women are more self confident, and more likely to have jobs or small businesses; their cooking draws on a much wider range of vegetables and plants; also, ironically enough, their songs and music are less Oriental than those which are currently in fashion in Crete. Some of the Ayvali Cretans can recite poems, songs and epigrams for hours on end. And all of them, down to the third and fourth generation, at least know one: *Kriti mou omorpho nisi, to fiori tou levanti* (Crete, my beautiful island, the flower of the Levant).

Ali Onay, a small, strutting and loquacious octogenarian, was in early 2004 the grand old man of the Cretan community on Cunda. In his Cretan expansiveness, he personifies some of these contradictions. His father was a wealthy Muslim merchant in the Cretan port of Rethymnon; the family were loyal, prominent Ottoman subjects whose only language was Greek. He has his own way of rationalizing this: his native tongue is not Greek but *Kritika* (the Cretan form of speech). In the version of history that he and his community have cultivated, the conquest of Crete by the Ottoman Empire in 1669 was a 'liberation' because it ushered in a more benign regime, for Muslims and Orthodox Christians alike, than existed under the previous Venetian masters. As for Kritika, he says it came into use in early Ottoman times for practical reasons. Crete was a place administered by Ottoman Muslims – who might be Arabs, Slavs or Albanians, as well as Turks – who often took Greek Christian wives. Kritika simply became a useful lingua franca. The Muslim people of Crete were not Turks (because that concept did not yet exist) or Greek; they were Ottomans who spoke Kritika.

As Ali Onay recounts his family story, he is by turns mischievous, triumphant, sentimental and tearful. 'Nobody in our community brought more money out of Rethymnon than we did,' he chuckles, describing how his father filled the posts of a brass bed with gold coins, and packed all their trinkets, embroidery and archives into wooden trunks, beautifully made from scented cypress wood. 'I will keep those trunks for the rest of my life because they remind me of Crete,' he declares, 'even though on the day I die my children will call the rag-and-bone man and say, come and get rid of this old tat.' His words about Crete – a mixture of fond reminiscence and scathing comments about Greek nationalism – are complemented in a poignant way by the contents of his home, which occupies two upper floors of a stone house off Cunda's central square. Not only wooden trunks, but tapestries, embroidery, a faded silk gown, some carefully framed documents, sepia photographs of men with high black boots and thick moustaches and an old map of the island; all these things celebrate and mourn the experience of life on Crete. Among his most precious heirlooms are eighty pages of romantic poetry, copied out by a maternal great-grandmother. They are in Ottoman script, based on Arabic letters, but the language is Greek.

As a child, Ali Onay says, he was conscious that his parents had close friends among the Christian Greeks of Rethymnon, but the family was also wary of the Christian community's political intentions. Ali says that for at least a decade before the exchange, his entrepreneurial father had seen clearly where the compass was pointing. He had closed down most of his business and converted a great deal of his wealth into cash. 'My father understood perfectly well that there was no hope for Muslims in Crete under Greek rule, and he was quite right.'

Ali Onay insists that the death-blow to Greek–Turkish co-existence in the region came in May 1919, when the Greek army asserted control of Smyrna and gradually occupied larger swathes of Anatolia. To drive home this point, the old man recalls his parents' horror when, while still living in Rethymnon, they heard tales of the atrocities that Greek troops were committing in Turkey. One of his parents' neighbours, a Greek Orthodox butcher, had a son who was fighting with the army on the Anatolian front. The boy came back wounded, with terrible stories of how his fellow soldiers had beaten and humiliated Turkish women. The boy's parents were shocked, and so of course were Ali Onay's parents. These stories from the battlefield had confirmed his parents' presentiment that it would soon become impossible for Christians and Muslims to co-exist anywhere in the region. 'This was sad because Christians and Muslims had lived together happily for four hundred years,' Onay insists. In keeping with the standard Turkish terminology, he distinguishes between the Rums – Ottoman subjects of the Greek Orthodox faith – and the Greek state, Yunanistan. When Yunanistan sent its army to invade Turkey (in 1919) it was not a foregone conclusion that the local Rums in places like Ayvali would abet the occupying army; but in fact they did, and therefore they had to pay the price. 'Unfortunately the Rums forgot the tradition of Christian–Muslim friendship after 1919. Before the Greek army came to Anatolia, the Rums were not nationalists, they were Christians who were loyal Ottomans. But when the Greek army came here and did terrible things to the Muslim community, and the Rums collaborated with them, then it was all over. If only those terrible things hadn't happened, the Rums would still be living here now.' That is Ali Onay's wistful riposte to the ghosts of Bishop Gregorios and all the local Greeks who died in 1922.

Was his father right, then, to conclude that there was no future for Muslims in Crete or anywhere in Greece? In fact, Ali Onay maintains, the family should have left even earlier; they should have heeded the advice of cousins who had already left Crete for Izmir or other parts of Anatolia long before the exchange. But for a man who insists it was right to leave Crete, he remains very attached to the place.

Ahmet Yorulmaz, the town's most eminent writer, gives formal expression to what might be called the ideology of the Cretan–Turkish community. Sitting in a seafront cafe, clad in the beret and cravat of a Mediterranean intellectual, he holds forth passionately on the history of

the port, and also of his ancestral homeland, Crete. He is expansive, elo-
quent but respectful of the official Turkish line. 'I am a pacifist, a
humanist, I want people to be free from aggression and militarism,' he
repeats over and over again, while being careful to add that in his view,
the best way to guarantee good relations between Greek and Turk is a
high and well-defined fence; in other words separation. He is sceptical
about the prospects for a deep reintegration, or reconciliation, between
Greeks and Turks. 'They still think we're barbarians – haven't you heard
the Archbishop of Athens using that word?' And he does not believe that
Turkey will ever be accepted by Europe. 'They simply don't want us, and
one day they will be honest enough to admit that. So Turkey must simply
fall back on her own resources, trade with anybody who wants to trade
on fair terms, but otherwise rely entirely upon herself.'

In his best-known novel, *Savaşin Çocukları (Children of War)* Yorulmaz
describes the life of Muslims in Crete before the exchange. As is required,
both by ideology and collective memory, the point is made that intercommunal violence had made life so terrible that escape to a new country
became an attractive option. But Yorulmaz, who was born in Ayvalik to
Cretan parents in 1932, allows himself at least one model of happy
Christian–Muslim co-existence on Crete: the Muslim hero is looked after
by an older Christian couple, as though he were their son. But that, so to
speak, was in the good old days. Once hatred took hold and relations
between the two peoples began deteriorating, separation was the only
solution. Whatever else they think of the architects of the population
exchange – Mustafa Kemal Ataturk and Eleftherios Venizelos – Greeks
and Turks should be grateful to the two leaders who disentangled them
and saved them from one another's wrath.

> It's understandable if a Greek resents Mustafa Kemal for throwing the
> Greeks out of Anatolia, or a Turk resents Venizelos for invading
> Anatolia . . . but really we should be grateful to both men because they
> saved the Greeks from the Turks, and the Turks from the Greeks.

Those are the views of Yorulmaz, the ideologue; but he has a genetic
memory which speaks to him in a different voice. He was once invited to
Chania, the Cretan port where his parents lived, to speak at a conference
organized by the town hall. And as the party was walking along the

seafront, past the old Venetian walls, 'I let the others walk ahead, and I broke down and wept, because the place was exactly as I had imagined it in my mind's eye.' Yet he remains unmoved by the Greek blood that flowed in Ayvali in the recent past: 'It was their own fault, the Greek army shouldn't have invaded . . .'

That is a central plank in Turkish nationalist thinking, used to justify the 'terrible things' that were suffered by the Greeks of Anatolia, especially in places like Ayvalik. Because the Rums had collaborated with the invaders dispatched by Athens, they had collectively forfeited their right to live in Anatolia; they should be thankful that most of them were allowed to escape to Greece with their lives. This unforgiving view is a sort of mirror image of the Greek-nationalist view which long used the word 'unredeemed' to refer to ethnic Greeks who lived outside the Hellenic state but might one day be incorporated – as though living under the authority of one's own nation was the only human redemption worth having. As Yorulmaz sees things, far from 'redeeming' the Orthodox Christians of Anatolia, the invading Greek army sealed that community's fate because it enraged the Turks and galvanized them to expel all Christians – military and civilian – from their land. He has a point, but this axiom – 'Whatever happened was all the Rums' fault' – also serves a psychological purpose; it prevents people from reflecting on the fate of the Rums as human beings.

A different version of Greek–Turkish history is told by the first contingent of newcomers who arrived in October 1923. They were Muslims from Mytilene, bringing their own mixture of memories of living among the Greeks. Before 1912, their island had been a prosperous outpost of the Ottoman empire, of whom about three-quarters were Greek Christians and the remainder Muslims whose first language was Turkish. Among the island's prominent families were Ottoman Greeks who had grown wealthy under the Sultan's tutelage; and sophisticated Muslim seigneurs who got on fairly well with their Christian neighbours. Where the Ottoman style of governance in Crete was often crude and violent – crushing the artistic life which had flourished under the Venetians – Mytilene in late imperial times was an example of refinement as well as interreligious co-existence, at least among the rich. Many of the island's poorer inhabitants – Christian as well as Muslim – had moved to Anatolia during the 19th century in search of greater economic opportunities. But by the standards of the region and the era, late Ottoman Mytilene was a civilized place.

That well-ordered world was shaken up after the Greek navy took over the island as part of the 1912 Balkan war. Before the regular Greek forces asserted control of Mytilene, irregular Greek fighters – in Turkish *çeteler* – were allowed in certain places to run amok; killing, robbing and intimidating the Muslim Turkish community. This was in accordance with a well-known pattern in Balkan and Anatolian warfare which recurred as recently as the 1990s in Bosnia and Croatia: politicians and generals send irregular soldiers of fortune to 'soften up' an area by terrorizing or expelling its population – while officially denying all responsibility for the 'excesses' which these supposedly uncontrolled elements have committed. Fortunately the tradition of Christian–Muslim co-existence on Mytilene was fairly well entrenched, and this acted at least intermittently as a restraining influence on the Greek ceteler.

The guardian of the Mytilene Turks' collective memory is Ferhat Eris, born on that island in 1911, and ever since October 1923 a resident of Ayvalik. He grew up in the prosperous village of Skalohori near the northern tip of the island, where a minaret still stands as a memorial to Muslim residents. In his early nineties, he reels off an unselfconscious mixture of good and bad memories. Fear of the irregulars overshadowed his early childhood, he recalls, but in part because their behaviour was so erratic and unpredictable. 'The Greek çeteler killed a couple in our village but mostly they were kept away by the local Greek Christians who insisted on protecting their neighbours.' Even with the bandits, he insists, you could never tell which way they would jump.

My mother and her sister were terrified when they ran into a group of Greek irregulars. They gestured at the baby my mother was carrying – my brother – and asked if it was a boy or a girl. My mother was too frightened to lie, so she blurted out the truth. But all the chief bandit did was offer my mother some walnuts and suggest that she mix them with her breast-milk to make the baby strong.

The family of Ferhat Eris were relatively prosperous livestock farmers. Like many of his Orthodox Christian neighbours, Ferhat's father had emigrated to the United States where he saved money and broadened his horizons. On returning to his home island, he insisted that his sons improve their linguistic skills by attending Turkish school in the morning, and Greek school in the afternoon. Intercommunal relations were good: 'We lived like brothers with the Greeks, we did business together and never did anything to break one another's hearts – at least until the Greek army landed in Izmir in 1919.' Even when Greek–Turkish tensions began rising sharply, because of events on the nearby mainland, there were friendships across the divide which remained robust.

Whether consciously or unconsciously, Eris mingles his happier reminiscences of co-existence with anecdotes that drive home the inevitability of separation.

One of our neighbours on Mytilene, a very dear, joyful man called Ismail Hocaoğlu, used to speak fondly of a close Greek friend; each was ready to protect the other and help him to escape in the event of trouble flaring up. But one day, on the eve of the exchange the Greek took Ismail to Mytilene castle and pointed out a group of Greek fighters, armed to the teeth. 'You should thank the leaders of Turkey for agreeing to the population exchange, because otherwise those fighters would be coming to get you,' the Greek warned his friend.

Ferhat Eris vividly remembers the final journey across the channel, on 15 October 1923. 'The Greek governor of the island told us, the Turks of Mytilene, that we must gather up our possessions and leave. The Greeks in our village cried when we left; we had been working very well with them, they had done us no harm.' Ferhat's father managed to take 300 sheep across the channel; a Greek officer initially tried to prevent the livestock being transferred, but an American observer intervened and insisted that all moveable property, which included farm animals and even pets, could be brought by the exchangees.

Exactly two weeks after their arrival, the Turkish republic was proclaimed by the victors in the Greek–Turkish war and the Eris family, along with 10,000 other Muslims from Mytilene, found themselves citizens of this new state. Ferhat sired thirty descendants; on the wall of his sitting room, decked out with magnificent embroidery in the Greek style, there is a photograph of one of his sons in his uniform as a Turkish air force officer. But the paterfamilias did not return to the island of his birth for another seventy-eight years, although it remains clearly visible from his apartment on the Ayvalik seafront. When he did finally go back, he was able to find a handful of elderly people who remembered his family. He instantly recognized his old house, and persuaded the locals of his bona fides by pointing out the pump which his mother installed, to the enduring benefit of the entire village.

Even if they brought away some moveable assets, in the form of coins, jewellery or livestock, the Muslims of Ayvalik saw their living standards tumble during the early years of their life in Turkey. Ali Onay's father began by setting up a soap-making business, and used a sailing boat to ply his produce up and down the coast; then he bought a simple olive press. But for some of the Muslims who came from Crete with no property at all, there was little choice but to queue up at a sort of soup kitchen established by Ali's father.

To this day, town politics in Ayvalik is strongly influenced by contrasting memories of things that happened in Greece immediately prior to the exchange. Ahmet Tufekci, the politician who dominated local politics for much of the past decade, is a strident Turkish patriot whose feelings are informed by some bitter family experiences. Shortly before the exchange, his home village in Mytilene saw one of the island's worst outrages by Greek irregulars. Some twenty Muslim villagers were packed into a coffee house and shot dead. Ahmet Tufekci's father was badly wounded in that incident and was lucky to survive.

These dark memories seemed to shape the local politician's outlook. When he was mayor he resisted proposals for the restoration of Ayvalik's former Christian churches, several of which are unused and in danger of collapsing – although there are conservation groups and Turkish entrepreneurs who would willingly finance such an effort. Tufekci, an old-fashioned populist, has insisted that, even now, 'the atmosphere is not right' for the restoration of Christian churches – and that in any case, the town has more pressing construction needs like schools and clinics. One of his rivals in municipal politics is a soft-spoken and thoughtful architect, Mujdat Soylu, whose family also came from Mytilene but apparently in somewhat happier circumstances. Soylu has tried to take the sting out of the question by arguing that churches, restored as museums, could be an important tourist attraction and source of revenue. But in the end, the issue cannot be disentangled from politics or history. Restored churches would remind every visitor, and every resident, of the multiple layers of pain which lie below the facade. Not just the pain of Muslims wrenched from the Greek homes, but also the pain of the Christians who built this port but have no place here any more. Soylu's sad conclusion is that eighty years on, 'it is still too early for people to remember what happened'.

CHAPTER 2

The road to Lausanne

Who first proposed the idea of an obligatory, almost total transfer of minorities between Greece and Turkey? Rarely in history has there been a proposal whose parenthood was so vehemently denied by all the interested parties, even though each side had its own strong reasons for wanting it to be accepted. In autumn 1922, during the international deliberations that followed Turkey's triumph over the Greek army, and the death, flight or imprisonment of virtually all the Orthodox Christians in Anatolia, the possibility of a massive, agreed population exchange was in every politician's mind. Each player in the diplomatic game wanted to be able to say that the actions of others left 'no other choice'.

Nobody played these games so skilfully as Eleftherios Venizelos, the quicksilver politician who first became prime minister in 1910 and dominated the Greek political scene, whether in office or in exile, for the following three decades. He had first risen to prominence in his native Crete as a leader of the faction which demanded full union with Greece and opposed the rule of Prince George of the Hellenes, who acted as high commissioner while the island remained under notional Ottoman sovereignty. Harold Nicolson, the British diplomat, once said that in the aftermath of the First World War, Venizelos and Lenin stood out as the only two great men in Europe. Venizelos could be moody as well as charming and his private thoughts were often hard to discern. But to this day, he remains a towering figure in the modern Greek political pantheon, admired from the centre-right to the socialist left.

Despite his country's terrible state, and the fact he held no public office, the moral standing of Venizelos was, in autumn 1922, at a zenith.

This was because the Greek military blunders of the previous year and a half had been on someone else's watch: they were the responsibility of King Constantine and the monarchists, who had thrown the Cretan out of office in a surprise election result two years earlier. Most of the Greek army's biggest successes, by contrast, could be ascribed to Venizelos. He had led Greece to victory in the 1912–13 Balkan wars, guided Greece into the ranks of the anti-Ottoman Entente and secured a mandate for Greece to occupy Smyrna as a reward. Because things only turned sour for the Greeks after he left the scene in late 1920, his reputation as a genius of Hellenic strategy was unblemished. So in September 1922, when a group of embittered, anti-monarchist officers seized power in Athens and expelled King Constantine, it was Venizelos whom they asked to represent the country in world affairs. More than most other Greek politicians, he was trusted and liked by the power brokers of the world. He was also better than most of his compatriots at reading the signs of the times, and at calculating what his country should do and say. In late 1922, these instincts told him that Greece should make the best of a bad state of affairs, use the exodus of Orthodox Christians from Anatolia to repopulate its newly won northern lands, and hence consolidate Greek control of the southern Balkans. He was adamant that Greece must bear in mind its long-term interests – which were assumed, in those days, to include a homogenous or ethnically pure population – while it struggled to cope with the immediate refugee crisis.

Admirers of Venizelos insist that he was a humanist as well as a strategist. At one point, when negotiations over the details of a mass population exchange were already in full swing, he made a dramatic statement that was intended to show people that he was aware of the human implications of large-scale, forced migrations. 'Stirred by the instinctive feelings of attachment to the land and homes where their ancestors have lived for centuries, the Greek and Turkish populations involved . . . are protesting against the procedure . . . and display their dissatisfaction by all means at their disposal,' he declared. This was one of the few statements at the time which acknowledged that a population transfer would cause, as well as alleviate, human pain. But his main Turkish interlocutor, General Ismet, instantly retorted that Greek diplomats had been the first to introduce the idea of an obligatory population transfer. Not so, Venizelos insisted; the real initiator had been Fridtjof Nansen, the Norwegian entrusted by the world community to deal with the vast refugee flows created by the First World War and its aftermath. Nansen, in turn, replied that in promoting a near-total exchange of religious minorities between victorious Turkey and defeated Greece, he was simply following orders. The instruction had come from the high commissioners of the four powers – Britain, France, Italy and Japan – who had a mandate to occupy Constantinople, pending the settlement of peace terms with the Ottoman empire and its successor.

Meanwhile Lord Curzon, the British foreign secretary, made some statements that epitomized the deeply ambivalent attitude of the great powers. They knew a compulsory population shift would cause suffering, but they wanted a settlement that minimally satisfied the geopolitical interests of all the governments concerned and therefore had a chance of lasting. Curzon called the idea of a compulsory population move, 'a thoroughly bad and vicious [one] for which the world would pay a heavy penalty for a hundred years to come', but he also acknowledged that there was no other option.

In truth, the idea of moving people in large numbers across the Aegean, with the approval of the world community, was supported in almost equal measure by Venizelos; by Mustafa Kemal and his military commander Ismet; by Curzon; and by Fridtjof Nansen, the Norwegian who established the principle that aid to refugees was an obligation for the entire world community.

Nansen in particular understood that part of his job was to absorb the moral and political cost of proposals that everybody backed but nobody wanted to sponsor openly. Long before Dag Hammerskjold, Bernard Kouchner or Bob Geldof, he was perhaps the first person in the 20th century to demonstrate the uses of a dynamic personality who could enter war zones and disaster areas as an all-purpose problem solver. A hero of Arctic exploration, Nansen was also one of the first people to prove that celebrity, in the modern sense, is a convertible currency: achievement in one area can readily open doors in many other different fields. As a young man, Nansen had fascinated the newspaper readers of Europe and America by showing them that the earth had not been fully mapped and tamed. He was living proof that even in the age of railways and cables, there were still parts of the world where people could only survive if they tested the limits of their endurance. One such place was the ice cap of Greenland, where the 27-year-old Nansen and five followers made a backbreaking journey, braving some of the coldest temperatures recorded on earth.

In the second half of his life, Nansen's restless, driven personality found its outlet in diplomacy. He used his access to the mighty in many countries to become a player in world politics and humanitarian affairs. His new calling was to alleviate the pain of millions of people who were left homeless and destitute by a decade of global war and revolution. His first missions were in the chaos of post-revolutionary Russia where, against the odds, he persuaded the communists to release 400,000 prisoners from Germany and central Europe. As one of the few westerners who could communicate with Russia's new rulers, he then became involved in efforts to relieve the famine which struck the Volga region in 1921. It was here, by most assessments, that he had his first failure. He was tricked by the Bolsheviks into becoming their advocate, without realizing that they had no real interest in saving peasants' lives. But Nansen was engaged simultaneously in another task which ended more successfully: caring for the welfare and legal status of hundreds of thousands of former subjects of the Tsar who had fled the Revolution and were now stateless. By lending his name to the 'Nansen passport' – an identity card for the stateless which the governments of the world were gradually persuaded to recognize – he established the principle that refugees were every nation's responsibility. The mandate for this work came from the League of Nations, an embryonic but ambitious organization which persuaded him to become its first High Commissioner for Refugees in August 1921. Merely by accepting this new job, Nansen boosted the prestige of a small Geneva-based body which would metamorphose, later in the century, into the vast international relief agency called the UNHCR. As the explorer – and his young, well-connected British advisor, Philip Noel-Baker – came to realize, organizations in their infancy have drawbacks and advantages. The League could offer him very little money or support, but its mandate – initially restricted to Russia – could, over time, be stretched and shaped in many different directions.

So at the age of sixty, Nansen was well qualified to be a broker between Turks, Greeks and others involved in the crisis unfolding on both sides of the Aegean. By early September 1922, Nansen was working at his modest office at the League's Swiss headquarters, and Russia was still his main concern. A few weeks later, he became a central actor in a new crisis, in which the geopolitical and humanitarian stakes were every bit as high. On 19 September, he received a cable from his deputy in Allied-occupied Constantinople, Colonel Procter, confirming what the world half suspected: hundreds of thousands of Greeks and other Christians from various parts of Anatolia were fleeing for their lives following the rout of the Greek army. Some had been evacuated on ships from the burning city of Smyrna, either to the nearby islands such as Chios or Mytilene, or to the ports of Piraeus or Salonika. Among these fugitives there was a high proportion of women and children, because wherever they could, the Turks had taken the Greek male population prisoner. Some refugees were crowding into the relative safety of the Ottoman capital, which was already filled with homeless Muslim Turks, left destitute by the rampages through Anatolia of the Geek army.

A humanitarian nightmare, as well as political chaos, loomed over the battered Greek state. This was because Mustafa Kemal, the new leader of the Turkish nation, insisted firmly that Christian minorities had no place in the republic he proposed to build. This implied that Greece, with an existing population of 4.5 million, would have to absorb at least 1.2 million refugees. It seemed entirely possible that the Greek kingdom, already exhausted by more than a decade of war, might simply collapse.

Nansen had little experience of the Greek world, although his assistant, Philip Noel-Baker, whose wife Irene was heir to a large estate on the island of Euboea, knew it well. Noel-Baker had been at Nansen's side during the Russian crisis; the young Briton, viewed as one of the great talents of his generation, had already developed a shrewd understanding of his mentor and knew how to make himself useful.

As the scale of the Anatolian crisis became clear, Nansen plunged himself into the affairs of the region. He became one of the central figures in negotiating the deal whereby Greece and Turkey deported their religious minorities, not by a unilateral act of force but by international agreement. His main partners were Venizelos, who had accepted the Greek government's plea to act as its international advocate; and Lord Curzon, a former Viceroy of India who was nearing the end of a glittering career and regarded Greek and Turk with almost equal contempt. Nansen had to settle for any interlocutors he could find among the victorious Turks; they showed a prickliness in dealing with the outside world that reminded him of the Bolsheviks.

The archival evidence shows that between Venizelos and Nansen, in particular, there was an almost complete identity of views. Both were men of the world, with sensitive political antennae and a sharp understanding of the way in which diplomacy, statecraft and humanitarian politics would intersect in the 20th century. Venizelos and Nansen had both been present at the Versailles conference in 1919; the former as a virtuoso performer and the latter as an observer, gradually caught up in intrigues over food aid from America to Russia. At Versailles, the Greek and the Norwegian had moved in different circles; but three years later, in the aftermath of the Turkish triumph, they found themselves exchanging long, secret messages, and mostly agreeing about how the refugee crisis should be contained.

Nansen's first move, while still in Switzerland, was to broaden his mandate. Brandishing a cable from his envoy in Allied-occupied Constantinople, Nansen persuaded the League to extend his remit so as to embrace the refugees of Anatolia. In theory, this was just a mission of mercy, but in Nansen's powerful hands it soon became intensely political. By early October, he was in the Ottoman capital, a place rife with intrigue and opportunism. The ancient city and a strip of land either side of it had been under Allied occupation – British, French and Italian – since 1920. For Britain especially, retaining freedom of navigation through the channel that runs through the city, leading to the Black Sea was an overwhelming strategic priority. The city was also the seat of the Sultan and the religious authorities who notionally held sway over the remaining Ottoman lands. But the army of Turkey's real masters, the nationalists gathered in Ankara under the leadership of Mustafa Kemal, was advancing confidently towards the historical capital. It was the fondest hope of many of the city's Turkish inhabitants, and the dread of its remaining Greeks and Armenians, that Ankara's forces would soon march in.

At the time Nansen arrived on the shores of the Bosphorus, there was still a possibility of renewed war between Turkey and the British empire. Before demobilizing his peasant army and letting them return to their fields, Kemal had pledged to assert control, whether by force or diplomacy, over Istanbul and also eastern Thrace, the southeastern corner of Europe. The British government, although divided, and disenchanted with its earlier support of the Greek cause, had made it clear that a unilateral Turkish advance would mean war. At one point, Britain's war minister, Winston Churchill, had issued an appeal to the British Dominions to prepare to fight for the freedom of the Straits. Only on 11 October did the military representatives of Turkey, Greece, Britain, France and Italy conclude an armistice which staved off the prospect of fresh international conflict.

A few days afterwards, Nansen and Philip Noel-Baker drove out of Constantinople and observed one of the immediate consequences of the armistice: the evacuation of eastern Thrace not only by the Greek army, but by the 250,000 or so Greek civilians who lived there. To the 800,000 or more Christians already fleeing from Anatolia, another huge contingent of refugees had been added – and virtually all of them were converging on Greece. Nansen described the scene:

> When at night we came on top of a hill, I thought I saw a whole city before me with its thousands of lights – it was their camps spread out over the plain, camp-fire by camp-fire, and there they were sleeping on the ground without shelter of any kind . . . They do not know where they are going and will find no shelter when they come . . .

Another description of the exodus from Thrace was written by a young American journalist, Ernest Hemingway.

> Twenty miles of carts drawn by cows, bullocks and muddy-flanked water buffalo, with exhausted, staggering men, women and children, blankets over their heads, walking blindingly along in the rain beside their worldly goods . . . It is a silent procession. Nobody even grunts. It is all they can do to keep moving.

Hemingway could also see that the human and political consequences of this exodus would continue to be felt for a long time to come.

> There are 250,000 Christian refugees to be evacuated from eastern Thrace alone . . . Nearly half a million refugees are in Macedonia now. How they are to be fed nobody knows, but in the next month all the Christian world will hear the cry: 'Come over into Macedonia and help us.'

While that passage from Hemingway's article in the *Toronto Daily Star* has been cited frequently by modern historians, very few seem to recognize the journalist's source: he was repeating a famous sentence from the Acts of the Apostles.

In fact, the Greek farmers who fled eastern Thrace were by no means the most unlucky of the 1.6 million or so people who were forced to migrate in one direction or the other in the aftermath of the Greek–Turkish war. Families were left intact and they had, at least, a few days to save their lives, and were able to bring some livestock and possessions with them. Nor was there anything irrational or unpredictable about the scale and speed of the Thracian exodus; it was the logical outcome of the armistice, whose precise terms had been disputed angrily between Britain and France before being presented to the Turks. With the new balance of power created by Kemal's successes on the battlefield, it was generally accepted that eastern Thrace must revert to Turkish control; but France favoured the Turkish demands for a virtually instant handover, while Britain held out for a little more time, to allow the Greeks – whether military or civilian – a more dignified and orderly departure, and to stave off nationalist pressure on Constantinople.

In the end, the treaty gave the Greek army fifteen days to move out, whereupon the Allied forces would have a month at the most to transfer the territory to Turkish control. As soon as these terms became known, the Greek inhabitants realized they had not a moment to lose: in the words of a desperate telegram to Athens from the outgoing Greek administration:

> The evacuation is taking place under the most tragic and catastrophic circumstances imaginable . . . In Silivri [now a seaside resort on the eastern outskirts of Istanbul] the fifteen-day deadline has been reduced in effect to three days, and the evacuation of the panic-stricken population in such an absurdly short timetable is technically impossible because all means of transport have been requisitioned by the army. There are clear indications that public order will be disrupted after the withdrawal of the army; you will have a picture of the appalling and frightful disaster which has descended on our hapless country . . .

While the concern of Nansen and Venizelos with the Greeks of eastern

Thrace was doubtless sincere, neither politician could spend too long lamenting their exodus; there was a larger picture to consider. While Nansen parleyed with the Allied overlords of Constantinople, and sought to establish contact with the Turkish nationalists who were strengthening their grip in the rest of the country, Venizelos was shuttling between London and Paris. Ironically, he was watching the collapse of his geopolitical ambitions from the European capitals where he had achieved his greatest diplomatic triumphs a few years earlier. Still, although he had no official status, except that of advisor to the unsteady new regime in Athens, he had a better grasp of what was really happening than many of his compatriots who were closer to the scene.

For the British, he was a familiar, if controversial, interlocutor. Lord Curzon knew him well. Even as the foreign secretary was wrangling with the French to secure a slight adjustment (in a pro-Greek direction) in the armistice terms, he told Venizelos the hard truth that the basic principle of transferring eastern Thrace from Greek to Turkish control had to be swallowed. Venizelos duly transmitted this message to Athens, where it was initially resisted by the officers who had recently seized control of Greece. As the hardline generals saw things, the Greek army in Thrace was relatively intact; after the unspeakable humiliation it had suffered in Anatolia, it could at least make a stand to prevent Turkey from re-entering Europe.

Venizelos was the only Greek figure with sufficient personal standing to counter this argument. He persuaded the generals that flexibility over eastern Thrace would earn Greece goodwill at the forthcoming peace conference. But when, on 13 October, Venizelos saw the precise terms of the armistice he had made his country accept, he was horrified. From the Greek embassy in Mayfair, the most Anglophile of Greek politicians wrote to Lord Curzon in a tone of bitterness over the short deadlines for the evacuation of Thrace – which, as he argued, could exposed hundreds of thousands of people to the danger of 'complete annihilation' unless they fled instantly.

> The tragic situation of these unfortunate people will be the more increased by the fact that the Turks have not been compelled to give any amnesty to those who, thinking themselves to be Greek subjects for the past two years either served in the Greek army or collaborated in the

Greek administration, and will now be prosecuted for high treason . . . and will be hanged . . . The Greek nation feels that in the hour of its misfortune, it has not been supported in its legitimate claims . . . Its chief fault for which it is so severely treated has been . . . believing the Great War to have been fought, among other things for the liberty of small nations.

Even as he remonstrated over the Thracians' plight, the Cretan's quick mind was already pondering the next moves. Painful as it was, the exodus of the large Greek population from the Thracian ports and farms on the European side of Istanbul, and their settlement a hundred miles further to the west, would have one beneficial effect from the viewpoint of Greek strategy. The evacuation of eastern Thrace would 'Hellenize' the area immediately to the west, where Greek-speaking Christians had previously been a small minority, easily outnumbered by Turkish- or Bulgarian-speaking Muslims and Christians who identified with Bulgaria. Fear of Bulgaria, which was keen to regain an outlet to the Aegean, and had made a secret diplomatic agreement with Ankara in mid-1922, was almost as strong in Athens as fear of the Turks. That was an added incentive to make a deal with Turkey which Greeks and Turks could accept, and which would keep Bulgarian territorial ambitions at bay. For all these reasons, then, a transfer of the Greek population from eastern to western Thrace could be a price worth paying. More important, the same principle – shifting populations in order to 'tidy up' the ethnic and political map – could be reapplied on a much larger scale.

That idea occurred almost simultaneously to Venizelos and Nansen. Even before witnessing the uprooted Thracian peasants camped out on a hillside, Nansen's practical instincts told him that since many of the Greek refugees were farmers, they must be resettled on agricultural land, and enabled to feed themselves, as rapidly as possible; the period in which they were dependent on handouts must be kept to a minimum. There was only one way in which the requisite amount of Greek land could be freed up in a short time, and that was to transfer to Turkey the Ottoman Muslim population of Greece, amounting to about 500,000 people. Hence the confidential letter sent by Nansen, from the Pera Palace hotel in Constantinople, to Venizelos in London on 10 October. He describes as 'indescribably grave' the situation of the refugees, numbering up to

750,000, who were already fleeing, or had fled, from Anatolia to Greece. Despite the best efforts of the Greek authorities and relief agencies, the new arrivals were inadequately fed, sheltered and clothed, and the resources needed to care for them even till the following summer were not available.

> The fundamental problem . . . is that of the ultimate fate of the refugees. Everyone appears to agree that it is hopeless to expect either that the Turks will agree to receive them again in Asia Minor, or that the refugees themselves would agree to go . . . They must, therefore, be set-tled elsewhere, and I presume it will be the purpose of the Greek government, either as a result of a treaty with the Turkish government or without such a treaty to settle them in the vacant lands of Macedonia and Western Thrace. So far as I understand the matter, it appears to me that the exchange of populations will be so lengthy and difficult an undertaking that in any case, vast numbers of the refugees will have to be settled on lands which are at present unoccupied and uncultivated . . .

Venizelos, for his part, saw no reason why the population exchange should be 'lengthy and difficult'. On 13 October, in between complaining to Lord Curzon over the cruelty of the armistice terms, he sent Nansen a cable asking him to 'endeavour to arrange that transfer of the population begin before signature of peace'. Two days later, Nansen secured his mandate from the high commissioners of Britain, France, Italy and Japan – the Allied powers overseeing Constantinople – to 'take all possible steps' to negotiate a population exchange 'as soon as possible, independently of the peace negotiations'. So it was technically true to say that Nansen was merely acting on behalf of the Allies when he promoted the two-way pop-ulation transfer; but it was a mandate which he had actively sought.

Although a certain amount of Macedonian land might be freed up by confiscating estates, either from private landowners or the church, it seemed to Venizelos that removing the Muslim population was not merely desirable but essential if the incoming refugees from Anatolia were to be resettled. An agreed population exchange was the only way this could be achieved. But what exactly did this mean? As a diplomatic instrument, it was not entirely new. During the previous decade, each new round of fighting over the spoils of the Ottoman empire in Europe had led to huge population movements, and in at least two cases, such movements had been endorsed and encouraged by the governments involved. As a result of the first Balkan war of 1912, hundreds of thousands of European Muslims had fled to the Ottoman empire. This in turn prompted the new Turkish regime to 'make room' for the newcomers by expelling Greeks from parts of the Anatolian coast. The second round of fighting, in which Turkey grabbed back some land from Bulgaria, left both Bulgarians and Turks on the 'wrong' side of a newly established border. So as part of their peace settlement, it was agreed that people on either side of the frontier within a fifteen-mile band could move to the states that claimed their allegiance.

One motive for the small-scale Turkish–Bulgarian 'population exchange' of 1913 (apparently the first time the term was used) was only disclosed by a Turkish diplomat many years later. Turkey at that time expected another war with Greece in which it hoped to recover Mytilene and several other Aegean islands. It was therefore keen to regularize its relations with Bulgaria and 'even out' the ethnic map. This affirmed an important principle in diplomacy. For countries that are keen to pick fights and expand their territory, it can be useful to have 'strategic minorities' beyond the national territory whose grievances can become an excuse for war. But when two countries are attempting to make peace, population swaps can be a useful of 'tidying up' the frontier and preventing any unwanted flare-ups over disgruntled minorities.

After the First World War, in which the Bulgarians were defeated along with their German and Ottoman allies, there was another small-scale population exchange, this time between Bulgaria and Greece. When Bulgaria was forced to give up western Thrace, which briefly served as its access to the Aegean, the territory's new Greek masters wanted to get rid of the Bulgarians who lived there. The Greek–Bulgarian population exchange of 1919, which was in theory voluntary, served as a handy way to make western Thrace a little more Greek.

On the eve of the 1914–18 war, a deal on a larger scale had been worked out in principle by Venizelos, as Greek prime minister, and Turkey's chief diplomat in Athens. Although it was never implemented, this accord would have exchanged significant numbers of Muslims in Greece's new, northern territories for Greeks then living in Anatolia. It is

easy to see why this seemed expedient. It would 'relieve' Greece of a large
and potentially disloyal Muslim minority and help to 'Turkify' the west
coast of Anatolia. At that point, apparently, Venizelos saw little immediate prospect of ever bringing western Anatolia under Greece's political
control.

So in autumn 1922, after Kemal's military triumph, this idea re-
emerged in a far more drastic form. Watching events in London, Venizelos
came to the conclusion that the compulsory eviction of Greece's entire
Muslim population (ideally with the consent of Turkey and the international community, but if necessary without) was the best way to absorb
the Orthodox Christian refugees and stabilize the country. Writing to the
Greek foreign ministry on 17 October, he observed:

> It is no exaggeration to say that the future of Greece hangs on whether
> a good or a bad resolution of this question is found. Failure will lead
> to disasters which one shudders to contemplate, while a successful solu-
> tion will enable us, within a few years, to recover from the terrible
> burdens which the war's unhappy outcome has imposed on us – and
> to ensure, despite the collapse of Greater Greece, the consolidation of
> a Great Greece – whose borders will never be secure unless western
> Thrace and Macedonia are established as Greek territories, not only
> politically but ethnically . . .

In other words, Venizelos already saw in the drama of the refugees an
opportunity as well as a problem. Although his vision of a Greater Greece
straddling Europe and Asia had evaporated, it should now be possible to
consolidate his earlier territorial gains, the northern Greek lands, by
replacing their Muslim population with Anatolian Christians. Moreover,
at least when addressing his own, rather desperate, compatriots, he was
very frank about how this result should be achieved.

> This means that without the immediate departure of the Turks in
> Greece, the problem of housing the [Christian] refugees will be insol-
> uble, and their final resettlement will also be virtually insoluble. And
> if Dr Nansen does not manage to secure the consent of the government
> of Ankara to this immediate departure, the [Athens] government must
> be prepared, as soon as the [Greek] evacuation of eastern Thrace is

completed within four or five weeks, to order the compulsory eviction of the Turkish population in Greece. We will request that this evacuation should be effected under the supervision of Dr Nansen, who will certify that it has taken place in the most civilized way. The departing [Muslims] must not only be allowed, but helped, to take all their moveable property with them. This task should be entrusted secretly to a committee headed by a senior official, which will determine the deadlines by which each province will be evacuated, starting with western Thrace, to be followed by western Macedonia and the islands . . . If, as I calculate, there are about 350,000 Turks in Greece – including western Thrace – then it would be possible to accommodate, in the houses they leave behind, up to 500,000 Christian refugees and perhaps as many as 700,000. It is obvious to what degree this eases the problem of the immediate accommodation for the [Christian] refugees; and the business of their definitive resettlement will also be facilitated, as refugees fill the vacuum which the departure of the Turks will create. From the start, basic care should be taken to ensure that rural communities [from Anatolia] are installed in rural areas, and urban migrants in urban areas . . .

Venizelos was not only advocating draconian measures; as a politician with a better than average sense of the international mood, he had clear ideas about easing the presentational difficulties that a forced eviction of Muslims would bring.

The government should be aware that our moral standing in the civilized family of nations has been terribly diminished as a result of the arson and other acts of violence which the Greek army allowed itself to commit in Asia Minor, acts which have been very efficiently exploited by Turkey's formidable and well-organized propaganda machine. We urgently need, therefore, to regain the moral esteem of the world, and the compulsory population transfer must be carried out in such a way that this measure – which in itself is assuredly a barbaric one – will more readily be accepted as an action of last resort, carried out with the care and sympathy of a civilized people for the plight of those who face compulsory transfer. Faced with the protests that this measure will undoubtedly arouse in foreign countries, I am prepared publicly to acknowledge the 'paternity' of this idea, and to defend it. Whatever remains of the prestige I have enjoyed internationally will help to moderate the indignation . . .

Venizelos, as this letter shows, had a very modern sense both of public relations and the politics of humanitarian intervention. He understood the game in which local actors must engage: advancing the interests of their own side (because nobody else will) while presenting to the world an image of sweet reason and disinterested humanism. Each party must denounce the actions of the other side as crimes not merely against its own people, but as outrages against humanity – while ensuring that its own actions, however ruthless, seem either reasonable or at worst, an understandable response to unbearable provocation. In his understanding of this imperative, Venizelos was every bit the equal of the nationalist power brokers of more recent conflict zones, from the Balkans to Afghanistan.

But what of Nansen, envoy of the international community? Was he shocked by the ideas that Venizelos was putting forward? It seems not. On the contrary, the idea of tough and swift action to stabilize the region, through a massive exercise in ethnic engineering, seems to have appealed to the Norwegian's penchant for grand strategy and practical action. Nor did Nansen need much encouragement to adopt the negotiating tactic advocated by Venizelos; in other words, induce the Turkish authorities to accept a negotiated two-way exchange by warning that the Greek government might otherwise expel its Muslim community unilaterally.

On the same day as he wrote his frank message to the Greek foreign ministry, the Cretan sent an almost equally revealing letter to Nansen in Constantinople, in which various ways of influencing the Turkish side were suggested. 'Perhaps if reasons of a higher order fail to persuade Mustafa Kemal' of the case for a two-way population exchange, said Venizelos, then, 'the Greek government under the pressure of unavoidable necessity will be very probably compelled to impose this migration on the Turks living on Greek soil'. An even more pressing concern for Venizelos was the fate of the Greek men who had been captured by the Turkish army as it swept through Anatolia. On this matter, too, he urged Nansen to pass on to the Turkish side the message that Greece was prepared to retaliate in kind.

With regard to the question of the release of males of military age, it might be possible for you, if the necessity should arise, to bring to Kemal's notice that if his attitude remains uncompromising, the Greek government remains uncompromising; the Greek government will proceed to take reprisals in the form of a male mobilization of the Musulmans in Greece. I sincerely regret to have to place before you these arguments of force, but to the Oriental mind these may possibly prove more effective should others fail . . .

How, then, did the 'Oriental mind' respond? In Allied-occupied Istanbul, where the Turkish nationalist writ did not yet run, Nansen had difficulty at first in finding negotiating partners who spoke for the Ankara government. Mustafa Kemal himself had no interest in holding face to face negotiations; he was far too busy dealing with the aftermath of victory and imposing his authority on a fractious coalition. But at meetings with Kemal's trusted lieutenants, Nansen seems to have used a version of the arguments suggested by Venizelos. According to his aide Philip Noel-Baker, Nansen put the following case to Refet Pasha, the governor elect of Istanbul:

The Greek government from sheer lack of living space might feel obliged to expel their half million Turks; if the treaty were made which he proposed, those Turks would be moved under the supervision of an international commission, the value of their lands would be impartially assessed and when they arrived in Turkey they would receive full payment for everything they had left behind. In any case, Turkey would need new citizens to fill the towns and villages which the Greeks had fled.

Having smashed the Greek army and driven the great majority of Orthodox Christians out of Anatolia already, the victorious Turks were in no mood for lectures from their defeated foes or their proxies. Moreover, the threat of unilateral measures against the Ottoman Muslims of Greece must have seemed to Ankara like so much bluff. If such action had been attempted, it would have provided the Turkish side with a plausible ground to march on into western Thrace, a region that was in the nationalists' sights, or to undertake further horrible retaliation against the

Orthodox Christians who remained in Anatolia. But the general principle of a negotiated Greek–Turkish population exchange had already been acknowledged as an attractive one by the Turkish nationalists; Venizelos and Nansen were pushing at an open door. As early as March 1922, Lord Curzon had been told by an envoy of Mustafa Kemal that: 'The Ankara government was strongly in favour of a solution that would satisfy world opinion and ensure tranquillity in its own country. It was ready to accept the idea of an exchange of populations between the Greeks of Asia Minor and the Muslims in Greece.'

At that time, with the Greek army firmly entrenched in the heart of Anatolia and no immediate threat to the region's Orthodox Christians, such an outcome would have seemed like a huge, gratuitous concession by the Allies to a Turkish nationalist government whose legitimacy Britain did not acknowledge. Lord Curzon replied to the envoy, Yussuf Kemal Bey, in a way that seems naive and poignant with the benefit of hindsight. While 'something was possible in this direction' such a transfer was not a complete solution because, 'the [Greek] population of Asia Minor was somewhere near half a million. For physical reasons such a large number could not entirely be transported and for agricultural and commercial reasons many of them would not be willing to go.'

By October 1922, the problem of 'willingness to go' among the Greek Orthodox of Anatolia, who in fact numbered closer to 1.5 million, had of course been settled. The great majority were either dead, captive or scraping an existence in Turkish ports or Greek refugee camps. But the March proposal was the first signal from Mustafa Kemal's camp that Muslims from Greece (and many other former Ottoman territories) would be welcomed and indeed encouraged to migrate to the new Turkish state that he wanted to build. He saw no compelling reasons, either strategic or humanitarian, to 'leave in place' the Ottoman Muslims who lived in Greece – with the significant exception of western Thrace, which some Turkish nationalists still dreamed of reclaiming through a plebiscite.

In early September 1922, when his forces were already chasing the desperate Greek army towards the Mediterranean, Kemal raised the idea of a population exchange once again. This time the proposal was in the form of negotiating instructions to his envoy Fethiye Bey, who was dispatched to London in order to give the impression that Ankara was open to armistice talks. In fact, as Turkish historians have noted with approval,

Fethiye's whole mission had an element of bluff; after its victories in the heart of Anatolia, the Turkish army had no incentive to lay down arms until it had driven the Greeks out of the region, including Izmir. But the proposals that Fethiye Bey brought to England were an accurate enough statement of Ankara's post-war demands. He called for massive reparations from Greece for physical and moral damage, the immediate transfer to Turkish authority of Constantinople and eastern Thrace – and for a population exchange. On 22 October Kemal confirmed this position: he sent Nansen a short cable announcing that the idea of an exchange was 'acceptable in principle' and inviting him to negotiate the details with his deputies.

On the lips of politicians who were prepared, in any case, to expel minorities unilaterally, what exactly did an 'agreed population exchange' imply? Each party to such an agreement was saying, in effect: I authorize you to expel, and send to my country, those of 'my' people – my ethnic kin or my co-religionists – who live on your soil. In other circumstances, I might regard such an expulsion as a hostile act, but by virtue of the deal we are now concluding, I will accept and facilitate this measure – and in return, I am obtaining your permission to expel 'your' people from my soil.

The other difference between unilateral expulsion and 'exchange' is that in the latter case, the governments co-operate to ensure some compensation for the people involved on either side. To put it crudely, mutually agreed exchange allows the governments involved to reap the 'benefits' of a unilateral eviction of unwanted minorities, without incurring the moral opprobrium.

To liberal western ears, the ideas of governments 'benefiting' from the removal of undesired minorities sounds repulsive. But most of the new nation-states that emerged from the ruins of the Ottoman, Austro-Hungarian and Czarist empires thought in exactly those terms. This raises the question of where the perceived 'benefits' of expulsion lie. Whether it happens in Idi Amin's Uganda, Nasser's Egypt or Serb-controlled Bosnia, the unilateral expulsion of a minority is often an act of pure self-interest and calculation on the part of nationalist factions or leaders who are struggling to consolidate power. Even when cloaked in romantic nationalist ideology, the main point about such an act is that it provides the leader with spoils which can be distributed to loyal supporters. In the case of an agreed exchange, the governments involved restrain their self interest; and at least in theory, mitigate the harm they are inflicting on the communities involved by guaranteeing their lives, helping them to take away some goods and obtain compensation for their fixed assets. In return, each state secures 'loyal' and dependent citizens, while ridding itself of potentially disloyal 'aliens'.

As of mid-October 1922, it seemed to Nansen that he could and must proceed quickly with a grand bargain between Greece and Turkey on precisely those lines. One reason for urgency was the obvious fact that the unilateral expulsion of Anatolia's Christians was grinding on. Turkey's ports were filling up with refugees who had been driven from their homes and were desperately hoping to be evacuated. This led pessimists on the Greek side to fear that the Turks had a diminishing incentive to regulate by agreement a course of action – the expulsion of all, or virtually all, Christians – which they were rapidly implementing anyway. But if Mustafa Kemal saw advantages in a negotiated accord, it was partly because he, like Venizelos, hoped for a lasting peace between Turkey and Greece; and also because of the argument which Nansen himself had used – the influx of Muslims from Greece would to some extent fill the demographic and economic hole left by the departing Christians.

In the third week of October, Nansen and Noel-Baker went to Athens to make sure the Greek leadership, guided from afar by Venizelos, fully understood and supported the idea of a population exchange overseen and indeed economically assisted by the League of Nations. Nansen anticipated with great prescience the role that would played by international financial institutions, like the World Bank and International Monetary Fund, in the latter half of the 20th century. He explained to the Greek foreign minister, Nikolaos Politis, how the League of Nations, by agreement among its leading members, could boost Greece's creditworthiness and help it raise the funds needed to care for the refugees. When Nansen presented the minister with a detailed written proposal, it became clear how desperately grateful Politis and his government were for help from any quarter, and what huge, almost childish faith they had in Nansen. 'Before I read this paper,' Politis reportedly said, 'I want to tell you that Greece accepts everything you propose. I don't need to read it to say that all Greeks know your friendship for our people, and our government has implicit faith in your wisdom.'

With the grudging assent at least of the Turkish nationalists, and the adulation of a desperate Greece, Nansen seemed well placed to clinch the accord. But at the end of October, he encountered a serious problem. His friends in Athens were assuming that Constantinople and its surroundings, in other words the area occupied by the Allies, would be excluded from the exchange – so that the 300,000 or more Greek Orthodox Christians, many of them very prosperous, who lived there could remain secure in their homes.

Kemal made no such assumption. For Turkish nationalists, the Ottoman capital's large population of Christians seemed to epitomize the foreign domination of Turkey's economy which they were determined to overturn. Furthermore, the Christians had discredited themselves in Turkish eyes by actively supporting the Greek nationalist campaign to annex western Anatolia, and to grab the city they longed to see restored as a new Byzantium. So the expulsion of the Christians on the Bosphorus was seen not merely as legitimate but desirable. As Mustafa Kemal's envoy Hamid Bey told Nansen on 31 October: 'the Ankara government only permitted him to negotiate on the basis of a total and enforced exchange of populations'. In other words, with Constantinople very much included.

When Nansen relayed this message to the Greeks, their reaction was one of dismay, and they made this clear. Nansen felt that the inclusion of Constantinople, with all its economic importance and historical resonance, in the population exchange was a pill the Greeks might have to swallow; but as Venizelos saw things, a fresh exodus into Greece from the banks of the Bosphorus would neutralize the anticipated 'benefit' of expelling the Muslim population. As he wrote from Paris on 1 November:

> The problem posed by the demands of the Turks for the eviction of our ethnic kin in Constantinople is dire. If tens of thousands of the Constantinopolitan Greeks are added to the tens of thousands who are already taking refuge on our soil, then the already very difficult problem of resettling them will become insoluble. Nor will the eviction of the Turks in Greece provide us with any relief because their numbers hardly exceed those of Greeks in Constantinople and the surrounding area.

Nansen, meanwhile, was advising the Greeks to accept the 'principle' of total exchange, including Constantinople, on the grounds that it was still desirable to secure an agreement as quickly as possible – and the Turkish side might be persuaded to make some exception for the Ottoman capital at a later date. If an accord was struck, the Turks might have to hold back from expelling the Constantinople Greeks, since compensating them for their vast property holdings would be too expensive; but if there was no accord, a large part of the city's Christian minority might leave anyway, with no right to sell or be compensated for their houses and land.

Even Venizelos could see that if the Turks were determined to expel all Christians without exception, there might at some point be no option but to regulate the process by treaty. But his immediate reaction was that Greece should harden its position. It should redouble preparations to expel the Muslims of Greece unilaterally (which might be easier in the current relatively fluid situation than later) while holding back Muslim men aged between eighteen and forty-five as hostages for the Greek men detained in Turkey. As a signal of its resolve, Greece should also make sure that its army had at least six battle-ready brigades. While renewed fighting was neither expected nor desirable, Venizelos apparently thought a show of strength might induce 'the Turks to show greater respect for us than they show to our former allies'. This was unusually blunt language for the Cretan politician. But he felt betrayed by the lack of response from Turkey – or anywhere else – to the goodwill he had shown over eastern Thrace. It was under his influence, after all, that the Greek army had agreed to evacuate that region, along with its Greek inhabitants, while largely holding back from the atrocious practices, including widespread burning of towns, which had so discredited their retreat from Anatolia.

The differences between Nansen, Venizelos and the Greek government in Athens should not be exaggerated. Nansen understood very clearly why the Turkish demand for including the Ottoman capital in a population exchange seemed impossible for the Greeks to accept; both for sentimental reasons – the fact that only months earlier, Greeks had been dreaming of reestablishing an empire with Constantinople as its capital – and for practical ones. So long as they remained in place, the Greeks of Constantinople were a bastion of Hellenic financial and commercial power. As refugees, they would be an unbearable burden on an already desperate homeland.

On 3 November, Nansen – who was still in Istanbul, waiting to see if the Turks would show flexibility – wrote a sympathetic letter to Politis, the Greek foreign minister. 'I have myself come to the conclusion that it would be impossible to negotiate an agreement between the governments of Greece and Turkey on the basis of a forced population exchange, including the city of Constantinople.' The Turkish demand for the city's inclusion had caused Nansen 'grave concerns' and he had conveyed this opinion to the Allies on whose behalf he was supposedly negotiating. This was in response to a letter from Politis which expressed indignation and above all fear over the political and psychological repercussions which the forced departure of the Constantinople Greeks would have in Athens. In accepting the principle of a population exchange, Politis revealingly made clear, the Greek side had initially imagined that the result would be almost entirely to their advantage. On the one hand, it would formally accept the expulsion of the Christian population from Anatolia and Thrace, which was in any case a *fait accompli*; but it would also secure the release from captivity of the Greek men whose dependents had already fled from Anatolia to Greece – and more important, it would rid Greece of its Muslim population, thus freeing up space for the newcomers. That, said Politis, was how Greece initially imagined things:

> It never entered our heads to suppose that additional Greek popula-
> tions, and in particular that of Constantinople, would be obliged to
> abandon their homes. Not only is Greece already saturated with
> refugees, and quite incapable of accepting any more . . . but the con-
> science of the nation would balk at seeing a Greek government – and
> especially the present one, which is only a provisional administration –
> accept the monstrous event which the mass exodus of nearly 400,000
> Constantinople Greeks would amount to . . . I feel sure that these con-
> siderations will find a profound resonance in your conscience as an
> impartial and civilized man – and that your generous spirit will insist
> on delimiting the proposed negotiations to the lines earlier foreseen.

Even as these feverish exchanges about the principle and the scope of a population transfer were in progress, a separate diplomatic game was unfolding over the location, and terms of reference for a broader peace conference. Initially Turkish officials insisted that their country's fate should be decided on their own territory, ideally in Istanbul. Only with great reluctance did they accept Lausanne, in neutral Switzerland, as a venue. Initially the British government insisted on inviting to the peace conference both the Sultanate and the new Ankara government, to the latter's intense irritation. But with every passing day, the authority of the Sultan was ebbing away and that of the nationalists was rising, even in the territory along the Bosphorus where the Allies were in charge. On 16 November Sultan Vahdettin – the thirty-sixth and last sovereign of the Ottoman Empire – told the British he feared for his life, and the following night he was spirited away from Istanbul by sea. This settled the question of who would speak for Turkey; as the Sultan fled, the nationalist delegation to the peace talks had already left by train for Switzerland, expecting the conference to open on 13 November. In fact it was delayed by another week; this intensified the Turks' suspicion that Britain, as host of the conference, was using the extra time to garner diplomatic support and deny them the fruits of their victory on the battlefield.

Nansen and Venizelos had hoped that a population exchange could be negotiated well before the peace conference started. The impasse over the Constantinople Greeks had made that impossible, but as the conference opened with a sonorous welcome from the President of Switzerland, it was widely understood that the fate of religious minorities in both Greece and Turkey was among the most pressing items on the agenda. As the diplomats exchanged niceties, every public space in Athens and the adjacent port of Piraeus, from theatres to government offices to royal palaces, was filling up with the ragged, destitute and sick migrants from the Christian communities of Anatolia.

CHAPTER 3

Lost brothers, lost sisters: from Samsun to Drama

We lived in the mountains. We were being killed, and we killed. We were being burned down, and we burned. In the end a truce was made in 1922, and we came down to Greece by sea from Samsun.

My sister was caught when the war ended. The Turkish army came to the place where we were. In the ensuing battle my sister, a young girl, was captured. A baker from Kavak took her and adopted her. He raised her as though she were really his child.

In 1961, when I went to Samsun, I found her. I had been looking for her since 1958. I wrote to the mayor of Kavak. He did what no Greek would have done for me. He told me in his letter that wars do thing like that; that whatever had happened, Turks and Greeks were brethren. He found my sister and gave her my letter, and we corresponded until 1961 when I went to see her myself. She didn't recognize me.

She had three daughters and a son. The boy was serving in the Turkish army. The oldest girl asked many questions about our whole generation: her grandfather, her grandmother, about her mother's other siblings. But they had all been killed. In the end she said to me: 'Oh uncle, our mother was a Greek woman, and she became a Turk. What does that make us?'

Michael Papadopoulos, interviewed in Kiriyia village
near Drama in 1964 by the Centre for Asia Minor Studies

Like so many towns in Turkey and Greece, the port of Samsun is distinguished more by the beauty of its natural surroundings, and by the richness and complexity of its historical associations, than by anything noteworthy in its modern appearance as a hub of commerce and industry. It was founded 2700 years ago in the space between two fertile deltas. West of Samsun, the 'red river' (in Turkish, *Kızılırmak*) gushes into the Black Sea after twisting through much of Anatolia; on the east side is the mouth of the 'green river' (in Turkish, *Yesilırmak*) which bisects some graceful old towns, as well as rain-soaked valleys which resemble Ireland or Wales. Towering above the harbour is the peak known as Agiou-tepe. This and other nearby mountains were the scene, in the early 1920s, of some of the fiercest and most proudly remembered clashes in the decade of war which led to the virtual separation of the Turks from the Greeks. In the town itself, one of the few impressive monuments is a giant equestrian statue of Mustafa Kemal Ataturk, who sailed into Samsun on 19 May 1919, determined to restore his country's honour and reestablish Turkish control over Anatolia. His mission was given added impetus by the anger felt among almost all Ottoman Muslims over the Greek occupation, just a few days earlier, of the port known by Turks as *gavur Izmir* (infidel Smyrna).

While Samsun could never match the sophistication or cultural life of that city, the modern histories of the two ports have features in common. In both places, commerce was once dominated by an extrovert Greek Orthodox community which burgeoned in the late 19th century and attracted immigrants from Greece. In both cities, this growing wealth was used to galvanize, and rehellenize, the less sophisticated Orthodox Christians of the nearby hinterland, who in some cases spoke nothing but Turkish.

By December 1922, Greek Samsun (or *Amisos*, to give the place its ancient Greek name) was vanishing as rapidly as Greek Smyrna had done three months previously. The final chapter of a struggle for control of the Black Sea mountains, and hence for the Black Sea coast, was unfolding, with human consequences that worsened by the day. Whenever they could manage it, well-armed men were slipping away by sea to Russia, and eventually Greece, after hiring or stealing boats. They were members of the Orthodox Christian guerrilla bands who had done battle, by the merciless laws of mountain warfare, with Turkish soldiers and irregulars for the last several years. At the same time, the unarmed members of their community – tens of thousands of women, children and old people – were staggering down the mountains towards the harbour, in the hope of being shipped to Greece or any other place of safety. Many of these people had been on the move, in terrible conditions, since mid-1921. That was when the Turkish nationalists, facing a Greek assault on their headquarters in Ankara, undertook the biggest of a series of internal deportations of Orthodox Christians in the Black Sea region. In some cases, guerrilla leaders brought their families up to the mountains with them, reckoning this was the only way to save them from exile. But only a small percentage of the region's Orthodox Christian population was holed up in these upland strongholds; most remained in their villages until they were burned out or marched away.

In this war, neither side had a monopoly of cruelty. The incineration of a Christian village was avenged, wherever possible, by the destruction of a Muslim one. Both sides engaged in hostage taking as a way of making money. If ransoms were not paid, the victims were killed. On both sides, the mountain warriors were heirs to an outlaw tradition whose origins were as much criminal and opportunistic as they were sectarian or political. They were warlords in a sense which the regional strongmen of modern Afghanistan would recognize.

By the end of 1922, their guns had fallen silent and peace talks were in progress in Switzerland. In the Samsun area, a sort of local truce had been in force since March 1922. This was agreed under pressure from tradesmen who complained that perpetual war had drained the region of its population and wrecked their business. But in the final quarter of the year, as the Turkish army prevailed elsewhere in Anatolia, there was a fresh drive to rid the Black Sea region of its remaining Orthodox Christians, whether armed or otherwise. The Christians, for their part, could easily see that escape by sea was their only hope. Yet the shipment of refugees from Black Sea ports was needlessly snarled up by mutual suspicion between Turkey and Greece. The Greek government had offered to send ships which would have removed the refugees for little or no payment, but the Turkish government would not allow this. As the Turks saw things, too little time had elapsed since the bombardment of that stretch of the coastline by the Greek navy. Britain was willing to help with an evacuation, but not on the huge scale that was needed. Ships from several other countries were prepared to take refugees away from Samsun, but only for payment. Some vessels were bringing refugees straight to Greece; but as Greek ports became inundated, others were leaving their human cargo in the care of the Allied military mission which was still occupying Constantinople.

A report circulating among aid agencies, including Britain's Save the Children Fund, gives a flavour of the situation in Samsun harbour in late 1922.

> Information dated November 27th places the numbers already arrived at this port from the interior at 30,000 [with] additional numbers arriving at the rate of 500 *per diem*. A British steamer was *en route* for Samsun on December 7th to remove 2500. On about the same date, two French ships, one Italian and four Turkish have arrived at Constantinople [from Samsun] in the last few days, crowded to their utmost capacity with such refugees as were able to pay seven Turkish pounds as passage money.

Another circular, dated 11 December, reports that:

> . . . the refusal of the Kemalists to permit Greek ships to embark Greek and Armenian refugees has resulted in a decision to employ British ships which will bring refugees from Samsun, Trebizond and other ports to Constantinople whence transhipment to Greek vessels for Greek destinations will be carried out. American naval authorities are unable to assist the enterprise, but are placing destroyers conveniently near the ports of evacuation to act as observers.

What lay behind these laconic notes were some furious and unseemly diplomatic battles. Everybody, including the Turkish authorities, wanted to get the Orthodox Christian refugees away from the Black Sea ports as quickly as possible; no country was willing and able to conduct the whole evacuation; and Turkey was wary of opening its territorial waters to erstwhile enemies. In the end it was Turkish ships who took many of the refugees away from Samsun, in conditions that were truly hellish, in part because so many people were sick before they boarded.

Among survivors and their descendants who now live in Greece, the

voyage from Samsun, and the long trek over the mountains which preceded it, are remembered in two different ways. On the one hand, there is
a romantic tradition which stresses the bravery of the Black Sea fighters
who held out to the end in their mountain hideouts, waging an unequal
battle with the Turks at a time when many voices on the Greek side
regarded their struggle in that region as a hopeless one. People recall with
admiration that these fighters eagerly accepted clandestine assistance from
the Russians, in 1915–17, and (albeit only spasmodically) from the Greek
army from 1919 onwards. By doing so, they effectively opened an additional front in a long war against the Turks which was waged by Russia and
the other Entente powers during the First World War; and then by Greece,
initially with the support of the Entente powers, after 1919.

That is one part of the story now told in Greece. Another strand of collective memory stresses the brutality of the evictions, and forced marches
over harsh terrain, which came to a head in mid-1921 but had been
imposed intermittently on the Orthodox Christians of the Black Sea
region since the middle of the First World War. This tradition often presents the deportations as a gratuitous act of sadism, part of a
long-premeditated plan to remove virtually all non-Muslim, non-Turkish
minorities from Anatolia.

It is not, in fact, logically possible for both traditions to be fully accurate. If it is true that Turkey, whether Ottoman or nationalist, faced a
lethal challenge from fighters who were co-operating with its enemies,
then the mass deportations, cruel as they were, were not gratuitous or
even egregious by the standards of warfare in the Ottoman or post-
Ottoman world. They were, by Turkey's lights, an act of self-defence,
based on the principle that mountain guerrillas are unbeatable as long as
the civilian communities that sustain them are allowed to remain intact.
The same principle was cited during the 1990s by Turkish generals fighting the Kurds, and in the early 21st century by Russian commanders
battling the Chechens. However terrible its consequences, the Turkish
masterminds of the 1921 deportation were neither the first nor the last
people to be guided by that iron logic: irregular fighters, with a modicum
of popular support, can never be defeated without removing the civilian
population that succours them. That is what any Turkish or pro-Turkish
historian, faced with Greek allegations, would invariably point out.

But none of this historical point scoring lessens the pain of tens of thousands of women and children who were marched away from hitherto peaceful villages. They were herded southwards for weeks on end, as far as the Kurdish-inhabited lands which now form the extreme southeast of Turkey, in conditions which only the hardiest survived. Whether by design or otherwise, the participants in these marches ran into Turkish armed gangs who abducted young women. Almost every family faced desperately hard choices over how best to protect its children: to leave them in the care of a local Turkish family, or to bring them on a trek over the mountains in which they might die of cold or exhaustion. In the case of families with daughters of marriageable age, there was an equally excruciating dilemma. Should they be 'married off' to local Turks, and hence guaranteed a life of relative security and comfort amid the community which was now dominant, or brought along on a march whose hazards included abduction and rape? Among descendants of those who did live through the ordeal and escape to Greece, there are vivid memories of the strange twists of providence that made possible their survival and eventual departure.

The following story was told in early 2005, by a middle-aged man in a northern Greek village where Turkish-speaking Christians from Havza, south of Samsun, settled in 1924. The speaker described the ordeal of his father, who was seven at the time of the mass deportations.

As my grandmother and the other members of her community were being marched through a Turkish village, they met a Turk on the road who pointed at my father, a small boy at the time, and said, 'Why are you bringing that child on the march with you? That child is going to die. Let me bring the child up and he will survive.'

So my grandmother, very reluctantly, entrusted her child to a Turkish foster father. My father was immediately washed, fed, dressed and given a new Turkish name by his benefactor. Then the Turk sent my father into a fenced-off courtyard to play with some Turkish children of his own age. My father played for a while, but then he began thinking about his mother and the other members of his family who were on the march. He managed to escape through the fence, and by a lucky chance he ran into his older brother who was also on the march, with a different group. My father was reunited with his mother who, cried when she saw her child, saying: 'I won't leave you again, either we will die together or we will live together.'

In the same Greek village, also in 2005, a man in his nineties, no longer able to speak very coherently, proffered an exercise book containing his own handwritten story. The tale is told in Greek, although his own native language, and the only language he remembered in old age, was Turkish. It sets out his recollections of the mountain trek, southwards from the Black Sea, in which he took part as a boy of around ten. He was part of a group of 8000 Christian villagers whose numbers had been reduced to barely 6000 through abductions, exposure and disease by the time they arrived in southeastern Anatolia. During a march of several months, they experienced blazing heat as well as severe cold. Every morning they would take a roll call in the heat of the sun; they thought this was a deliberate trial of their endurance. At one point, they were looked after by 'unfortunate Armenian women who had gone over to the Turks; they brought us bread and water'. At another, they camped out by a lake and caught enough fish to ease their hunger. High up in the mountains, the marchers reached a ruined monastery where the six priests amongst them conducted a service and 'we took communion, giving thanks to the good Lord for having preserved us so far'. Finally, after crossing the Euphrates river, they were fed by members of the American Red Cross; but this last part of the journey, in the autumn of 1921, was also the most dangerous, because the marchers were warned by their Turkish taskmasters that they would pay a terrible price if the Greek army succeeded in its bid to capture the new Turkish capital. A message was sent westwards with the warning that if the Greek army ever marched into Ankara, Greek Orthodox captives would be killed in retaliation. 'They told us to pray to our God that the Greek army should not take Ankara. Finally word came that the Greek army had retreated, and so the infidels or *yavurlar*, as the Turks called us, should be spared.'

The failure of the Greek assault on Ankara – later described in great and bitter detail by Prince Andrew, the father-in-law of the present British Queen – had many consequences. One consequence, it seems, was the survival of a group of refugees, originally from the Black Sea but later deported to the banks of the Euphrates, who subsequently made their way to northern Greece.

In 1922, at the time when desperate Greek Orthodox refugees were pouring into Samsun in the hope of being shipped away, there were many impediments to survival, not least the fact that the people arriving on the

Black Sea coast were already in poor physical shape. In places like Izmir and Ayvalik on the west coast of Anatolia, by contrast, the suffering of civilians had come to a climax only in the final weeks of the Turkish–Greek war: Muslim Turks were burned out of their homes, Orthodox Christian men were taken prisoner and their families bundled onto boats for Greece. So in the Aegean region, the deported Christian families were in reasonable health at the time of their expulsion; their biggest source of anguish was the loss of their menfolk and the fact that in most cases they feared destitution on arrival in Greece.

For their counterparts in northern ports like Samsun, things were worse. Deportation by sea was only the latest in a long series of miseries which had weakened their bodies and left them in an acutely vulnerable state. On arrival in Samsun many of them had to take labouring jobs to earn enough money to pay the fares for their transportation. A deadly bottleneck developed as Orthodox Christian families fled or were moved in ever greater numbers from the interior to the Black Sea coast. In some cases this involved trekking northwards on the very routes they had been herded along the previous year. The Turkish authorities warned that unless the unwanted Christian refugees could be taken away swiftly, they might be redeported, to an unknown fate in the interior.

Around the same time, the main ports of Greece were becoming saturated as refugees arrived from western Anatolia. Many had initially taken shelter on islands like Mytilene or Samos, then moved to Piraeus and Athens in search of work and shelter. The only place for Black Sea refugees to seek any real succour was Allied-occupied Constantinople. In that city, a large, successful Greek community remained more or less intact, although some of its leading members had taken flight after the Turkish victories of September 1922. But as the schools, church halls, and public buildings on the banks of the Bosphorus were transformed into refugee camps, almost uncontrollable epidemics of smallpox and typhus soon broke out. Some were already ill when they arrived, and so quickly did the refugee crisis worsen that it was not possible, at first, to organize quarantine in an effective way.

Samsun's transformation, in late 1922, into a point of embarkation must have seemed extraordinary to anyone who had survived the various changes of fortune which the city had undergone in the past few years. In 1919, when Mustafa Kemal sailed into the port, sent by his Ottoman masters on a mission to pacify the region, it looked a most unpromising place to start his own nationalist campaign. The small British garrison was attempting, somewhat half heartedly, to enforce the peace and disarmament terms imposed on the Ottoman empire. The town's trade was again in the hands of Greeks who had grown rich as dealers in tobacco and hazelnuts, the mainstays of local agriculture and industry.

The Samsun Greeks were adaptable characters, because circumstances gave them no other choice. During the First World War they saw a terrifying ebb and flow in their affairs, especially after the spring of 1916 when the Russian army occupied the land immediately to the east – this sent thousands of Turkish soldiers, irregulars and civilians fleeing westwards, and it redoubled the disdain of the Turkish authorities for a minority which was suspected (rightly in some cases) of actively working for a Russian victory. It was announced that wherever Orthodox Christians failed to report for military service (which in practice meant forced labour) or deserted after joining up, their whole community would be held responsible. This provided an excuse for a first round of village burning, and that in turn whetted the appetite of Christian warlords to take revenge. In October 1916, one of the leaders of the Christian irregulars was spirited away on a Russian ship and sent back with a consignment of guns. In early 1917, many of Samsun's prominent Greeks were sent into internal exile; one of the city's central squares, now distinguished by a modern clock, became a place of public hanging for any Greek guerrillas who were caught. At one point, virtually all the adult males in Samsun had fled their homes; many took to the mountains and joined the irregulars.

There were fierce contests for control of the Agiou-tepe mountain. One of the biggest backers of the Greek guerrilla cause was a stridently nationalist Orthodox bishop, Germanos Karavangelis. Earlier in his life he had been a keen sponsor of Greek fighters in their struggle against the Bulgarians for control of Ottoman Macedonia; and he was confident that similarly assertive tactics could be used successfully in northern Anatolia, even though a glance at the map would suggest that the Hellenic cause had much less hope in a place so far from the Greek kingdom. But in one sense, Germanos was right to see the conflicts over Macedonia, and over the Black Sea coast as connected. In the aftermath of the 1912–13 Balkan wars Samsun was one of the many parts of Anatolia where Muslim refugees from the Balkans arrived and demanded accommodation. Sometimes they insisted on being housed in hitherto Christian villages. The newly trans-ferred Bishop Germanos urged the Black Sea Christians to resist these incursions by force; and the downwards spiral of Christian–Muslim rela-tions in the Ottoman world, both Balkan and Anatolian, took another twist.

The activities of Bishop Germanos only intensified the dislike har-boured by the Turkish authorities for a new, more nationalist variety of Orthodox Christian hierarch, and by extension for their flock. But at the end of 1918, when the Ottoman empire and its allies accepted defeat, the local balance of power in Samsun changed abruptly in favour of the Greeks. The British garrison freed some jailed Greek fighters. Greek mer-chants and other fugitives came back to the port, and they in turn encouraged the return of Greek families who were originally from the southern Black Sea coast but had migrated to Russia in the 19th century. Even Bishop Germanos came back after a period of exile and resumed his enthusiastic support for an active, armed campaign to wrest control of the Black Sea region from Turkey.

That is why Samsun could hardly have been a less propitious place for Mustafa Kemal to begin his campaign. He realized that himself. After taking stock of the local situation, he travelled up the 'green river' to the spa town of Havza, where Muslim Turks were in the majority, and started organizing the first of many protests against the recent Greek occupation of western Anatolia. For every Turkish child who learns about his coun-try's foundation, the rest is glorious history: a growing military and political movement which faced down the British, discredited the treach-erous Ottoman government in Istanbul, won the sympathy of the French and Italians and finally smashed the Greeks.

Three and a half years after his Samsun landing, Kemal had indeed forced all his challengers, whether local, regional or imperial, to recognize him as master of a new Turkish state. His first concern in late 1922 was to consolidate this victory, both at the negotiations in Switzerland and in the everyday life of war-ravaged towns like Samsun. While he and his leading supporters had differences over many things, such as the pace at which the old Ottoman order should be dismantled, they were broadly agreed on one matter: there would be no place in the new state for the Christian minorities who, from their point of view, had served as a fifth column for Turkey's would-be occupiers.

That, at any rate, was the theory. A more practical problem, left for the rest of the world to deal with, was posed by the sick, desperate people who crammed into Samsun port, leaving behind mountains strewn with ruined Christian settlements and wrecked Muslim ones – in a region where for most of the previous century, people of the two faiths had tended the same animals, cooked the same food and played the same music. The Orthodox Christian families who emerged from this world were known in their new homeland as Pontic Greeks, after the Greek word *Pontos*, meaning sea. They still form a distinctive community in Greece, cultivating a dialect which has certain ancient Greek features and differs too sharply from the standard speech of Athens to be comprehensible by anyone but a philologist. In a country with little tolerance of local difference – because the things which unite all Greeks are deemed on ideological grounds to be more important than whatever minor things may divide them – the Pontic Greeks stand out as jokers in the Hellenic pack. They have a reputation for being lively, irascible, flexible, creative and stubborn. Like the Irish in England or the Poles in America, they are sometimes the butt of jokes, usually feeble ones, which credit them either with slow wits or a perverse kind of logic. But they take this in their stride, with the confidence of people who have no doubt that they are much cleverer than their detractors. It is worth noting that almost all the attributes which are ascribed in Greek popular lore to Black Sea people are also ascribed to Black Sea people in Turkey. In Turkey as in Greece, it is a commonplace that 'Black Sea people are different', and this difference is described in strikingly similar ways.

Yet for anyone seeking to recapture the culture and collective memories of the Orthodox Christians of the Black Sea region, the present day city of Samsun offers little immediate evidence. Guidebooks acknowledge that the port was founded by colonists from Greece in the 7th century BC who called the town Amisos. However they are reluctant to acknowledge that anyone who claimed a Greek heritage, or used the name Amisos, has lived in the area more recently. Greek and Christian history has been airbrushed away from the local heritage as successfully as the Muslim faith has been erased from places in present day Greece where it was once predominated, such as the northeastern town of Drama.

Drama now tells the visitor a different story: it hides the fact that Muslims once lived there, but glories in the way that it welcomed many newcomers from places like Samsun. There is a feverish, bustling intimacy about the life of this higgledy-piggledy town, quite prosperous for no immediately obvious reason, which lies midway between mountain wilderness that leads to Bulgaria and the pine-forested Aegean coast. In the shops selling expensive baptismal dresses, designer track suits and flashy gold crosses, and across the large expanses of concrete that cover the old town centre, there seems to be a perpetual flow of repartee which suggests that most of the town's 40,000 or so residents know each other well.

Only on closer inspection does the social geography and recent history of the place start to become clear. At the beginning of last century, Drama was an Ottoman garrison town. It was a way-station for soldiers and other subjects of the Sultan as they travelled from Istanbul to the western fringes of the empire on the Adriatic. In 1911, on the eve of the Balkan wars which wrested the area from Ottoman control, there were 11,000 Muslims and only 2500 Orthodox Christians living in the town. This meant that the overwhelming majority of its Ottoman-era residents were forced to leave under the population exchange, while most of its current residents descend from Orthodox Christian refugees who arrived from places like Samsun in the early 1920s. With a near completeness that is rare even in northern Greece, this place literally swapped populations. Among today's Greek residents, the commonest place of origin is the Turkish Black Sea coast and its hinterland; in other words, Drama is essentially a Pontic Greek town. If the town's commercial and social life has more vim and sparkiness than you would expect in a smallish town, that is a product of the Pontic Greek world.

Although it has long since been cemented over, there is a stream running through the town centre, roughly north–south, which used to divide Drama into an Ottoman quarter on the eastern side, and an Orthodox Greek quarter (complete with a Byzantine fortress) to the west. Only on the 'Greek' side have a few buildings with some historic interest and aesthetic appeal been left intact. There are some agreeable ponds, parks and chestnut trees, and some handsome stone buildings, up to four storeys tall, painted a light shade of ochre. These are the warehouses where tobacco, the town's mainstay both before and, to an even greater extent, after the population exchange, was stored and processed. On the eastern, in other words, formerly Muslim, half of the town, not a single old building is left. In the town centre, a very sharp eye can detect the occasional Ottoman inscription on a crumbling stone wall, denoting one of the dozen or so inns that used to be one of the town's main features.

So powerful was the impact of the population exchange that it is still possible to classify Drama's neighbourhoods by the origin of the refugees who settled there in the 1920s. On the eastern (ie ex-Ottoman) side, one district houses families from eastern Thrace, the region whose Greek residents fled in October 1922 under the indignant gaze of Ernest Hemingway. Another neighbourhood houses people who left western Thrace, fleeing the Bulgarians. On the main road that leads westwards out of the town, there is a district that bears the sonorous name of the emperors of Trebizond who commanded the southeastern corner of the Black Sea: Komnini. Both there, and all over the remainder of the town and in the surrounding villages, it is the Black Sea people who predominate.

One consequence of this Pontic heritage is that most families in Drama have raw and painful recollections of the exodus; the sort of memories which can still inspire an attitude to Turkey and Turks which is wary, often embittered, but at the same time profoundly ambivalent. People in Drama think of Turkey as a country and a landscape to which they continue to be connected, despite themselves.

Every other household in Drama has a story of an immediate forebear who survived the marches against the odds: by bribing a Turkish guard, by doing some job or favour for his Turkish captors or else by joining the relatively small number of Christian armed bands which held out until a chance arose to escape by sea. In many cases, there are family memories of young women and girls who were left behind; under varying degrees of duress, they married Turks or were fostered into Turkish families.

By mid-1923, the centre of Drama was becoming a squalid refugee camp as fugitives from Anatolia's chaos crowded in from different directions; people knew the region's Muslim majority was about to be deported, leaving plenty of housing and land for refugees who were in desperate need of both. As in many parts of northern Greece, things did not work exactly as planned. One of the immediate results of the exodus of the Muslims was to allow the locally powerful, and their friends, to grab the town's best housing. Over the remainder of the decade, tens of thousands of farming families, mostly from the Black Sea, were settled on land round Drama, and in the town itself hundreds of simple brick houses were built – two rooms either side of a central corridor, with an earth lavatory in the garden. Some of these structures still stand, though they have been converted into much more comfortable dwellings, with court-yards and flower beds and spaces to sit in the sunshine and enjoy some neighbourhood gossip.

One of the links between the old life in Samsun and the new life in Drama is the tobacco plant. The region around Drama had produced an abundant harvest of dark, sweet Oriental tobacco long before the refugees arrived. In this part of the world, many a well-endowed monastery or wealthy Ottoman Muslim landowner had enjoyed windfalls in the 19th century thanks to surges in the world price of tobacco or cotton. What the Black Sea refugees brought was a fierce determination to coax tobacco out of the toughest of ground, in places where arable farming was virtually impossible. These included the mountain above Drama whose name, Falakros or Bald, reflects its harsh and stony terrain.

In the region of Drama, as in many other parts of Greece, the telling of the local epic is the self-imposed task of retired schoolteachers, who form a bridge between official versions of history and the collective mem-ories and lore of the people who grew up with them. Anybody in Drama with some interest in the town's affairs can reel off the names of two of them: Mr Vassilis (Hadzitheodorides) and Mr Savvas (Papadopoulos). Both are familiar and well-liked figures in the town, respected for the books that each of them has produced on the people of the area and their Black Sea heritage.

'Mr Vassilis' and his brother Theofylaktos, an equally prolific author, have documented in astonishing detail the story of a highland village called Perasma, between Drama and the Bulgarian border, where they were brought up in the 1930s by their father George. George had been a substantial landowner near Samsun but later found himself tending a tiny tobacco farm in the northern Greek mountains. If the second and third generations of Black Sea refugees seem dogged, almost fanatical in their determination to keep alive memories of the old country, the old way of life, it is because of the extraordinary changes of fortune, and the sense of having emerged alive almost by a miracle, that every family seems to carry. Vassilis and Theofylaktos are one example of this.

Their village of Perasma was established by a group of twenty-five fam-ilies who described themselves as Amisinoi, people from Amisos, present day Samsun. In fact, some came from towns and villages near Samsun, others from places much further east; but they were all Pontic or Black Sea Greeks, speaking similar dialects and carrying a similar jumble of memories. It was during the seaborne exodus from Anatolia that they banded together as a group and started looking for new ground to settle. The spot they found is a place of thick forestation, fast-flowing streams and formidably harsh winters, not dissimilar to the highlands immediately to the south of Samsun. As the two brothers, Vassilis and Theofylaktos tell the story (from a robustly Greek point of view, of course) it is a place where Orthodox Greeks and Muslims alike used to face perpetual danger from Bulgarian raiders and bandits. When the Muslims (with whom they co-existed only briefly, and more or less happily) were moved out under the population exchange, the settlers from Samsun were left to face the Bulgarians alone. Having found a bolt hole in Greece, many Perasma families were forced to leave again as many as four times during the remainder of the 20th century: because of the onset of the Second World War, because of destruction and mass abductions by Bulgarian Axis forces, because of the civil war between Greek government forces and communists, and finally – in the 1990s – because the electricity authority confiscated land to build an artificial lake. In 1944, much of the village was burned by the Bulgarians, and many villagers, including nine-year-old Vassilis, fifteen-year-old Theofylaktos and their mother spent several months in Bulgarian captivity. After each temporary evacuation, the villagers stubbornly returned. Only from 1960 onwards, when people in northern Greece started going to Germany in search of work, did the settlement begin to empty out. Today only four of its two dozen family homes are regularly occupied.

In his seventieth year, Mr Vassilis is a small, dignified man with a grey pencil moustache and understated gravitas. He is not just a teacher but an educational bureaucrat; for a time he was responsible for the Greek schools in Germany. For at least some of the emigrants from northern Greece in his care, moving to Germany brought them in touch with their heritage in ways that no pedagogue ever planned. They have found that the Pontic Greek dialect and Pontic music continue to flourish, powerfully and unselfconsciously, among certain Turkish-born residents of Frankfurt or Düsseldorf who originate from the mountain valleys which the Black Sea Greeks also call home.

Back in his native Drama, Mr Vassilis is one of the few people who knows about the location of Drama's Ottoman inns. He can also point out the site of one inn that was taken over in the 1920s by a legendary Pontic Greek chieftain who turned his Christian name, Stylianos, into a half-Greek, half-Turkish *nom de guerre*, Istyl-aga. This building, now replaced by featureless modern apartments and shops, once served as the headquarters of an 'Association of Armed Leaders and Warriors of Pontus' where Istyl-aga and others preserved the memory of their mountain war. These martial traditions (including the practice of bringing women and children up to the remote hideouts which served as headquarters) were put into action once again during the Second World War. The revival was especially dramatic in the central part of northern Greece where some Pontic chieftains joined the anti-German resistance while others lent their services to the pro-Axis, anti-communist side. In places like Perasma, where the occupier was not only fascist but Bulgarian, it seemed obvious how Greek patriots should fight – against the Axis.

Describing his own family story, which is also the history of the twenty-five householders who ended up in Perasma, historian Vassilis recalls that like many fugitives from Samsun, they made their landfall on the west coast of Greece. This was because the ports of Piraeus and Salonika were full and ships were being redirected to any harbour in Greece that would accept them. George, the father of Vassilis, arrived with his companions on the island of Lefkada, where the travellers' bedraggled appearance and their unusual dialect of Greek came as a shock to the local people who were seafarers, fishermen or cultivators of stony terraced farms. Some Black Sea Greeks recall that these encounters with the Ionian islanders were marred by differing levels of religious devotion. While the Ionians were certainly good Orthodox Christians, they were not as pious or as careful to avoid swearing as the newcomers from Samsun, who saw their Christianity as a precious embodiment of their communal identity.

But in the case of George Hadzitheodorides and his companions, there is no recollection of quarrels over religion. The Lefkada islanders are remembered as decent hosts who looked after the refugees to the best of their ability and gave them odd jobs to do, but could offer little by way of long-term employment or economic prospects. So the party of boat people from Samsun moved on, initially to the western Greek port of Preveza, where they found the natives somewhat less friendly. The authorities urged them to move to the northeastern regions where Muslims would soon be moved out, and refugees were being encouraged to move in. They marched on to Salonika, where they found a chaotic mass of refugees searching for lost relatives, and thence to Drama, which presented a similar spectacle on a smaller scale. The local police advised them strongly to go at least a few miles northwards, towards the mountains and the Bulgarian border; the government had strategic as well as humanitarian reasons to see those slopes settled by loyal Greeks. That was how Vassilis and Theofylaktos and three other children came to be born in Perasma, at a time when the Muslim exodus had left a modest abundance of economic assets – watermills, fruit trees, and fields where a resourceful Pontic farmer could coax out some tobacco of the sweet Basma variety.

Soon after settling in Perasma, several families managed to track down lost children or close relatives in orphanages in other parts of Greece, from Athens to the island of Syros; a community was reassembling. What they could not do, at first, was reestablish contact with friends or family members who had been left behind, to an unknown fate, in Turkey. It was not until twenty-five years later that this sort of family reunion became possible.

For the refugees in places like Perasma, life had other compensations. When tobacco prices were good, especially in the late 1930s, its farmers enjoyed a modest bonanza, and the successful sale of the harvest would be celebrated with exuberant sessions of music and dancing. But Vassilis and his brother also remember how precarious life was. If the tobacco buyers who inspected the newly harvested crop in late autumn were dissatisfied with a farmer's produce, a family could face financial disaster; the best it could hope was to sell the rejected leaves at knockdown prices the following spring. That was the fate which their father suffered one year. But having been a seigneur in his Black Sea homeland, George Hadzitheodorides was a dignified man. His personal honour came dramatically (and for the family, disastrously) to the fore in a discussion with a Greek government official over the compensation he was entitled to claim for the land and property he had left behind. The proud refugee pointed out that his family had been respected gentry in the Samsun region for over 200 years. He insisted that apart from his estate, where the family name was inscribed on every bridge, he should be entitled to claim some compensation for the £3000 he had left in an account in the Ottoman bank. When the need for some documentary evidence was pointed out, the old man lost his temper and began speaking of his sufferings in Anatolia as though they should exempt him from any such bureaucratic details:

How dare *anyone ask proof of a man who was hung upside down by his legs till he was nearly dead, and then transported with 1,800 other people to the depths of southeastern Turkey, where all but 350 of them perished . . . How* dare *an inspector speak thus to a man who had returned from this trek to his home village, only to find that virtually all his relatives had died?*

At the end of this impassioned conversation, the family's application for compensation lay crumpled in a wastepaper bin. That is one of the things that historians Vassilis and Theofylaktos (who lives in a refugee district of Athens) recall about their father; they relish the memory with cussed Pontic pride.

The Black Sea Greeks brought with them not only a dialect but an extraordinarily rich oral tradition: a tradition of theatre, folk poetry, epigrams, fables and complex social rituals, which in certain villages near Drama has remained weirdly intact, in a kind of timewarp. Recording and celebrating one such timewarp has been the life's work of another literary schoolmaster-cum-ethnographer, known to his former pupils as Mr Savvas. Sporting thick spectacles and an old-fashioned trilby hat, Savvas Papadopoulos has filled a small shelf with careful studies of the fiddlers, the priests, the amateur midwives and the purveyors of folk medicine who peopled his childhood and kept alive the memories of a place about 900 miles to the east.

His village is Mavrovatos, a collection of flat, single-storey houses with red-tiled roofs, surrounded by fields of rice, cotton and corn, just a few miles south of Drama. It was established in the 1920s by a community which until shortly before had lived under the Tsar. Their previous home was Karakurt (in Turkish, black wolf) on the easternmost edge of Anatolia, near the fortress town of Kars. This area had been under Russian control between 1878 and 1918.

The families who eventually washed up in Mavrovatos had some experience of migrating in response to political circumstances. Around 1880, they had moved eastwards from the Pontic mountains to Karakurt because they deemed it safer, and perhaps economically more advantageous, to live under the Russian empire than under the Ottomans. But the Tsar's authority brought its own difficulties: the villagers remembered a hard struggle to ensure that local schools taught Greek letters as well as Russian. What prompted this community to leave its eastern Anatolian home was not the Greek–Turkish war but the 1917 Bolshevik revolution, and the chaos which ensued throughout the Tsar's former dominions. This prompted the Russian army to withdraw from the regions adjoining Turkey, allowing the Ottoman forces to march back in and reconquer land they had lost to Russia four decades earlier.

Immediately after the 1918 Armistice, as local lore tells the story, the Karakurt community hoped it could live peacefully under Turkish rule, because the incoming Turks assured them they bore no grudge against the 'Rums' or Greeks; it was only the Armenians they wanted to hunt down. At one point, Turkish troops were billeted on Karakurt and local people duly fed and accommodated them. A few of the soldiers started demanding girls, and the locals complained about this to their commander. At that point, in the revealing words of one Mavrovatos villager, recorded by Savvas the teacher: 'The commander was furious, he said: "These people are feeding you as much as you can eat, aren't you ashamed to behave like that?" And he summoned other soldiers and told them to beat the offenders. We reckoned the commander must have been a secret Rum . . .' In the reminiscences of Black Sea Greeks in particular, this last line – '[he] must have been a secret Rum' – is a recurring one, cited whenever a Turkish officer or bureaucrat behaves with unusual kindness towards a 'Rum' or Greek Orthodox Christian. At least sometimes, this explanation is probably accurate.

Despite these relatively happy moments of Turkish–Greek encounter, the Karakurt people were quickly caught in the middle of Turkish–Armenian fighting. As one villager artlessly recalled: 'Our people sometimes found themselves with the Turks, sometimes with the Armenians. But once the Turks saw some of us with the Armenians, they didn't want to have us around any more.' So the embattled Greeks fled northwards to places that that were still under Russian control, and eventually to the north coast of the Black Sea. From there, they sailed in small groups to Greece. Wherever in Greece they found themselves, the

Karakurt exiles went to extraordinary lengths to reassemble their community and reconstitute their old way of life, with its elaborate customs for betrothal, marriage (a ritual that lasted many days, with carefully assigned roles for every member of the two extended families) and funerals.

As Papadopoulos describes it, the influx of refugees into the Drama region, and the appropriation of land, was a more spontaneous, unregulated process than official versions of history would suggest. In Mavrovatos the newcomers simply squatted in an underused estate which had belonged to an absentee Greek, rewarded with land after the 1912 Balkan wars; before that the landlords had been Turkish beys.

When the first boatload of Karakurt people sailed into nearby Kavala, the authorities tried to settle them in the mountains, but they felt insecure there, complaining that there were too many 'other races' – presumably Muslims, native Greeks or Bulgarians – so they descended *en masse* to the lands which became Mavrovatos, and dug in. Two stone mansions which had once belonged to the local estate were taken over and turned into living quarters. The refugees liked the fact that there were not too many others around; and the proximity of a malarial, mosquito-ridden swamp seemed to reduce the likelihood of undesirable neighbours. Once it had reestablished itself in a new place, the old Karakurt community steadily drew in its former members. Savvas Papadopoulos recalls how his mother was induced to rejoin her fellow villagers.

In 1922, my mother was a pretty thirteen-year-old with cropped hair, living with her mother and five siblings in the refugee settlement of Kalamaria on the Salonika seafront, where the family had recently arrived. She was spotted by a wealthy Salonikan gentleman who turned out to be the prefect of the city and took her into his household as a kind of domestic help, almost an adopted daughter. The governor later married and he and his wife both grew fond of their young protégée. He even offered to take my mother's entire family under his wing; he would find them all jobs in the city hall and a good 'Turkish' house, in other words a property vacated by the Muslims who were departing. But this obstinate refugee family had other ideas; they were determined to rejoin their fellow villagers who had settled these muddy fields south of Drama.

In the end it was a tragedy that prised my mother away from her benefactors. There was a fight between the Karakurt villagers and another Pontic Greek community which had moved in nearby. Our village went to attack the other side with pitchforks, and it might have ended with a few cuts and bruises. But there was a single shot from the other village which killed my mother's older brother, who was eighteen at the time, stone dead . . .

By that time, my mother had grown attached to her benefactor, and he had promised to find her a good husband. But when her surviving relatives came to tell her of her brother's death, she immediately succumbed to pressure and agreed to rejoin her family. The city governor was infuriated, saying that as soon she arrived in the village, this promising young sixteen-year-old would be married off and made to sire a dozen children who would live, if they survived, in grinding poverty. That is just what happened, and my birth in 1928 was one of the consequences.

Poignant as this story sounds, it is one that recurs in various forms among Black Sea reminiscences. There are many accounts of young girls arriving in Greece as refugees and somehow escaping the clutches of their extended families, only to be lured back, usually by some trick. This story is unusual in that a real tragedy, rather than an invented one, was used to entice an errant family member home.

Like every Black Sea ethnographer worth his salt, Savvas Papadopoulos has made a couple of field trips to the lands of his ancestors. His travelling was done in the 1980s, when Turkish–Greek relations, and the political climate inside Turkey, were quite tense. In this sort of atmosphere, travellers are instinctively cautious about new acquaintances and unplanned encounters. But then or even now, a native speaker of Pontic Greek could hardly journey along the north coast of Turkey without being conscious that in certain places, his own tongue is being spoken. When this happens, glances are exchanged, people mutter the word '*imeteros*' (which in ancient and Pontic Greek means 'one of ours') and conversations begin.

On his own travels, Mr Savvas has had his share of memorable encounters, though he is sensible enough to be hesitant about publicizing the details. Such meetings invariably have a strong emotional resonance for the Greek interlocutor, while for the Turkish one, they can be awkward or even dangerous, especially if the Pontic Greek returns to say, Salonika and proclaims with great enthusiasm that he has rediscovered his enslaved brothers and sisters in a forgotten Turkish valley. In a Turkish state which remains highly sensitive to questions of identity and culture, the last thing many of these 'brothers and sisters' want is to be 'rediscovered' by anybody, least of all by people who are bent on claiming them as would-be citizens of another country.

Among the cooler headed members of the Pontic Greek community, it is understood that there is another reason to be relatively discreet about the contacts they maintain with people who still live in their ancestral lands. Some of the current residents of Samsun and other Black Sea towns are not just their 'brothers and sisters' in a purely figurative or cultural sense; they are literally brothers and sisters, or at any rate close family members who were somehow separated in the turmoil of Anatolia's decade of war. Among divided families who are anxious to remain in touch, across the barriers erected by passports, flags and armies, the less said about politics, and the less said in public, the better.

But the fact that certain things are left unsaid does not make them less significant. When families in Drama gaze eastwards to Turkey, they are looking, on the one hand, at a place where they or their immediate forebears suffered almost unbearable pain and in some cases, inflicted pain in revenge; but they are also looking at a place where many of their close family still live. Samsun and Drama, the two tobacco towns, are divided by blood, but also united by blood.

CHAPTER 4

Who goes, who stays: the Lausanne bargain

Despite the comprehensive terms of the Turkish–Greek divorce negotiated in Lausanne, there are a number of places where to this day, people who call themselves Turks and people who call themselves Greeks continue to live side by side. In every case, these exceptions are the result of diplomatic bargains that were struck in a Swiss lakeside hotel, after long and difficult haggling, in January 1923.

One such place is Greek Thrace, which is still home to at least 100,000 Muslims. Most of them speak Turkish as a mother tongue and regard themselves as ethnic Turks; others speak Pomak, a dialect close to Bulgarian; and a few are Roma or gypsies. Over the past eight decades life has not been easy for these Thracian Muslims, who stayed in Greece while their co-religionists in other parts of the country were expelled. But apart from a handful of minor flare-ups, Thrace has not been the scene of any serious Christian–Muslim conflict. The Thracian landscape is still studded with minarets and church towers, crescents and crosses, erected by communities in active but rarely violent competition with one another.

The Thracian Muslims have often been caught between the suspicion of the Greek state, which long regarded them as a stalking horse for a hostile power, and Turkish nationalists, who dreamed of using them in exactly that way. In recent years, the economic lot of this community has improved, as it reaps the benefits of Greece's membership of the European Union, and as various forms of discrimination once practised by the Greek state (to do with building permits, professional licences and land transactions) are removed. In villages in the extreme northeast of Greece, near Bulgaria, the atmosphere is one of intense Muslim piety. Women of all ages cover their heads, and life is regulated by the muezzin's call to prayer. Compared with the modernity of western Turkey, such places feel like a throwback to the Ottoman past. In the region's main towns, Kommotini and Xanthi, Orthodox Christians and Muslims rub shoulders warily and uneasily; there is little social intercourse, and cross-community marriages are rare and generally discouraged by both sides. But the towns' minority neighbourhoods, once identifiable by their primitive, tumbledown houses, have in the more liberal climate of recent years seen a rapid sprouting of new apartment buildings, complete with satellite dishes that allow people to follow the fortunes of their favourite Turkish football teams.

About 200 miles to the east, in Istanbul, there should in diplomatic theory be a Greek Orthodox minority of comparable size. In practice, the city's once thriving Orthodox Christian community has dwindled to less than 2000, most of whom are elderly. As recently as the early 1950s, the community was still large and relatively prosperous, but it left in two big waves. One came in 1955, a time when Turkish–Greek tension was seething over the future of Cyprus. With covert encouragement from the Turkish government, a mob ran amok in the city's Greek neighbourhoods, wrecking churches, graveyards, businesses and homes; much of the city's Greek heritage was destroyed. Then in 1964, another time of high emotion over Cyprus, the Turkish government expelled several thousand Greek passport holders who had been residents in Istanbul. This triggered the departure of a much larger number of ethnic Greek families, and the community's size and economic power plummeted.

Despite this decline, the Istanbul Greeks have managed, by the skin of their teeth, to retain control of quite a number of communal institutions, such as schools and churches. By far the most important institution is the Orthodox Patriarchate, whose holder is by ancient tradition regarded as the first among equals in the hierarchy of the eastern Christian Church. The present Patriarch, Bartholomew I, is the 270th holder of an office which dates back 1700 years. He has gained a worldwide reputation as a campaigner against environmental pollution, although he has to tread a careful path in his native country. A fluent Turkish speaker and law-abiding citizen of Turkey, his movements and activities are closely monitored by the Ankara government, which refuses to recognize him as anything other than a local bishop, responsible for the tiny Istanbul flock. He resides in a dignified but modest wooden building on the shores of the

Golden Horn. The surrounding neighbourhood used to be populated by wealthy and influential Greeks, but it has degenerated into a slum. In many different ways, Bartholomew I presents an extraordinary mixture of strength and weakness. He is a cleric who commands global esteem, but his local congregation is dwindling towards non-existence.

About 500 miles southeast of Istanbul, there is a place where Patriarch Bartholomew might have kept a flock, if things had turned out differently at Lausanne – one of the few regions of Anatolia where the Orthodox Christians seemed, initially, to have a good chance of remaining, even when the great majority of their co-religionists were being deported. This is the strangely beautiful landscape of Cappadocia, whose giant cone-shaped rocks, made of crumbling volcanic tuff, had been used since the earliest Christian centuries as places of worship or monastic retreat. In this region, the Orthodox Christians were mainly or solely Turkish-speaking, although the Greek language had regained some ground in the late 19th century as prosperous local Christians built schools and hired teachers. Unlike Izmir, Ayvalik or the Black Sea, this region was far from any major battlefield and had been spared the terrible blood-letting which in so many places had destroyed whatever mutual trust existed between Christians and Muslims. In the small towns and villages of Cappadocia, the two communities were very close in everything except faith. Religion was not, of course, a trivial difference in Ottoman society but in this area, it was not a cause of hatred either.

As it turned out, the Cappadocian Christians too were forced to migrate to Greece and adapt to a country which shared their religion but was very strange to them in other respects. But despite the enforced separation, the old symbiosis between Turks and Greeks, Muslims and Christians in Cappadocia is not entirely dead. Of all the Orthodox Christians who were forced to migrate to Greece, there is no group that retains such fond and relatively unsullied memories of the homeland as the Cappadocians; and there is no part of Anatolia where Greek visitors, especially those who originate from the region, are made so welcome.

In a tiny but once wealthy Cappadocian village known in Greek as Sinasos and in Turkish as Mustafapasha, a powerful emotional link still exists between the Orthodox families who left the place in 1924 (and now live in Greece or the United States, but pay nostalgic visits to Cappadocia as often as possible) and the Muslims who still live there. Here, as in the

Black Sea region, emotional bonds are reinforced by blood ties; at the time of the exchange, half a dozen Greek Orthodox women managed to stay behind in Sinasos, by marrying Muslim men and adopting Islam. Part of the town's current population descends from Slavic-speaking Muslims who were deported from northern Greece in 1924; but these 'new arrivals' are treated with a certain reserve by the longer established Muslim families, who look back nostalgically to the time when the village was three-quarters Orthodox Christian, and very rich – thanks to fortunes made in Istanbul by Christian Sinasos boys made good, as ship chandlers or caviare traders.

Small wonder, then, that all Greek Orthodox visitors to Mustafapasha are warmly received. These include the Patriarch, who in recent years has managed to make a brief annual stopover in the town, just long enough to conduct a service in one of its well-built churches, where the only living worshippers are his own entourage and any Greek Orthodox who happen to be passing. For the Patriarch, whose activities are so closely circumscribed by the authorities, such visits test the limits of the permissible. But ironically, the fact that no Orthodox Christians now live in the town, or indeed anywhere in Cappadocia, makes these Patriarchal visits easier for the government to stomach, and less of a challenge to the secular Turkish state. An Orthodox Patriarch of any kind is still viewed with suspicion in some Turkish quarters; but a Patriarch without much of a flock is apparently viewed with a greater degree of tolerance.

A large but unsettled Muslim community in Greek Thrace; a tiny Greek Orthodox community in Istanbul, led by a cleric of high international stature; a non-existent Christian community in Cappadocia. In each of these places, the present state of affairs has its roots in the arguments that were conducted in Switzerland by a prickly Turkish general, a sharp-minded Greek politician and an irascible British aristocrat.

The Lausanne conference opened on 20 November 1922. It brought together the representatives of Turkey and all its First World War adversaries, with half a dozen other states, including America, acting as observers. They gathered in the faded luxury of the Hotel du Chateau at Ouchy, near Lausanne, on the shores of Lake Leman. Despite this tranquil Alpine setting, it seemed at times entirely possible that a breakdown at Lausanne would lead to fresh hostilities.

The Lausanne conference was both an end and a beginning. It was the final episode in a decade of conflict over the future of the Ottoman heart-land. For imperial Britain, it marked the end of a period when its ability to manipulate events in the Near and Middle East, through a mixture of diplomacy, economic might and military power, seemed beyond question. And for the British foreign secretary Lord Curzon, a master practitioner of that imperial diplomacy, it was the closing episode in a glittering career.

For the new, republican rulers of Greece, the conference put an end to the wild dreams of reconstituting the Byzantine Empire – the so-called *Megali Idea* or Great Idea – which had dominated and distorted the external policies of the small Hellenic state during its first century of existence.

For Turkey, the conference signalled the end of a real empire, not an imaginary one; and the emergence of a new, secular republic which aspired to be compact and uniform rather than sprawling and diverse. The founder of that republic, Mustafa Kemal, had already succeeded in one long-desired objective, just a few days before the conference began: the Ottoman government, discredited by its fawning relations with Istanbul's western occupiers, had ceased to exist. But within Kemal's inner circle of allies and comrades in arms, there was dissent and jealousy. The Grand National Assembly in Ankara, which he had set up only two years earlier as a new source of legitimacy and power, could not be relied upon to back him unconditionally. Nor could he fully rely on his close companions from earlier stages in his military and political campaign; each had his own claim to a just reward. Finally, as his envoy to the Lausanne peace conference, Kemal sent his most trusted military commander: the small stubborn figure of Ismet Pasha, who had led the Turkish nationalists to their first military victories in 1921, and overseen their final victory in 1922. Relations between Ismet and the prime minister Hüseyin Rauf Orbay were strained, yet it was from Hüseyin that Ismet was supposed to take his negotiating instructions, subject to the approval of the Ankara assembly. Meanwhile the second-ranking member of the Turkish delegation in Lausanne was named as Riza Nour, a sharp-tongued doctor who often outdid his comrades in the intensity of his dislike for Anatolia's Christian minorities. These internal rivalries help to explain why no Turkish official involved in the Lausanne negotiations felt much inclination to 'take risks for peace' or make any move which others might construe as weakness before the western world or the Greeks.

In any case, no-nonsense pragmatism came naturally to Ismet, a soldier whose inexperience of diplomatic niceties was seen as a virtue. He could be relied on to dig in his heels to ensure Turkey's peace terms were met. The central demand was an end to any arrangement or regime which seemed to compromise Turkey's independence. So there could be no question of accepting the existence of minorities with any special privileged status, guaranteed by foreign powers; nor should foreign powers expect to have any economic privileges, as they had enjoyed under the so-called capitulations which gave their agents and representatives virtual immunity from Turkish law. Under the instructions that Ismet received, there were certain proposals which the Turks must not even agree to discuss at Lausanne; chief among them was the idea of carving out some of Anatolia's territory to be a homeland for the Armenians.

For Lord Curzon, the dominant personality at the conference, the biggest priorities were freedom of navigation between the Black Sea and the Mediterranean – in other words, through the Straits, which the new Turkish state would control; and also the future of Mosul, in present day Iraq. In a geopolitical game that sounds quite familiar in the early 21st century, the oil-rich Mosul region had been occupied and appended to the existing British protectorate of Mesopotamia immediately after the First World War. In 1922, no less than in 2003, Turkey feared that a favourable regime for Mosul and its Kurdish population, under Anglo-Saxon protection, would stoke the separatist aspirations of its own Kurdish citizens. While Lord Curzon wanted to keep Mosul under British tutelage, Ankara's political masters were determined to enfold that territory within their own, newly emerging borders. France and Italy, meanwhile, had other bones to pick with Turkey. Having lent their tactical support to Kemal's campaign against the Greeks, the French and Italians hoped to be rewarded by economic privileges of the kind which western powers had enjoyed in the old days. Curzon was almost as wary of his French and Italian allies as he was of the Turks. To the Turks, it often seemed that the western powers were ganging up to deny their country the fruits of its sacrifices on the battlefield; but viewed from inside, the western camp too was fractious and quarrelsome, with Britain perpetually suspicious that France and Italy were making separate deals with Turkey in order to secure some financial or diplomatic advantage.

Right from the start of the conference, an abrasive atmosphere was created as Lord Curzon's denunciations of Turkish misdeeds met with a prickly and defiant response from Ismet and his team. On 1 December, during the first full-blown discussion of prisoner and minority questions affecting Greece and Turkey, the foreign secretary alleged that Turkey had been responsible for the removal, by killing or expulsion, of 1 million of its ethnic Greek subjects. He reasoned as follows: in 1914, the Greek population of Anatolia had been 1.6 million. By the end of the First World War, some 300,000 of these Ottoman Greeks had died or fled. By summer 1922, this figure had risen by another 200,000. Since the Turkish victory in September, another 500,000 Greeks had been killed or driven out – so his best guess was that 5–600,000 still remained. Many of these were males aged between fifteen and sixty, who were being prevented from leaving, and in many cases had been hauled off to captivity and forced labour.

In retrospect, Lord Curzon was overestimating the number of Greeks who remained in Anatolia; it is unlikely that they then numbered more than 300,000. But from his own viewpoint, he succeeded in one important aim, which was to make a harsh moral case against Turkey and put it on the defensive in the most public of arenas. However, Ismet Pasha seemed unbowed. He confirmed that Turkey wanted all Greeks to leave Anatolia as soon as possible. It had recently extended the deadline for their departure to 13 December, which was less than two weeks away.

Earlier that day, the conference heard a report from Fridtjof Nansen, who painted a stark picture of the humanitarian disaster which the Greek exodus from Anatolia was causing. Nansen's report also made plain what he (and others who were less keen to endorse the proposal openly) saw as the only appropriate response: an agreed population exchange, on the grounds that 'to unmix the populations of the Near East will . . . secure the pacification of the Near East'. In other words, the Greek exodus from Anatolia – which was taking place anyway, in the most horrible conditions – must somehow be regulated and formalized, while the Muslims of Greece should be expelled to Turkey in order to 'make room' for the refugees who were flooding into Greece.

Liberal opinion in the western world recoiled in horror at the idea that Turkey's expulsion of its Christian subjects should be accepted and indeed validated by international treaty. The *New York Times* reported from Lausanne that a 'black page of modern history' had been written on 1 December. The report went on:

Ismet Pasha stood before the statesmen of the civilized world and admitted that the banishment from Turkish territory of nearly a million Christian Greeks, who were two million only a few short years ago, had been decreed. The Turkish government graciously allows two more weeks for the great exodus. The statesmen of the civilized powers accepted the Turkish dictum and set about ways to get those thousands of Greeks out of harm's way before they should meet the fate of 800,000 Armenians who were massacred in 1910 and 1917.

A day later, an editorial comment in the newspaper put the rhetorical question:

Is this to be the end of the Christian minorities in Asia Minor – that land, where, thirteen centuries and more before the Turk first came to rule it, Paul had journeyed as a missionary through its length and breadth, and where the first 'seven churches that are in Asia' stood, to which the messages written in the Book of Revelation were sent?

To modern ears, this blast of indignation sounds like a voice from another age. It harks back to an era when the western establishment was disposed to favour the cause of Christianity over other faiths; and to sympathize more keenly with Christian victims of war than with other victims, including those who had suffered at the hands of Christian powers. To some eastern Christians, the editorial stands as a token of the hypocrisy of a western world which laments loudly over the fate of its co-religionists but in the end will accept the *faits accomplis* created by war. In any case, behind the smokescreen of British and American indignation, and Turkish defiance, a deal was rapidly taking shape. Nansen's proposal to 'unmix the people' of Greece and Turkey, whether the people wanted this or not, had gained widespread acceptance. Only the precise terms remained to be settled. Nansen's call for a Greek–Turkish population exchange was seen as 'manna from heaven' by one Turkish delegate, the feisty Riza Nour. In his memoirs, which provide a revealing insight into Turkish nationalist thinking at the time, Nour recalls that 'we had wanted to put the population exchange proposal forward, but did not dare to do so'; hence the delight in the Turkish camp when Nansen grasped the nettle first.

But the degree of assent which Nansen's call for 'unmixing' already enjoyed was probably not obvious at the time. Even though they liked the content of his proposals, the Turkish envoys to Lausanne had insisted, on procedural grounds, that the Norwegian should not deliver his report to the 1 December session of the conference in person; it had to be read out by somebody else. Only the following day, at a meeting of a newly formed sub-committee on prisoners and minorities, did Nansen have a chance to speak in his own name about the pressing 'humanitarian' case – as he put it – for a general, compulsory population transfer between Greece and Turkey. The next day he left for Norway. A week later, he was presented with the Nobel Prize for Peace: not only for his assistance to prisoners of war and famine victims in Russia, but also for his 'present work for the refugees in Asia Minor and Thrace'.

If Nansen's support for a compulsory exchange of minorities across the Aegean (not only as an emergency measure, but as a sort of strategic choice) posed any moral problems, the Nobel Prize committee were untroubled by them. Nor were any qualms expressed by the western nations who had given Nansen a mandate (initially to look after prisoners) and encouraged him to use it creatively. As Nansen's biographer, Roland Huntford, observes, 'It was the first time the Powers had exploited an international civil servant to legitimize their actions.'

Back in Lausanne, there was intensive bargaining throughout December and early January over the scope of the population exchange. Lord Curzon backed Eleftherios Venizelos in his insistence that the Greek population of Constantinople be exempted. The Turks were equally adamant that this wealthy, dynamic community be included. For Ankara, getting rid of the Constantinople Greeks, who had formed nearly half the city's pre-war population, was one of the main 'benefits' that a population exchange seemed to offer. A closely related Turkish demand was for the expulsion from the shores of the Bosphorus of the Orthodox Patriarchate. When the Ottoman imperial system was at its height, the Patriarch had been one of its linchpins; he enjoyed enormous administrative and tax-raising powers over the empire's Orthodox Christian subjects, whether Greek or not. In return he was supposed to 'deliver' the loyalty of the Christians to the Sultan, and of course pass on a substantial share of taxes. But the founders of the new, modern Turkish polity insisted that such an institution, with a history of acting almost as a state within a state, could have no place in a country where minorities (insofar as they were tolerated at all) would be taxed, conscripted, educated and held to account in the same way as any other citizen.

The Turkish nationalists also had more specific grievances against the Patriarchate. Since December 1921, the Patriarch, Meletios IV had adamantly supported the Greek cause in the war. A modernist in theological matters and friend of Venizelos, Meletios had worked unstintingly to win moral and material support (including the support of western churches) for the Greeks of Anatolia, especially after the tide of military affairs turned against them. For the victorious Turkish nationalists, expelling the Greeks of Constantinople and removing their religious leader were closely related aspirations – and both were presented, in the early stages of the Lausanne talks, as non-negotiable demands. On 16 December, Ismet formally submitted a demand for the Patriarch's expulsion. It was argued that 'religious' institutions which had a quasi-political role could have no place in the new Turkish state – whether these institutions were Christian, Muslim or anything else. Under the old Ottoman system, the roles of monarch and spiritual leader, or caliph, of the Muslims had been vested in a single person, the Sultan. But a few days before the Lausanne meeting, the last Ottoman sultan had fled his capital in a British warship: political and religious authority would never again be combined in a single figure. This new separation between God and Caesar must apply to Christians as well as Muslims; and since the Orthodox Patriarchate was incorrigibly political, it must leave its ancient residence on the shores of the Golden Horn.

On 4 January the Turkish delegation reaffirmed its insistence on the removal of the Patriarch and his office with even greater vehemence, putting emphasis on the political role which Patriarch Meletios had played as a standard bearer of the Greek cause during the recent war. There was a hint that unless Turkey won satisfaction on this point it might withdraw concessions in other areas, and insist on an early, unilateral expulsion of all Greeks from Constantinople. At the same time, if the Greeks did agree to the removal of their spiritual leader to some other place, such as Mount Athos, the monastic community in a nearby region of Greece, the Turks might be willing to allow a greater number of ethnic Greeks to remain in the Ottoman capital. With some tenacity, the British delegation insisted, both publicly and privately, on the right of the Patriarch to keep his ancient see. Lord Curzon instructed his assistant, Harold Nicolson, to visit the Turkish delegation and make it plain how strongly people in England felt about the highest office of the eastern Christian world, and how badly the Archbishop of Canterbury and the British establishment as a whole would view any move against this historically important office.

How much people in England really knew about the Patriarch, or how much Curzon cared about the matter, is open to question; but the foreign secretary did clearly have a sense that any obvious mishandling of Greek and Turkish questions could have a high domestic cost. It was only a few months since the career of Lloyd George, the veteran Liberal prime minister, had foundered because his almost unconditional faith in the Greek cause, and in Venizelos, was seen to have been discredited. To a foreign secretary who was sensitive about his place in history, it must have appeared that British acquiescence in the expulsion of a bishop from a see that dated from the dawn of the Christian era could easily rebound against him and ruin his reputation.

In a proposal which Venizelos and the Greeks readily accepted, Curzon suggested that the Patriarch's role should in future be purely religious. All 'political and administrative' functions would be taken away. But on those terms, the prelate must stay. On 10 January, Lord Curzon publicly warned the Turks that 'a shock would be delivered to the conscience of the whole Christian world' if the Patriarchate were expelled. By that time, however, a bargain had been struck behind the scenes. Ismet Pasha duly declared that 'as supreme proof of its conciliatory dispositions' – and as long as the Patriarch's role was a strictly spiritual one – the Turkish side would renounce its demand for the expulsion of the Patriarchate. With characteristic bluntness, Riza Nour's memoirs explain how the Turkish delegation reconciled itself to this concession. Allowing the Patriarch to remain in place would be a way of 'keeping the snake in his hole' – in other words, the Turkish authorities would be able to keep a careful eye on him. If the religious leader were permitted to decamp to Mount Athos, he would then be able to 'spread his poison' more easily; this was the Turkish doctor's acerbic comment.

This deal helped to ease the way towards a broader one: on the exemption not only of the Patriarch, but of his local flock – in other words, the Greek Orthodox people of his home city – from the population exchange. From the Turkish point of view, an Istanbul Greek community whose religious leader was barred from involvement in politics would be less threatening to the new Turkish state, and slightly easier to tolerate. The Turkish delegates to the peace conference were also reassured when they successfully laid down that the Istanbul Greeks, like all other religious minorities, must be subject to military service exactly like all other citizens. At the start of the conference, the western powers had argued strongly for Christians to be exempted from the Turkish army. But on this matter, too, Riza Nour voiced Turkish thinking at its bluntest: as long as they were subject to conscription, the young men of the Istanbul Greek community would have a strong incentive to emigrate; and within a generation, this factor alone would sharply reduce the size of the minority. So it made sense for Turkey to cave in over the retention of the Istanbul Greeks, in exchange for other concessions.

These concessions, moreover, would have to be substantial from the Turkish perspective. Stripping the Greek Patriarch of all administrative functions, and subjecting his flock to military service, would not be sufficient. In return for allowing 100,000 or more ethnic Greeks to remain in Istanbul, the Greek side was induced to make a directly comparable gesture; the exemption from the population exchange of the Ottoman Muslims in western Thrace, whose numbers at that time were roughly similar. For Turkish nationalists, this was a sensitive region. According to the National Pact of 1920, which had laid out the size and structure of the Turkey they were fighting to create, the future of western Thrace must be decided by a plebiscite – in which there was a high probability that region's Muslim majority would opt to join Turkey.

At the time of the peace negotiations, most other demands in the National Pact had been met, and Kemal was under pressure to win satisfaction over western Thrace too. The region itself, a narrow coastal plain rising to a mountainous wilderness, was seething with tension. The Greek refugees who had streamed in there from eastern Thrace a few weeks earlier were now squatting wherever they could; and the Greek police and army were busily evicting local Muslims to make room for them. On both sides of the new border, troops were massing. On the Turkish side, some of Kemal's militant supporters were insisting that western Thrace should not be conceded to Greece without a fight. In Athens, meanwhile, some of the military officers who had seized power in September were still dreaming of reclaiming eastern Thrace. As a further source of tension, the most recent masters of western Thrace, the Bulgarians, remained bitterly resentful at their loss of their access to the sea. Their prime minister, Alexander Stambolitsky, was hinting that Bulgaria might make a unilateral dash for the Aegean.

For all these reasons, there was a convergence of interest between the ultimate masters of Greek and Turkish diplomacy: Venizelos in Lausanne, who held no formal office but was the leading figure in the Greek world, and Mustafa Kemal in Ankara. Both leaders wanted to nail down a settlement, over both borders and populations, as rapidly as possible; a settlement that would leave both countries as 'satisfied' rather than expansionist powers, with enough spare energy to concentrate on reconstruction and fend off the designs of countries which were left unsatisfied by the post-war settlement. For Kemal, conceding western Thrace to Greece, but with its Muslim population intact, seemed a workable basis for a settlement that would satisfy both Athens and his own supporters. At the same time, Kemal seemed willing to agree unconditionally with the shipment to Turkey of Muslims from the remainder of Greece, despite the protests from some Muslims in Salonika, who had little wish to move to another country. The Turkish leadership had resolved to 'gather in' whatever remained of Islam in most parts of Greece, whatever the feelings of the ordinary people involved.

In part because of the humanitarian crisis at home, Venizelos was also at pains to finalize a Greek–Turkish deal as quickly as possible. He did not want the bargain to be held up by broader and more intractable disputes between Turkey and its erstwhile adversaries: with Britain over northern Iraq and access to the Black Sea, and with France and Italy over economic privileges. By late January, two months after the Lausanne conference had opened, there was no sign of a breakthrough on those broader issues. The Turks were exasperated by Lord Curzon's arrogance, and the feeling was mutual. Meanwhile the British were infuriated by what they saw as underhanded and sneaky behaviour by the French and Italians, aimed at currying favour with the Turks. Tempers had also flared over the question of an Armenian homeland. Every time a delegation of Armenians was given a hearing, the Turkish delegates walked out in protest. The United States, acting as an observer in Lausanne, felt obliged to keep the cause of the Armenians on the agenda because of the strong feelings in liberal American circles about the plight of the eastern Christians, especially the

Armenians. The Turks did not want to alienate America, a growing power with which the Ottoman empire had not been at war, and a promising economic partner which could be played off against the Europeans. But they were determined not to be swayed by America's pleading on behalf of the Armenians.

Doubtless Greek politicians felt some sympathy for the plight of the Armenians, as fellow victims of Turkish fury. Greece had been sheltering tens of thousands of Armenian fugitives, along with hundreds of thousands of its own kin, since the Turkish victory in Anatolia. But ultimately Venizelos was not prepared to let the fate of the Armenians obstruct a Greek–Turkish deal which was in both states' interest. From the start of the Lausanne meeting, there was a broadly similar sentiment in the Turkish delegation. They felt a bilateral population transfer was strongly in their interest. It is worth asking why this was so, given that Turkey was bent on the eviction of all or almost all of its Greek Orthodox population, whatever happened. The best answer is probably this: although the net result may be the same, there is a big difference between unilateral expulsion, and expulsion with international consent.

As seems clear from the cable traffic between Ismet in Lausanne, and Hüseyin Rauf in Ankara – a set of documents which has become a classic text of modern Turkish history – the Turks assumed from the start that complaints from Britain and other western powers about the fate of the Ottoman Christians served a purely cynical purpose. By berating the Turks for preparing to expel all Christians from their territory, the Allied politicians were merely trying to whip up anti-Turkish sentiment in their home countries, and to increase the pressure on Turkey to give ground over the questions that they really cared about: Iraqi oil and freedom of navigation in the case of Britain, economic privileges (such as tax exemption and legal immunity for their nationals) in the case of France and Italy.

That was how Ismet saw things. On 23 November, a couple of days after the conference opened, the Turkish envoy advised his government that, 'they [the Allies] are talking about our intention to expel all Christians; I said this is not true . . . I think we will have great difficulty over the minorities issue.' But surely – as any third party reading this cable traffic might reasonably object – it was a simple statement of fact that Turkey had already embarked on a plan to expel all or virtually all its

Christian population. Was it not the case that the victorious Ankara government had given the entire Greek Orthodox community (or in practice, its womenfolk, elderly and children) a matter of weeks to leave the country – while able-bodied male Orthodox Christians had been detained and hauled off to labour gangs? In his statement of 1 December, Ismet did not deny this basic fact. As he made clear, the only concession Ankara was willing to offer its undesired minority was an extension by a fortnight of the formal deadline for its departure.

Even as it spelled out this position, the Ankara government remained sensitive to suggestions that it was behaving with gratuitous cruelty by removing 'all Christians', or even all religious minorities, from its soil. The best defence against such opprobrium lay in Greek, and hence international, assent. From the moment that Greece, as the main protector of the region's Orthodox Christians gave formal approval to the idea of removing most of them from Anatolia, there would be much less justification for Lord Curzon, the editorial writers of the *New York Times* or anybody else to complain.

In any case, as Ankara stressed, expelling all Greek Orthodox Christians did not quite amount to expelling all Christians. First of all, it did not automatically cover the Armenians, who had doctrinal differences with the mainstream Orthodox Church. Whether any Armenians at all would be allowed to remain in the new Turkish state was a separate question. Second, the expulsion policy did not cover the small number of adherents of western Christianity – Roman Catholics and converts to various forms of Protestantism – who lived in Turkey. More controversially, the Turkish government's initial view – maintained at least until the end of 1922 – was that Turkish-speaking Orthodox Christians living in Cappadocia should be exempt from the general exodus. The status of this community was a critical issue for any Greek–Turkish settlement, and for the future of Turkey. They numbered at least 50,000 and possibly as many as 100,000. Because they had lived more or less peacefully with their Muslim neighbours, it could hardly be argued that co-existence between them and Islam was impossible.

In some ways, the Turcophone Christians of central Turkey were the mirror image of the Greek-speaking Muslims of Crete. Both these communities were living proof that in real life, as opposed to nationalist theory, the difference between 'Greeks' and 'Turks' is not a sharp or simple contrast. Nationalist historians have argued whether the Cappadocian Christians were 'really' Greeks, by virtue of their religion, or 'really' Christian Turks. But both these positions have more to do with ideology than the real lives of ordinary people. An Ottoman Christian peasant in a Cappadocian village was subject to the authority of the Greek Patriarch in certain areas of his life; not only his religious life but his education – if he received any – as well all the rites of passage governing birth, marriage and death. But he was also a subject to the Sultan and a speaker of the same language as most of the Sultan's Anatolian subjects: in other words, Turkish. To ask whether he was 'really' Greek or 'really' Turkish is to pose an almost unanswerable question, given that the very words are now used in senses that did not really exist in the 19th century.

At that time, identities in Cappadocia were evolving rapidly and in confusing ways. In some places, a local Greek dialect, as curious and ancient as the Pontic one, was dying out in favour of Turkish. In others, Hellenic culture and language was being reintroduced by well-endowed Greek schools. Nor could any simple distinction be made between Christians in Cappadocia who were Turkish in their speech and way of life, and those in Istanbul who were clearly Greeks. Some of the wealthiest Orthodox Christian families in Greek Constantinople were led by merchants from Cappadocia who had gone to the big city and become more Greek in the process. It is not just that there were many points on the Turkish–Greek spectrum; individuals and families were perpetually moving in one direction or another along that spectrum and creating new realities. That is the best answer to anyone who asks what the Cappadocian Christians 'really' were, with the implication that there are only two possible answers – Greek or Turkish – and that they are mutually exclusive.

Ideology aside, the Cappadocian Christians seemed to pose a practical dilemma, and conceivably an opportunity, for the victorious Turkish nationalists. They did not want to have Christians living in central Anatolia if their lives were subject to a politically powerful Greek Patriarch. But if their connection with the Patriarch of Constantinople could somehow be broken, then the presence of Turkish-speaking Orthodox Christians would not only be tolerable; it might offer some positive advantages to a Turkish government which felt under attack from the Christian world, and wanted to show its determination to create a secular state with room for many faiths, including Christianity, so long as all their adherents were loyal to Turkey. So it apparently seemed to the new Turkish leadership, whose senior members devoted a remarkable amount of attention to the affairs of the Cappadocian Christians, at a time when their military victory over Greece was barely complete.

On 15 September 1922, a congress of a new, self-proclaimed Turkish Orthodox church was held in the city of Kayseri. Its prime mover was a maverick Orthodox priest with Turkish nationalist connections called Papa Eftim. This initiative, which clearly enjoyed some high-level support, was a direct challenge to the authority of the Orthodox Patriarchate of Constantinople over the Christians of Anatolia. Its message was that Muslims and Christians could, after all, live together in Cappadocia as long as they had a common loyalty to the language, culture and ethnic identity of the new Turkish state. Until his death in 1968, Papa Eftim continued to be a gadfly who enjoyed intermittent but never unconditional support from the highest levels of Turkish officialdom. In October 1923, an hour before the Allied occupation of Istanbul was ended, he led an invasion of the Greek Patriarchate and successfully demanded the expulsion of six bishops and the replacement of another; but if the intention was to establish full control over the Orthodox Church in Anatolia, and to destroy the old Patriarchate as an institution, it failed. By 1926, Papa Eftim had managed to secure control of two important churches in the Galata district of Istanbul where many people from Cappadocia lived. For the rest of his life he resurfaced intermittently, at times when the Turkish government wanted to make life harder for the Greek Patriarchate, only to be reined back whenever the authorities felt better inclined towards the Greeks. Curiously enough, many procedural details in the development of the 'Turkish Orthodox church' are mentioned in the cables sent to General Ismet in Lausanne from Ankara. The issue was clearly seen as important.

As of mid-December 1922, the policy of 'hiving off' the Turkish-speaking Christians of Cappadocia (both from the Patriarch's authority, and from the proposed Greek–Turkish population exchange) seemed to be gaining plausibility. Lord Curzon observed on 15 December that despite the general move to drive Orthodox Christians out of Anatolia, 'there will, I suppose, remain the reconciled Ottoman Greeks numbered at about 50,000 persons'. ('Reconciled Greeks' was only one of many different ways in which people attempted to describe the status of this elusive category of people, the Cappadocian Christians. Another, more commonly used term is *Karamanlides*, although this refers in particular to their practice of writing and publishing in Turkish with the Greek alphabet.) A day later, Venizelos concurred with the foreign secretary, predicting that, '50,000 Turkish-speaking persons of the Orthodox faith would stay [in Anatolia] in any case'. On Turkey's behalf, Ismet seemed happy to confirm these assumptions. He argued that the community in question had never asked for any privileged status, and was unlikely to do so in future. Subject to that proviso, both the Turkish-speaking Christians and any other religious minorities were welcome to remain.

In other words, both the Turks and every other party to the Lausanne negotiations were initially confident that the Cappadocian Christians would be exempted. If they had indeed been exempted, then the self-proclaimed Turkish Orthodox church would have had an entirely different role. Instead of being a largely fictitious structure whose main purpose was to harass the Greeks, it could potentially have been transformed into a robust and significant body of worshippers, serving as living proof that there is no incompatibility between loyalty to Turkey and belief in Christianity. When the movement began, that is presumably what some of its supporters expected. Turkey itself would be a different sort of state if it had been able to accommodate a substantial number of Orthodox Christians as full and loyal citizens who did not claim any particular connection to any other country; the Turkish republic's claim to be secular and tolerant would be far more plausible.

So it is worth asking why, in the end, all the bewildered Turkish-speaking peasants from the villages of Christian Cappadocia, as well as their wealthier and more sophisticated cousins from the nearby towns like modern Urgup or Kayseri, were packed off to Greece, bringing their icons, their deep piety and earthly remains of their favourite saints. It turned out that no party in Lausanne was prepared to put up a diplomatic fight to keep the Cappadocians in their homes, where they would almost certainly have preferred to stay. It seems that for both Turkey and Greece, the deal that was struck over the Patriarch must have changed the calculus. From the viewpoint of Greek diplomacy, it was clear that if the Cappadocian Christians had remained in place, they would not have been subject in anything like the old sense to the authority of the Greek Orthodox Patriarch. First because the Patriarch himself had been stripped of all but his strictly spiritual power, and second because the Cappadocians would probably have been resubordinated to the new 'Turkish' hierarchy, sponsored by Papa Eftim. For the Greeks, whether secular or clerical, the existence of a large Christian community in central Anatolia, under the sway of Eftim, would have been thoroughly undesirable. For one thing, it would have raised Eftim's significance as a thorn in the Greek Patriarch's side and possibly boosted the maverick priest's hopes of simply taking over the Patriarchate. If the alternative to all that was to bring all the Cappadocian Christians to Greece, then it would have seemed, from a Greek point of view, a vastly preferable one.

For the Turkish side, the mere fact that the Patriarch was to remain in Istanbul, albeit with severely circumscribed powers, may have increased the urgency of removing as many as possible of his potential flock. Whatever the Turkish authorities did, some Christians in Cappadocia would remain loyal to the Patriarch, and Greek Orthodoxy would therefore continue to have a toehold in the very centre of Turkey. Here again, a total deportation may have seemed a more prudent alternative. More fundamentally, neither Turkey nor Greece wanted to do away altogether with the old logic which connected Orthodox Christianity and Greekness on the one hand, and Turkey and Islam on the other. Turkey could potentially have made a move in that direction by supporting Papa Eftim's movement more wholeheartedly and keeping his potential flock, the Turkish-speaking Christians, in their Cappadocian homes. But to have done that would have been unbearably provocative to Greece, and to the Greek Orthodox community in Istanbul, who believed that their devotion was the prime guardian of Orthodoxy. Moreover, keeping tens of thousands of Christians in the country's interior would have made the construction of the new Turkish republic that much harder. For all its secular, anti-religious rhetoric, the new Turkish state would not go entirely against the grain of the Muslim faith which the great majority of its people practised. If the new goal was to convince people to serve the Turkish republic at least as devotedly as they practised Islam, this would be much easier to achieve if there were not too many religious differences among the republic's body of citizens.

In an ideal Turkish world, the Greek–Turkish population exchange would not have been the only one. During the opening days of the Lausanne meeting, the Turkish prime minister Hüseyin Rauf sent several cables to Ismet, urging him to seek agreement on 'exchanging' the Armenian population. In other words, to find some way of ridding Turkey of its remaining Armenians by consent rather than arbitrary force. Ismet quite accurately replied that there was nobody with whom such an exchange could be negotiated; the short-lived Armenian republic had been reduced in size, and incorporated into the Soviet Union. As the impossibility of swapping the Armenians for anybody else became clear, so too did the attractiveness of the Greek–Turkish deal. The Anatolian Greeks, at least, were one category of 'disloyal' citizens who could be expelled with the freely given permission of Greece, the one state in the world which claimed responsibility for their welfare.

The Greeks and Turks proved justified in their fears that their own bilateral tradeoffs might become entangled in broader diplomatic issues. By the end of January 1923, there was no sign of a global settlement between Turkey and the western powers. Matters were complicated by the growing tension between Britain and France. In mid-January, French troops had occupied the Ruhr region of Germany in a unilateral move of which London disapproved. After devoting ten weeks of his time (the Christmas holidays included) to the Lausanne negotiations, Lord Curzon had by late January put together a draft agreement which was promptly rejected by the Turks – and indeed by the French. In early February, the conference was suspended as Ismet Pasha went to seek further instructions from Mustafa Kemal and the Grand National Assembly.

But this did not stop the Greeks and Turks from working hard on the matters which most immediately concerned them – the exchange of prisoners, and of populations. On 30 January, Venizelos and Ismet signed the deal providing for a 'compulsory exchange' of Greek Orthodox Christians for Muslims, with effect from May. The only exceptions were the Orthodox Christians of Istanbul who had been established in the city since 1912, and the Muslims of western Thrace. The formal implementation of the exchange did not start for nearly a year because it took a long time – until July – to negotiate a broader Lausanne treaty regulating Turkey's entire relationship with the rest of the world. But as of the end of January, one thing had been made grimly clear: while traditional Ottoman society, with its peculiar, arbitrary mixture of cruelty and fairness, had allowed Christians and Muslims to live together, the modern states which were emerging from the Ottoman world would not.

CHAPTER 5

Hidden faiths, hidden ties: the fate of Ottoman Trebizond

Today's Trabzon is a throbbing Turkish port, flourishing as it always has on trade and transport and links with Russia. There is little hint of bourgeois refinement about its neon-lit kebab houses, or the stadium which is home to a famous football club. Yet it was here that the bourgeois life of the late Ottoman empire, a world in which Greeks played an outstanding role, flourished with brilliance for a few decades before its extinction. In the photograph albums of families who now live in northern Greece (or Marseilles, or Manhattan) there are scenes of men in frock coats and women in dark silk dresses, travelling by carriage to villas on the forested outskirts of the town; as dignified, elegant and doomed a world as Russia on the eve of the revolution. This world came to an end on a snowy day in early January 1923 when most of the Orthodox Christian families who still lived in the city were told they must leave their houses within an hour, bring whatever they could carry, and gather near the harbour.

Within a few days, they had been transported to disease-ridden refugee camps in Istanbul. From there, if they survived, the uprooted Greeks were taken to their notional homeland. A few members of their community stayed on in northeastern Anatolia after that mid-winter evacuation. They were mostly Russian subjects, and protected by the close relationship between Soviet Russia and the Turkish nationalists. And even after the coastal areas had been cleared of Christians, some remained in the mountainous hinterland for another year.

The January 1923 exodus took place as the convention on the Greek–Turkish population exchange was being finalized in Lausanne. By the end of January, the wording of the convention had been settled, but it was not ratified until the following autumn. If the convention had any effect at all on northeastern Anatolia, it probably helped to ensure that a relatively high number of Orthodox Christians from this area got out alive. But their departure was hardly well regulated or orderly. In any case, over a period of several years before the final exodus, the Greek bourgeois world had been vanishing and a new Turkish nationalist order was being constructed. The villas of the bankers were emptied, and eventually turned into museums; the trees lining their avenues were chopped down for firewood; the churches were pulled down or made into Muslim places of worship – just as a transformation in the other direction, from mosque to church, was taking place in northern Greece.

The Greeks of the eastern Black Sea liked to trace their presence in the area to the arrival of colonists from the Aegean around 700 BC. Greeks called the city they founded *Trapezous* or *Trapezounda*. It is now known to the world by its Turkish name of Trabzon. When speaking, in English, of the city's past, the most neutral name is perhaps the English version, made famous by Rose Macaulay's comic novel, *The Towers of Trebizond*.

This is a place where Greek culture, in the broadest sense, flourished over many centuries. The frescoed biblical scenes in the church of Haghia Sophia – now a museum, restored by art historians from Edinburgh in 1957 – are evidence that the Greek spirit flowered with particular brilliance in the 13th century. But because of its location, far from the main centres of Hellenism, the Greek population in the area has always formed a world apart; a world which had to find its own way of co-existing with other peoples, armies and rulers with a stake in this region. Like Istanbul, it was conquered by the Ottomans in the mid-15th century; but a web of intermarriages and alliances between the local ruling family, the Comninos dynasty, and the new Muslim masters helped ensure that the Greek monasteries of the nearby highlands retained their estates, and their role as co-proprietors of the region.

From the 17th century onwards, the silver mines, another institution under Christian management, provided a new lease of economic life for the Greek Orthodox community. These mines helped to sustain the peasants who prospered in the mountain valleys south of the port. The more successful of these peasants and traders moved down to the coast and found a niche in the thriving economy of Trebizond. During the final decades of the city's life as a cosmopolitan entrepot, the Greek minority acquired wealth as shipowners, merchants and bankers, and translated this wealth into schools and hospitals. It helped that the city formed one end of a trade route that led over the mountains to Tabriz in northern Persia; it became an intermediary in trade with Tsarist Russia.

A glance at the map would suggest that the Greeks of Trebizond and its hinterland – as an isolated pocket of Greek wealth on Anatolia's eastern edge – must be doomed in any final confrontation between Muslim Turks and Orthodox Christians. And so it proved. But the surprising thing about this Hellenic outpost's final years is how long Ottoman society persisted; how relatively durable a subtle and partially secret web of relationships between Greeks and Turks proved to be, even when it was breaking up elsewhere. Involved in this network were bishops, businessmen, politicians, soldiers and gangsters.

In Greek parlance, Trebizond and its surroundings are called eastern Pontus, while the ports of Samsun, Giresun and Sinope and their hinterland are known as western Pontus. When Greeks who originate from western Pontus recall their final years in Anatolia, their memories are largely of war, death and forced marches. Such things happened in eastern Pontus too, but among Greeks who came from there, there is a higher proportion of positive or at least bitter-sweet recollections. These memories reflect the prosperity and dynamism and cultural attainments of the Greek community on the eve of its departure; and also the intricate, and sometimes hidden forms of symbiosis between Christian and Muslim, Greek and Turk, rich and poor, to which Trebizond gave rise.

Some differences between the histories of western and eastern Pontus in the early 20th century are obvious. Trebizond was captured by the Tsarist army in spring 1916, and the Russian success in eastern Pontus enraged the Turkish authorities in western Pontus, where intercommunal warfare intensified and the government began the first of a series of mass deportations of Christian civilians. After the Ottoman defeat in 1918, Samsun found itself in the eye of the gathering storm. This was the place where Mustafa Kemal began his campaign to place the whole of Anatolia under Turkish authority, while it was in nearby Giresun that an irregular fighter and warlord of exceptional ruthlessness, known as Topal Osman, launched a wave of terror against the Christian population.

There was another significant, but less obvious difference between Samsun and Trebizond on the eve of the population exchange. The religious leaders of the Greek communities in the two places were very dissimilar characters. The senior Orthodox cleric in Samsun was Germanos, the warrior-bishop who had commanded irregular fighters in Macedonia and believed confrontational tactics would work in the Black Sea region too. In Trebizond by contrast, the leading Orthodox bishop, Metropolitan Chrysanthos Filippidis, was a subtle and conciliatory figure; a person who could respond nimbly to changing geopolitical circumstances – and believed that in a many-sided conflict it was worth building up moral credit with all parties. As soon as the First World War broke out, Chrysanthos approached the Turkish governor of the city and promised that his flock would remain loyal Ottoman subjects – assuaging the Turks' well-founded suspicion that the Christians' loyalties lay with Russia.

The other Christian minority, the Armenians, suffered atrocities which seem in Trebizond to have been particularly severe. According to testimonies given by Turkish officials and doctors at a trial conducted by the Ottoman authorities in 1919, many local Armenian children were poisoned, drowned or killed in other ways while their parents were being marched southwards. Having seen at first hand the collective punishment which the Ottoman authorities imposed on 'disloyal' communities, Chrysanthos worked to ensure that the Greeks were not subject to deportation; and that when they did receive orders to join labour gangs, their tasks were relatively light.

In spring 1916, he had to turn his diplomatic skills in a different direction. As the Ottoman army retreated and the forces of the Tsar marched into Trebizond, it was the bishop who formally transferred the city to Russian control. On the face of things, this implied 'liberation' for the Christians, enslavement for the Turks. But during the occupation, Chrysanthos laboured to ensure that local Turks and Muslims did not suffer unbearably. He also followed the revolutionary movement that was sweeping all the Tsar's dominions, including Trebizond. As early as mid-1916, he is said to have received a warning from Grand Duke Nikolai Nikolayevich, the Russian commander, that the Romanov monarchy's days (and hence Russia's participation in the war) might soon come to an end. With the encouragement of the Grand Duke, the bishop took soundings in the Ottoman capital about a separate Russian–Turkish peace, aimed at thwarting Britain; but neither the Turks nor their German allies seemed interested.

In February 1918, when the Russians finally left Trebizond, many of the local Greeks fled with them – fearing the cause of Orthodox Christians in northeastern Anatolia was lost. Among those Greeks who stayed, there was a brief surge of optimism at the end of 1918, after the Ottoman empire's defeat by the Entente – but Chrysanthos was too good a diplomat to see this relief as anything but short-lived. If he had a flicker of hope, it lay in the fact that Trebizond had always been a separate world. Since Byzantine times, it had been a place where Greeks and Turks alike moved to a different rhythm, and struck compromises not attainable anywhere else. While he shared the dream of a Pontic Greek state, with or without some association with Greece, Chrysanthos realized sooner than most how hard it would be to attain. When, at the Versailles conference in 1919, the Greek delegation floated the idea of an Armenian-dominated state which also included Trebizond, Chrysanthos and his flock were instinctively suspicious – perhaps because they sensed that linking their fortunes to the Armenians implied all-out hostility to Turkey, a state of affairs which the Pontus Greeks might not survive. His first preference was a Pontic Greek state with a strong and politically equal Turkish population, established with the consent of Mustafa Kemal and the Turkish nationalists. Only when the Turks turned him down did he open negotiations with the Armenians, which never bore fruit.

From 1920 onwards, Chrysanthos and his flock were concerned only with survival. Even as the Greek bankers and shipowners fled the city and its prosperity faded, there was a desperate effort to draw on whatever endured of the local tradition of intercommunal co-existence. When representatives of a more militant Greek view, sponsored by the pugnacious Bishop Germanos, arrived in Trebizond to propose a broadening armed uprising, they were given a cool reception. Matthaios Kofides, a local Greek politician and former deputy in the Ottoman parliament, asked the visitors tartly whether they proposed to stay around during the armed struggle they were urging the Greeks of Trebizond to launch. On getting a negative answer, he told his guests: 'So you expect to watch Trebizond burning through your binoculars . . .'

Around the same time, another war-hungry group travelled east to Trebizond in the hope of fomenting violence: a gang of cut-throats dis-

patched by Topal Osman, the bandit chieftain who had already terrorized
Greeks and Armenians in western Pontus. Initially they demanded 400
uniforms. When this was refused, they returned in an even uglier mood
and start robbing houses in the Greek neighbourhood. But it was Yahya,
a Turkish gangster and kingpin of the harbour, who saw the intruders off;
they were trespassing on his patch. Yahya was no gentler a character than
Topal Osman, but he maintained certain relationships with the Greek
community and was prepared, for a consideration, to help them escape
by sea to Greece or Russia.

In more respectable Turkish circles, too, it often seemed that Trebizond
was exasperatingly different from other places. It was one of the early
strongholds of the Turkish nationalist movement, but its local representatives were unwilling to bow to Kemal's authority.

In the end the challenge to Kemal from restive Muslim residents of
Trebizond was neutralized by a grisly series of events that came to a head
in March 1923. First Yahya was murdered in mysterious circumstances,
near the local army barracks. This killing exacerbated the discontent with
Kemal and his leadership that was already being voiced by an emerging
opposition within the Ankara assembly, in which deputies from
Trebizond featured prominently. One of these deputies, Ali Sukru, dis-
appeared after lending his weight to the opposition cause. It soon
emerged that he had been killed by Topal Osman and his gang, who were
doubling as bodyguards to Kemal. Sensing that his relationship with
Osman had become a liability, Kemal sent an army unit to arrest him, and
Osman was killed in the ensuing shootout. Kemal then had to move
swiftly to contain the surge of local pride which attended the burial of Ali
Sukru in his home port. In the end, Kemal was received with lavish hon-
ours in Trebizond and presented with a luxurious house which had once
belonged to a Greek banker; but it took some time for him to bend that
obstinate coastal community to his will.

Well before this happened, the local Greeks put up a final rearguard
action to save whatever it could of the old, cosmopolitan traditions of the
harbour. The terminal moments in the life of Greek Trebizond have been
described by Dimitris Fillizis, an engineer who managed to outlast virtually all his compatriots by offering the Turkish authorities help with
reconstructing the city's port and aqueduct. As Fillizis recalls, 'we [Greeks]
avoided gratuitous provocation of the Turks', even after the Ottoman

defeat of 1918. They made sure, for example, that the Greek Red Cross hospital, of which the Orthodox Christian community was immensely proud, was open to Turks as well as Greeks. The leading citizens of the city would organize what they called 'fraternal symposia' which brought together prominent Turks and Greeks. At least one wealthy Turkish dynasty – the Nemli-Zade family – seems to have been well accepted by the town's Christian elite and shared its comfortable life. But Fillizis tells a revealing story of what happened when a group of Greeks called on a wealthy member of the Nemli-Zade clan and sought advice on improving the intercommunal atmosphere. The response took the form of a grim fable: a fox proposed to a cock that they should be friends, unless the fox could discover three defects in the cock. The cock agreed. The fox proceeded to denounce the cock for his ugly red comb, his sharp claws and his raucous screech; and gobbled his companion up. The moral was that those who want to pick a fight will always manage to find a pretext. And in the end, Nemli-Zade's pessimism was justified.

For a while, the fact that the Turkish authorities in Trebizond were not fully aligned with Mustafa Kemal gave the local Greeks some room for manoeuvre. But as the Turkish nationalists gained strength all over Anatolia, and turned the tide in the war, things worsened for the Greek community in the northeast. A large number of the region's Greek men were sent to labour camps in Erzerum, hundreds of miles to the south. Among the few who escaped this fate were those, like Fillizis, who were doing useful work for the local authorities – and the several hundred who had Russian passports.

In mid-1921, when the Orthodox Christians of western Pontus were being deported in huge numbers, several prominent Greeks from Trebizond, including Kofides the politician, were hauled off to the town of Amasya and along with scores of their co-religionists, hanged for treason. Things changed faster than even the savviest of locals could grasp: Kofides' initial reaction to his arrest was naively calm – he had enjoyed excellent relations with his Turkish colleagues in the Ottoman parliament and he was sure that they would testify in his favour. That turned out to be a false hope. But Kofides' feeling that he had many Turkish friends was not all self-delusion, and it had one beneficial effect. His execution caused anger among the Muslims of Trebizond and they refused to hand over any more of 'their' Greeks to the gallows.

In the months which followed, Fillizis himself had some narrow escapes, thanks to long-standing relationships with local Turks, high and low. His friend Panos Panayotides, described by Fillizis as 'especially popular' with local Muslims, was arrested after the authorities discovered a crude optical telegraph in the Greek Club; the device was apparently bought by Panayotides in the hope of making a magic lantern. In any case, the suspect was released after pleading from friends in the local Turkish business community. At a later stage, Fillizis himself was apprehended during a round-up of the remaining Christian men, but the town's governor ordered his release because the engineer was doing vital work for the municipality. Some of the newly detained Greeks were employed in labour of a more demeaning nature. They were told to dismantle the fortress of the Comnenos dynasty, who had ruled the place before the Ottomans, and use the rubble for road building.

Although he is a restrained narrator, Fillizis lapses into elegy as he describes wandering around the churches of his home city and seeing icons smashed, vestments torn and frescoes desecrated. Entering his local church, he remembered his childhood efforts at chanting prayers he hardly understood, and prostrating himself before icons in the pious Orthodox fashion. He remembered 'the mellifluous voice of our dear Father Prodromos, the priest of our parish who was so dignified and educated, and I felt sorrow over the vanity of the world, the vanity of vanities . . .'

As the moment came for his own departure – apparently some time in late 1923 – his wife and a woman friend paid a final visit to the Greek graveyard, and were stoned by local urchins. 'To be fair, though, the Turks of our region were in general good and kind people . . . and they had a great fondness for their Greek compatriots *because they thought of us as kin . . .*'

That last assertion is a surprising one, and goes to the heart of the mysterious relationship between Greeks and Turks which existed in this part of Anatolia, even more than elsewhere. Both among the townspeople of Trebizond and in the villages of its hinterland, sometimes known as the Pontic Alps, the social barrier between Christians and Muslims was high but not impermeable. There were many extended Christian families in which some branches converted to Islam. This led to a rupture of relations between the cousins who followed different faiths, but the breakdown was rarely total. It was true, of course, that changing religion had consequences which went far beyond the realm of private belief. Converts to Islam became eligible for the army, but exempt from the taxes and tithes to the church which Christians were required to pay. In the 19th century, Christians had the advantage of being able to travel freely to Russia and seek their fortunes there – but also the disadvantage of being suspected, in Ottoman eyes, of being a vanguard for the Sultan's enemy. In part because of the continuing power of the region's Christian monasteries, and the Christian-operated silver mines, the peasants of the Pontus retained both the Greek language and the Christian faith to a greater extent than their counterparts in other parts of Anatolia. In some ways, the Greek language remained more durable than the Christian religion. Despite the strength of the region's Christian institutions, there were many speakers of Pontic Greek who did switch to Islam, and in some cases embraced the new faith with the convert's fervour.

There were also tens of thousands of people who seemed to straddle the two worlds: the crypto-Christians, people who outwardly appeared to be Muslim but secretly practised the rites of Christianity. While many things about the history of the crypto-Christians remain mysterious, it is well documented that several thousand of them threw off their Muslim attributes and declared their Christian identity around 1860, after the Ottoman empire – under pressure from its British and French allies – issued a decree that allowed greater religious freedom. Among the people of Pontic Greek descent who now live in Greece, there is a significant minority whose forebears of, say, four or five generations back were people who appeared, to the outside world, to be Muslim Turks. That is not an easy thing for today's Pontic Hellenes, so passionately attached to their Greekness, to accept – but the story of the crypto-Christians has been graphically recounted by a Salonika-based writer, George Andreades.

A passionate amateur historian and activist in the Pontic Greek community, Andreades struck a particular chord with a book describing the true story of a divided Pontic family, in which a woman living in Ankara, of Christian origin but fostered into a Turkish family during the 1920s, met up with her blood relations in central Greece. Treading on even more sensitive ground, the writer has explored the strange world of the crypto-Christians by revealing his own family story.

To recreate the shadowy crypto-Christian culture, Andreades draws heavily on reminiscences from his grandmother, Aphrodite Grammatiko-poulou, who died in 1955 after spending the final part of her 88-year life as a refugee in northern Greece. Virtually illiterate but endowed with a prodigious memory, the elderly lady saw herself as the guardian of a story that was much older still: that of her great-grandfather who was assumed by almost everybody to be a mullah, known as Molasleyman. On the face of things, at least, Molasleyman was a talented villager of modest origins who grew up in the Kromni valley, in the upland area south of Trebizond. He was born in 1767, when the nearby silver mines were an important source of employment and relative prosperity.

He left for Istanbul at the age of sixteen and returned to his native highlands at twenty-two, having received a grounding in Arabic, the Koran and Islamic law; enough to impress the local Ottoman authorities and be recognized as an Islamic judge. But at some point in his life, the mullah was drilled in religious knowledge of another kind: he was also a Christian priest who maintained a chapel in his basement, full of icons and candles. One of these icons, a depiction of St John the Baptist with angel's wings and carrying his own severed head, is a precious family possession in the Andreades family apartment in Salonika.

In his secret crypt, the 'mullah' apparently carried out scores of baptisms and weddings, perpetuating a world of extraordinary and subtle deception. The crypto-Christians – as patriarchal in their social organization as all Ottoman communities – had a system for 'taking' brides from their fully Muslim neighbours. Once the marriage contract had been sealed, the Muslim girl, rarely more than fourteen years old, would undergo a secret baptism, overseen by her future in-laws, and then be forbidden all further contact with her blood family. At the same time, the crypto-Christians would avoid 'giving' their own daughters to fully Muslim families if at all possible. As Anthony Bryer, one of the greatest academic experts on the Pontus region, has pointed out, this community had found a way of breaking the process whereby Greek Christians in Anatolia progressively lost 'their language, their religion, and their daughters' to the Muslim Turks. Instead of 'giving' daughters to Islam, they reversed the process, albeit by an elaborate and exhausting form of subterfuge. Molasleyman himself, faced with pressure from a wealthy Muslim family to hand over his own daughter as a bride, quickly approached a poor family of crypto-Christians and asked if they would provide an alternative son-in-law. This hastily betrothed pair – the mullah's thirteen-year-old daughter and his friend's seventeen-year-old son – produced two more generations of crypto-Christians. It was only the mullah's great-grandchildren who were able to live – in the second part of their lives, at least – as open Christians.

Molasleyman died in 1843, at the age of eighty-three, and was buried as a Muslim, in the Islamic cemetery of Trebizond. As family lore has it, the mullah had gone to the town to see whether the time was ripe for the community to reveal its Christian affiliation. But the local Christian bishops said it was not, and their caution was confirmed when, in a notorious case, an Armenian who had embraced Islam was hanged for reverting to his original faith. According to the Andreades family story, their clerical forebear died of shock on hearing the news of this execution, which effectively crushed all remaining hope that he could serve openly as a priest. This situation in the Trebizond region changed dramatically after the 1856 decree which was supposed to provide freedom for religious minorities and prompted tens of thousands of people to come out into the open as Christians, and seek the protection of the European powers.

The reasons for this initiative are still disputed, as are the motives of the crypto-Christians in general. One theory holds that by keeping their Christian practices secret, they were not merely concerned to hide their affiliation from the Ottoman authorities; they also wanted to avoid the stern hand of the local Christian bishops who had enormous power over every aspect of the social and educational life of their people, and did not hesitate to use it, by levying extra taxes and dictating exactly where and when schools should be built. Sceptics have suggested that the advantages of secrecy were overturned in the mid-19th century, as Russia tried to draw the region into her sphere of influence, in part by making herself the protector of the region's Orthodox Christians and encouraging the open practice of Christianity.

Among the sceptics were the British consuls in Trebizond who thought the mass conversion to open Christianity was a strategy to avoid service in the Ottoman army. Until shortly before, they noted, people registered as Muslims could avoid army service by working in the mines; now that loophole had been closed. So the people in question had decided that it was worth paying the taxes which the Christian clergy levied on their own flock, if by doing so they could avoid Ottoman military service and enjoy the other advantages of being Christian – such as access to an excellent education system, and the right to emigrate to the Russian empire. Andreades believes the truth about his forebears lies somewhere in the middle: they were both idealists who maintained a secret Christian faith when it would have been far simpler to abandon it, and opportunists with a keen sense of where the wind was blowing. Keen, but apparently not infallible: they were called up for service with the Ottoman army (as though they had never ceased to be Muslim), and as a result migration to Russia accelerated. If the intention of the 1856 decree was to clarify, once and for all, the status of the Ottoman empire's religious minorities, it did not succeed.

In any case, the strange story of the crypto-Christians was still unfolding six decades later when the Greek Orthodox community of Trebizond lived out its final moments. Particularly in the town itself, the division between Christians and Muslims was never simple or absolute, however much the impression of a straightforward dichotomy was cultivated by political and religious authorities on each side. There was a grey area which the crypto-Christians occupied.

The elusive quality of relationships between communities and faiths in the Ottoman twilight emerges clearly in the testimonies which have been gathered from elderly Greeks in very recent years. The impressive longevity of Pontic Greeks, and the sharpness of their memories, have made them a rich resource for lovers of oral history. One lucid account of 'religious ambiguity' in Trebizond and its surroundings, during the early 20th century, was provided by a certain Spiros Yakoustides, in an interview at his apartment in Salonika in 1997. He was 101 at the time he shared his reminiscences with Eleni Ioannidou, a diligent Greek social historian.

As the old man recalled, his family came from the mountain village of Imera – a place where Greek-speaking Christians had enjoyed a prosperous and relatively peaceful life, living largely on the remittances sent by menfolk from Russia. However, he spent most of his childhood in the port of Trebizond. His father had moved to the Georgian spa town of Borzhomi, part of the Russian empire, shortly after his birth; and his mother died in 1901, a year when infectious diseases took a heavy toll on the Black Sea coast. He therefore grew up with a paternal aunt in the port, attending its fine Greek schools.

We lived in a district known in Greek as Exoteicha, which means outside the walls. Most of the people there were Christian Greeks, but there were also some Turks. We had Turkish friends and neighbours who used to take me hunting for hares. But in some cases, I realized they were crypto-Christians. For example there was a baker called Ali-efendy. I understood he was a crypto-Christian when I saw him make bean stew without oil [in other words, in conformity with the Orthodox Christian rules for Lent] at a time when Christians were fasting. And when I realized this, I said, 'Don't worry, I won't give you away . . .' And after that, he would give me as much credit as I wanted at the bakery . . .

There was another neighbour with the same name, Ali-efendy. He had a shop selling butter and cheese, and he was a crypto-Christian too . . .

At the time I was born, my father was the manager of a drapery store which belonged to his in-laws, my mother's family. Their surname was Eleftheriades, but they had been crypto-Christians in previous generations. The head of the Eleftheriades family had the Turkish name of Nisan but he was also known [by the Greek Christian name of] Nikolaos . . . My uncle Christos was a builder who had a reputation for working very swiftly and skilfully. He took me around and taught me his trade. When I was a teenager he took me up to the monastery of Panayia Soumela. [This is the greatest of the region's monasteries, an extraordinary structure carved into the side of a cliff.] Some of the Turks living near there were crypto-Christians, and they protected the monastery. With my own eyes, I saw about ten or fifteen of them taking holy communion. There were many crypto-Christians and they protected us; if it hadn't been for them we'd have been slaughtered. For example, there were a lot of crypto-Christians in the police. During Holy Week [the week preceding Easter], they used to put a guard on our churches, and refuse to allow any Turks in, just in case anybody tried to desecrate our ceremonies. At Easter itself, there was a crypto-Christian who would watch our church to make sure nobody would bother us.

Having left school, Spiros Yakoustides worked briefly as a letter-writer and book-keeper for a leather merchant in his home port; and then – although he is vague about dates – paid a brief visit to his father in Russia (presumably around 1921–2) to see whether it was worth settling there. It was from there that he travelled to Greece. He then lost all contact with his father and has no idea where or when he died.

His kinsman, Yannis Yakoustides, who was born in 1908, gave an equally cogent account of his early life, at the age of ninety-two. His most vivid memories are of the mountain settlement of Imera, where he could sense, even as a child, that this was a prosperous place in rapid, probably inexorable decline; not so much because of Greek–Turkish, or Christian–Muslim, conflicts but because of the attraction of migration to Russia with its huge opportunities.

I was born in Imera in 1908, and my father left for Russia in 1911. Almost all the men were emigrating, leaving their families in the village so that the children would get a Greek education. Once they arrived in Russia, they would set up shops and bakeries and send money home. They found the Russians were simple-hearted people; when you sold things to them, they would pay whatever you asked . . . [Even if there had been no world war] our village would not have lasted another century . . . At the height of Imera's prosperity there were 400 households . . . but at the time of the population exchange there were only 120.

My relatives and I were part of the last group of people to leave Imera, in January 1924. I had a good schooling in the village, at least for the first five classes, and then [in 1921] all our teachers here exiled to places like Erzerum, in terrible conditions. All the remaining men were deported, except elderly people like my maternal grandfather. At the age of thirteen I was too young to be deported, so I was made the village clerk and I kept the job until we all left in January 1924. One of my jobs was to tell the village ladies whose turn it was to cook for the Turkish policeman who kept a vague sort of eye on the village. They fed him well; in our orchards, we had apples, pears, plums and we also grew vegetables like cabbage and potatoes. And our women would cook some delicious dishes: for example they would boil beetroot and fry it with fresh butter and eggs.

The order for the last remaining families to leave Imera came in the middle of winter, when the land was covered in snow. When we got about half-way to the sea, they tried to make us go back . . . but how could we have gone back? Our homes had already been emptied, and the local Turks were waiting to take them over. They kept us there fifteen days but we were able to send a forward party on to Trebizond to demand permission to proceed. Finally we were allowed to continue our journey, and we reached the port after another three days' march. There we stayed in a hostel with many rooms that belonged to the monastery of Panayia Soumela; that's what saved us. We had some rugs and we had also brought a cow . . . because my mother had stomach troubles and the only thing she could digest was fresh cow's milk. But in the end we had to sell the cow and we used the money to buy tickets on an Italian ship . . .

In Imera, we had a well-organized market with ironmongers, hardware shops, general stores . . . but the settlements in nearby Kromni were more scattered, and they couldn't produce anything. If you tried planting olive or fruit trees there, they wouldn't have grown. So quite a lot of the Kromni people went to Trebizond and worked for the city hall, as road workers or watchmen.

There may be a clue here as to why the town of Imera remained openly Christian, while the neighbouring Kromni district – and people from there who moved to Trebizond – tended more towards crypto-Christianity. Imera was prosperous and isolated enough to keep its faith; the Kromni people needed work and had to make compromises. But religious ambiguity was present in Imera too; not because of crypto-Christians, but because of the handful of locals – perhaps ten households – who had converted to Islam.

Yannis Yakoustides encountered his Muslim neighbours again when, during the 1980s, he and his relatives paid a couple of return visits to Imera. They found that some parts of the town remained inhabited, though most of it was derelict. On the first trip, in 1986, a Muslim villager who was an acquaintance of the family took him back to the old Muslim neighbourhood and laid on a feast for the visitors. They sat on the floor and reminisced, in Pontic Greek, about the old times. Some of the local Turks assumed the Greek travellers were coming to look for buried coins or treasure which they had left in their gardens, but the visitors replied that they wouldn't have done anything so stupid.

In view of the extreme dangers they were facing – including the ever present possibility of mass deportation – there is something remarkable about the fact that Pontic Greek children, growing up in the mountain villages of northeastern Anatolia on the eve of the exodus, were left with very happy memories of the world which they abandoned. In this matriarchal environment, the women were efficient enough farmers, and competent enough in the essential skills of motherhood, to maintain their community's life and give their children a sense of security. One vivid story of a Pontic childhood in the last days of Imera was offered to the author by George Siamanides, who in early 2005 was a humorous and intelligent widower of ninety-two, living in an apartment on the Salonika seafront.

I was born in 1912, in a mountain valley where for many centuries, Greek-speaking Christians had made an excellent living from farming, trading and mining. On the wings of an eagle, my home town of Imera is only fifty miles southeast of the great port of Trebizond but thanks to its altitude, over 4500 feet above the sea, the climate is different. Trebizond in July can be humid and oppressive; but in our highland home, the air in summer tastes like wine, and as soon as you fill your lungs with it, you feel all your ailments are being cured. That was why rich people from Trebizond, including my cousins, would spend their summers with us. And those of us who lived in Imera all year round were resilient. From November to April, we were enveloped by thick snow, and our livestock were kept indoors. But in spring, as the sun grew stronger, the fields around us turned into a carpet of rich and scented foliage. It was a perfect environment to raise cattle and sheep, and a paradise for youngsters. When I close my eyes, I can still recall the aroma from the blue flowers that wafted down from the meadows above our house. I can taste the milk from our three cows, and I remember the tang of the butter which we preserved in wooden vats, long before the age of refrigerators. The hay smelt of flowers, the milk smelt of flowers, the butter smelt of flowers; all our produce was of high quality thanks to the fodder provided by nature.

In my imagination, I can still hear the rivulet that cut through our valley, with a small pasture, thick with clover, on one side. As children we used to dam the stream with stones – and make a pool where we could splash about, revelling in every moment of the precious sunshine. And in my mind's eye, I can still see poplars with silvery leaves and steep hillsides, with tiny chapels at the top, appearing and then disappearing as the clouds scudded round them. Immediately above our house, there was a shrine at the top of a hill called Panayia Eremitissa – the hermit, or desert-dwelling Mother of God. On 15 August, the whole community would gather at the peak to commemorate the Dormition of Mary – and prepare for the rigours of winter.

We were not sophisticated Christians: some of our priests were simple folk, even though our community was led by powerful and well-educated bishops. But the feasts and customs of the Christian calendar were embedded in our life. Imera was almost entirely Greek-speaking and Christian; the only exception to this was a group of ten households, about an hour's walk from Imera which retained the Greek language but had converted to Islam. For some reason, they were much poorer than us, and we kept them at a distance, although they were related to us by blood.

Our village was in decline by the time I reached consciousness; but it was still a healthier environment for a child to grow up than anywhere else I have seen. The place in Europe it resembles is Switzerland. Our house was in a small settlement called Livadi, about half an hour's walk from the main town. At the height of our prosperity, there were about 350 houses in Imera, and perhaps 60 in Livadi.

But by the time I left, most of these dwellings had been abandoned. Yet we were not poor. Of course, we had no electricity or motor vehicles or any other modern convenience. But by the standards of rural Anatolia, we were a progressive community. During the first two decades of the twentieth century, Imera was devoid of able-bodied men. My father and all his male contemporaries were away in Russia earning their fortunes. Boys would marry young, sire children and then set out for the furthest reaches of the Russian empire, finding opportunities in that turbulent but exciting world. With the money they earned, they would return to Imera and build handsome two-storey houses of chiselled white stone. And these 'local boys made good' would pay for schools and churches which enhanced our community and amazed our Turkish overlords.

Among ourselves we spoke the Pontic dialect of Greek, but at school we learned the official Greek that was cultivated in Athens and Constantinople. We called ourselves Romioi *– the old word for Greeks in the Ottoman world – but Greece itself was remote from our consciousness. The country that loomed in our imaginations was Russia.*

One family of brothers from Imera, the Efthyvoulis boys, had a bakery in the Siberian city of Chifa which turned out 1000 loaves a day. In 1913, one of them was murdered – and they made him a beautiful tombstone with an epitaph in elaborate Greek. To this day, I wonder who they found to pen such flowery language. Other lads from Imera were involved in supplying the Tsarist army during the Russo-Japanese war of 1905; and others still engaged in small trading along the Amur river which divides Russia from China. Another boy from Imera was working in Irkutsk when during one of the many rounds of the Greek–Turkish war, fighting erupted in Crete. This lad got the idea that he should go to Crete and fight. For all of us, Greece was a distant place; but some of our youths must have had romantic ideas about the Greek national cause.

The patriarch of our family, though I never met him, was my great-grandfather Hadziyangos Fostiropoulos. He was a trader and money lender, whose name – beginning with 'Hadzi' – tells us that as a young man, he made the pilgrimage to Jerusalem. In photographs, he appears as a handsome and forceful character, wearing a velvet jacket, baggy trousers and clogs with pointy toes.

His sons built on his success and founded a bank.

Hadziyangos married twice. His first wife bore him three children, including my grandmother Efthymia, another daughter Eleni and a son, George who married into a shipping family from Chios and was among the creators of the Fostiropoulos bank. After his first wife's death, Hadziyangos married a younger woman with the lovely name of Chrysanna.

So my grandmother Efthymia found she had a stepmother who was her junior by many years; but the two women got along very well. Chrysanna, in turn, bore four sons and a daughter. Two of those sons worked in the bank – Constantine or 'Costas' in Trebizond, and Socrates in Batumi, the Georgian port which was part of the Russian empire. Another of Chrysanna's sons, Diomides, married a wealthy woman from southern Russia who owned 100 hectares of fertile land in Kuban. He was the playboy of the family; he enjoyed the large mansion and handsome carriages that he acquired by marrying well.

I hardly knew my uncles; the women who looked after me in my early life were grandmother Efthymia, my mother Sotiria, my sister Sophia and my aunt Sophia, the wife of Costas Fostiropoulos.

From time to time my father would bring money from Russia. He was dogged by bad luck. Once, near the end of a journey back from Russia, he was robbed of 120 pounds, a small fortune. He was only a few miles short of our house.

The strong ladies who dominated my childhood did a good job of sheltering the youngsters of the village from the turbulence raging around us. We used to accompany these ladies as they brought the cows up to their pastures in springtime, and we helped as they gathered up the hay and leaves to feed the livestock in winter.

Was I aware that a world war was going on? Did I know that our stretch of

the Black Sea coast was taken over by the Tsar's forces in spring 1916 – and
then abandoned, because of the revolution in Russia, in 1918? I do remember
the Tsarist occupation because one day, Russian soldiers came to our house
demanding food. They discovered the stable where our prize cow, Silky,
lived – and tried to take her away. But the cunning creature knew what the
Russians wanted. She lay down on the ground and refused to budge, even
when the soldiers beat her.

One of the few grown-up men still resident in the village was my
grandfather Dimitris Siamanis, a weatherbeaten old fellow, a retired
merchant, who was bewildered by the international crises that were
disturbing, and would ultimately destroy, our little Shangri-la. 'Accursed be
the dogs that turned our world upside down,' he used to mutter to himself.
But he still took pride in the comfortable house – it had cost him 120
[Ottoman] pounds – where we all lived. We had double windows to keep us
warm in winter, and oil paintings of hunting scenes on the wall.

After the Russian withdrawal in 1918, it was anybody's guess what would
happen to us. As Kemal's army established its authority across Anatolia, they
put on trial some prominent Greeks from Trebizond who were suspected of
supporting the campaign to create an independent Pontic state. My uncle, the
banker Costas Fostiropoulos, had to go into hiding and was charged in his
absence. Eventually he was acquitted after some Muslim business associates –
Turks who worked for the Ottoman Bank – testified in his defence. But he
had already spent a long time on the run: I remember how in 1920, he paid a
clandestine visit to the village and called on my grandfather, Dimitris
Siamanis.

He imparted the news that for the time being, the risk of deportation for
the whole community seemed to be receding. 'Siamani, we've been saved . . .'
I remember him saying. As an eight year old, I only half understood, but I
knew this was good news. I know it must have been in 1920 because my
grandfather died in January 1921.

Two years later, after the Greek army suffered its final defeat, we found
ourselves in mortal danger again. One day in January 1923, all the Greeks
who still lived in Trebizond were rounded up and transported by sea to
Constantinople. One of them was my older sister Sophia. She had married
and lived well in a handsome two-storey house in the port, though her
husband was in exile. On the day of the expulsion order, she was given fifteen
minutes to gather everything she could and go to the harbour. Of all my

*family, her story was the most tragic. Her infant child died in her arms
during the voyage; and she remembered this until her death in Salonika, in
March 2004, when she was 101.*

*Amazingly enough, our mountain community soldiered on a few months
after the evacuation of Trebizond. My family went on tending its animals,
and holding services in the one church still functioning. The school had
stopped its lessons, but I remained a voracious reader. By the age of ten, I had
gobbled up the novel by Victor Hugo,* Les Misérables.

*As I pored over my books and enjoyed one final summer amid the sights,
sounds and scents of Imera, the grown-ups were making plans to leave. They
knew that the great powers were negotiating a population exchange between
the Muslims of Greece and the Christians of Turkey; and reluctant as they
were to leave the mountains where our forebears had lived for centuries, they
saw the exchange proposal as a sort of salvation. But we did not wait to be
evacuated by the League of Nations; we simply chose a moment when we
reckoned we could leave, at our own expense, in reasonable safety.*

*As they planned their departure, my kinsfolk had certain advantages: they
were an extended family, with members in many different places, and the
fortunate could help the less fortunate. By mid-1923, the main branch of the
Fostiropoulos bank in Trebizond had been sequestered, but a department was
still functioning in Constantinople and my uncle Costas was there. Somehow
he sent messages and money to the village. For those of us who were still
hanging on in Imera, the main asset during those final months was a purse
containing 300 pounds which was carefully transferred from one family
member to another. For a time the purse was in the care of Chrysanna; then
Chrysanna gave it for safekeeping to my grandmother Efthymia. Chrysanna
trusted her stepdaughter, who was older than herself, more than anybody
else.*

*Finally the moment came for my aunt Sophia – the wife of Costas – to
take a large group of family members away from the village. So it was her
turn to take charge of the purse, and it was duly handed over. Sophia was a
capable woman, then aged around thirty. She sold her own livestock and
hired enough horses to bring her party on the steep winding road down to
Trebizond. In all, the party she assembled consisted of twenty people, of
whom the majority were youngsters – including myself.*

*Each horse carried two toddlers in baskets slung on either side of the saddle;
but I was old enough to walk. My mother and two younger sisters stayed*

behind for another month or so. I don't remember feeling frightened by the journey. When we arrived in Trebizond I saw the sea close up for the first time, and was excited. But most of the businesses and mansions owned by Greeks had been boarded up. The only Greeks who had been spared were the ones with Russian passports; the Turkish authorities didn't dare to touch them. We stayed for several days with one such person, a lady called Mrs Zachariadou whose maid was a deaf-mute. I can still picture the poor girl gesturing to her mistress to inform her that a large group of people had come to stay.

My aunt bought tickets for a cargo ship and we began our journey along the Black Sea coast. The change of environment did not suit me; I had headaches, and Aunt Sophia tried to soothe the pain by placing an onion on my forehead. But I was still curious enough to observe closely as we stopped at Giresun and took on a cargo of hazelnuts. A bag of nuts broke open and I ran after them as they rolled around the deck.

When we arrived in Constantinople, a young lad who was travelling with us was arrested by the Turks. But compared with many of the Black Sea Greeks who left Turkey around that time, our fate was not bad. With the help of uncle Costas and the family bank, we boarded another ship for Piraeus, and then sailed on to Salonika.

That was when our trials began. We found ourselves in a former army camp, used by French colonial troops during the First World War, where there were millions of lice. It was a moonscape, with not a tree in sight. We remembered our mountain valleys and we cried. But there were compensations as well as trials, as we accustomed ourselves to life in Greece, which was really a third-world country in those days. For one thing, we ran straight into my father and his sister: with Russia now firmly in the hands of the Bolsheviks, their adventures in that country had come to an end, and they struggled to start a new life in Greece.

My poor father never succeeded in Greece. For most of his life he had been travelling backwards and forwards between Russia and our home village – and he enjoyed his adventures in Russia. He had some cousins who had grown rich in the Crimea, and he used to joke to us about their pretensions. After the First World War, he went from Russia to Greece and tried making his fortune there. But nothing quite worked for him. At one point he set up a cafe with an Italian partner; but he complained that everything about Greece was unfamiliar – down to the cheap copper coinage – and it never presented as many opportunities as Imperial Russia once did.

My father's final attempt to make money in Russia was in 1922, when he and his cousin Yangos went off to Batumi to see if they could take advantage of Lenin's New Economic Policy. But they failed; by the time I was reunited with him in Salonika, he was starting from scratch again. We lived in Panorama, which is now a prosperous suburb but was a desolate place then. People would walk several miles to find jobs in the city centre. Typhus and other infectious diseases took a terrible toll among the refugees. But somehow the cycle of life continued; boys and girls fell in love, and we almost revelled in our poverty.

Soon after we arrived in Greece, we moved to the town of Naoussa, where my teachers were amazed by my reading abilities, and they put me straight into the fifth class.

But it was hard for the family in Naoussa. The native Greeks mocked our dialect and suspected our political affiliations. Of all ridiculous things, they accused us of being communists, and of turning Greece communist. There was a great irony about this – when so many of our fellow Pontic Greeks were suffering under the Soviet regime.

In Greece I have lived through turbulent times – invasion, dictatorship, civil war – and I rejoice that my grandchildren are now growing up in prosperity and peace. Through every trial, I have been sustained by the memory of the place where I grew up: its trees, its flowers, its solid stone houses and its perfumed air. I remember the men who laboured in Russia to sustain us, and above all the women who guided me as I took my first steps on the mountainside, and opened my eyes to the beauty and danger of the world around me.

But I still feel it was necessary for us to leave. Our only protection in Turkey was the isolation of our village and the good relations which people like my uncle enjoyed with his Turkish colleagues in the bank. But we never had any real security. For example, if we were robbed as we went from one village to another, who could we turn to for help? We had no protectors. I think we did the right thing when we came to Greece.

What makes this story unusual is the unspoken fact that young George Siamanides had hardly ever met a Turk or a Muslim before leaving Anatolia; this in turn reflects the fact that his home village was almost entirely Greek and Christian and physically isolated from the reach of the Ottoman authorities. But even in Imera, the fact that a handful of local families had become Muslim, while retaining the Greek language, served as a reminder of the possibility of religious and ethnic ambivalence. For many other Greeks from this region, especially those from the town of Trebizond, this and other kinds of ambiguity were an unavoidable feature of the world they left behind.

Ali Onay, the grand old man of the Cretan Turkish community on
the islet of Cunda, formerly Moschonisi

Ferhat Eris (right) now the doyen of 'Mytilene Turks' in Ayvalik,
with his father Ali and brother Mithat

Vedia Elgun (centre, seated) with her father Ali Esraf Ertan, a wealthy lawyer and landowner from Salonika, and her mother Kamile. Vedia's three sisters and brother are standing in the background

Vedia Elgun, a grand and loquacious Turkish lady whose family were once wealthy landowners near Salonika

Raziye Ogus, a grand old lady in her nineties who nurses memories
of a comfortable childhood in the Greek lakeside town of Yannina

Fatma Gültekin, a great-great-grandmother

Hüseyin Çetin, a Turkish citizen born in 1914

A Greek high school teacher in Trebizond and her pupils

Music students at the Greek High School of Trebizond

Wealthy Greeks on an excursion to the outskirts of Trebizond, where many of them had villas

Bishop Germanos Karavangelis,
a sponsor of militant Greek nationalism
in Macedonia and Samsun

Chrysanthos Filippidis, a bishop of Trebizond
who was also an artful diplomat

The great monastery of Panayia Soumela,
the spiritual heart of Christian Pontus

The cathedral of Ayia Sofia in Trebizond, now a museum

CHAPTER 6

Out of Constantinople

In many ways, the pulsating, nerve jangling, smoggy mega-polis of modern Istanbul would astonish a person who last saw it in early 1923, when it was the shrunken, war-ravaged capital of a dead empire. As the months ticked by before the ending of the Allied occupation, promised in October of that year, Turkish nationalists grumbled at the British, French and Italian forces who swaggered down the central thoroughfare which was then called the Grande Rue de Pera and is now known as Istiklal Caddesi (Independence Avenue). The nightclubs were full, and the refugee camps brimmed with fugitives from the Turks, the Greeks and the Bolsheviks.

Since then, the city's population has expanded by a factor of 30. It has recovered its old position as by far the biggest conurbation in the south-eastern corner of Europe, with 15 million residents spreading in every direction, mostly in cement blocks that look ready to crumple when the region is finally struck by the big earthquake everyone expects. Along with the decadence and hedonism that has never been absent, there is a new influx of rural conservatism; pious bearded men and headscarved women rub shoulders with designer-clad youth.

But of course, the city's defining features have not changed. Approaching the Bosphorus by sea, the traveller's eye is still caught by a vast square building with stone walls, small windows, and towers at each corner. This is the Selimiye barracks, which dominates one headland of the Asian shore. In early 1923, this forbidding edifice became a link in a chain of human misery, connecting the Black Sea ports of Samsun and Trebizond with the overstretched Greek harbours of Piraeus and

Salonika. Selimiye first caught the western world's attention during the Crimean War when it became a makeshift hospital for British soldiers. This was the place where Florence Nightingale pioneered the modern principles of nursing, as she carried her lamp round four miles of beds and browbeat officers into improving the sanitary regime for the wounded tommies.

By March 1923, conditions at Selimiye were much worse than they had been in the direst moments of the Crimean campaign. An even larger number of sick, despairing people – Anatolian Christians this time – were crowded into its endless corridors, awaiting succour. More than 8000 at one point, hundreds of whom were dying every day. There were no beds, no figure with the authority of Florence Nightingale and for a time it seemed there was little hope of stemming the epidemics of smallpox and typhus that were raging through the dank fortress, infecting doctors and nurses alike. Selimiye had turned into a charnel house because of a bottleneck that was developing in the flow of unwanted Orthodox Christians from Turkey to Greece. From mid-December, the Turkish authorities began forcing boatloads of Christians from the various Black Sea ports to set sail westwards. By January the main Greek ports were overflowing and the government in Athens said it was unable to accept any new arrivals, partly for fear of importing disease. This led to a pile-up of refugees in Allied-occupied Constantinople, where the local Greek community, in between fretting about its own future, had to pool its collective resources to care for the new arrivals as best it could. Every Greek-owned space in and around the city was filled with destitute people – the seminary and monasteries on the Prince's Islands, every Greek school, the showpiece Greek hospital of Balikli. But still it was not enough. At times, ships filled with sick passengers were left listing off the coast for days before a way could be found to let them land without infecting too many others. After every other available space was filled, the Allied authorities decided that Selimiye should be opened up to refugees; but for many of them, the barracks turned out to be a deathtrap rather than a place of safety. On 6 March the *Manchester Guardian* described the scene in grisly terms:

A hundred dead were counted in the [Selimiye] barracks, two-thirds of these having lain beside the living for several days. Fifty had died in one room. The refugees assigned to the task of grave digging, being the only ones allowed outside the camp, abandoned the barracks, horror-stricken, and fled.

On 31 January, a day after the population exchange was agreed in Lausanne, Venizelos had complained that the Turkish authorities were violating the spirit of the accord by proceeding with unilateral expulsions (of which 3000 people, recently driven out of Trebizond were only the latest example) rather than waiting until May, the earliest date when the population transfer was supposed to start. The Turkish delegation insisted that the people pouring out of their country's harbours were leaving voluntarily, while Greece was evicting Turks from Western Thrace and persecuting Cretan Muslims. The diplomatic climate began to worsen. In February, after the Greek government had formally closed its harbours to new arrivals, it was quietly but firmly rebuked by western embassies in the region. They anticipated, correctly as it turned out, that Turkey would retaliate by imposing even harsher conditions on the 100,000 or so Greek Orthodox men and boys whom it was holding captive as forced labour.

In the background, there was a deterioration not only in the Greek–Turkish climate but in the broader prospects for peace between Turkey and its former adversaries. On 3 February the Lausanne negotiations were suspended after Turkey rejected a draft text for a comprehensive treaty which had been presented by Lord Curzon in a spirit of take-it-or-leave-it peevishness. So the Turkish, Greek and other Balkan representatives returned to the febrile atmosphere of their homelands, hardly knowing whether renewed war or uneasy peace was in prospect. It was true that the most powerful figures in the Turkish and Greek worlds, Kemal and Venizelos, retained a strategic instinct which often enabled them to see beyond day-to-day crises. But their countries were still in ferment; in neither state did the government's writ run effectively, and in neither nation had war fever entirely subsided.

When the Turkish delegates returned to Ankara, they immediately sensed the ultra-patriotic mood. Whereas in Lausanne, the Turkish negotiators had often seemed stubborn and bloody-minded to their western interlocutors, the suspicion among Ankara's parliamentarians was that their delegation had been far too soft. These sceptics had grave reservations about the agreement on population exchange, struck only a few days earlier. The Lausanne negotiators were pleased to have secured a 'right to remain' for the Muslim population of western Thrace; but many politicians in Ankara thought their country should go further. It should simply press for the annexation of that territory. So on this and many issues, Mustafa Kemal had to find ways of assuaging a powerful nationalist backlash while finding a realistic basis for further negotiations with the Allies.

The Greek authorities, meanwhile, faced pressure of a different kind: a refugee crisis which brought the shattered Greek state, and Greek society, to the brink of collapse. In the end the crisis was contained, in the nick of time, by an international aid operation. As it was, thousands of the refugees who arrived in Greece in the course of 1923 died prematurely because of infectious diseases, poor nutrition and the exhaustion and trauma of the journey. The number might well have run into hundreds of thousands if there had not been massive external assistance. Yet this aid would have been far more effective, and averted more suffering, if the western nations had been better co-ordinated, and less preoccupied with outmanoeuvring one another in the race for influence in the newly established Balkan order.

Turkey also faced a daunting humanitarian task. It had to rehouse hundreds of thousands of its own citizens who had been burned out of their homes by the retreating Greek army, or put to flight during the Greek atrocities of summer 1921. But the new Turkish government was determined to deal with this challenge, as well as the impending one posed by an influx of Muslim 'exchangees' from Greece, without much external assistance. Even though their financial and administrative resources were very limited, the nationalist authorities in Turkey were so zealously attached to the ideal of unfettered independence that they preferred to do things their own way. Western charities had acquired a dubious reputation in Turkish nationalist eyes because they seemed more concerned about the fate of Ottoman Christians than of Muslims whose needs were also acute. It was therefore laid down that any role played by western relief agencies in Turkey would be of limited scope and strictly on Turkey's own terms.

In Greece, there were no qualms about seeking as much external help as anyone was prepared to provide. So desperate was the situation that the Athens government would have turned its entire public health and welfare system over to foreign hands if such a service had been on offer. But the process whereby Greece sought, and other countries provided, an emergency injection of aid was snarled up by geopolitical and human rivalries among the potential donors, who fell into two main categories. One line of assistance was provided by the government, relief agencies and ultimately the public of the United States. Another came from Britain and the other European nations which were trying to breathe life into the League of Nations.

Both the Americans and the League agreed that Greece needed emergency assistance immediately, and longer-term help with resettlement as soon as possible. But as almost always happens when relatively rich countries get together to reconstruct relatively poor ones, some unpleasant games of 'pass-the-parcel' were soon being played. Each side wanted the prestige and diplomatic leverage that went with leading a reconstruction effort; and each side seemed concerned about being manoeuvred into paying more than its share.

In the immediate aftermath of the Turkish victory, when it became clear that over a million Anatolian Christians were looking to Greece for shelter, it was above all the American government and American aid agencies which responded to the challenge. Public opinion in the United States was already sensitive to the sufferings of 'Near Eastern Christians' – a catch-all term to include Armenians, Greeks and various Christian communities of present day Iraq and eastern Turkey – thanks to the activities of American missionaries, teachers and relief agencies.

The words and deeds of these envoys remain highly controversial. Turkish historians have often accused them of being indifferent to the suffering of Turks and Muslims, and of spreading anti-Turkish propaganda with an agenda that was as much geopolitical as altruistic. Nor is the work of American relief agencies much remembered in Greece, perhaps because people do not care to look back on periods when they were vulnerable and humiliated. But in the United States, there are many families of Greek or Armenian descent that trace the survival of a grandparent or great-grandparent to an American hospital or soup kitchen in the depths of Anatolia.

In the aftermath of Izmir's capture, a wide mixture of imperatives guided American policy. On the one hand, American diplomacy and American business saw great opportunities in the emerging Turkish republic. The fact that the United States was a relative newcomer to the region, and was not tarnished in Turkish eyes by association with the strategic games which western Europeans had been playing there for centuries, could only help. The Americans had never joined the Entente in the war against the Ottoman empire. They had helped Britain and France defeat the German Kaiser, but never taken up arms against the Sultan.

The opening this presented for Washington was keenly sensed by Admiral Mark Bristol, the influential American envoy to Turkey. Bristol is generally treated as a hero by Turkish historians, and demonized in Greek and Armenian accounts. It is certainly true that during and after the capture of Izmir, he took trouble to suppress accounts of the story which showed Turks in a bad light. It was at his behest that American ships in Izmir harbour were instructed, at the height of the conflagration, not to do anything which might be construed as aid to the Greek enemy; they were to protect and rescue American citizens and property, but not local Greeks or Armenians. He was a person of robust views on racial questions. He was an Anglophobe who also regarded the Greeks as 'about the worst race in the Near East' and did not care much for the other religious minorities of the region. 'Armenians are a race like the Jews; they have little or no national spirit and have poor moral character,' he once wrote.

Despite his prejudices, the historical record clearly shows that the admiral was a supporter of the campaign to relieve the plight of the Anatolian Christians, both Greek or Armenian, during their exodus from Turkey and following their arrival in Greece. As long as they did not engage in 'anti-Turkish' propaganda, Bristol backed the American relief agencies in their efforts to assist the Christian refugees – especially after they had been removed from Turkey. When the Turkish authorities imposed a prohibitive tax on the import of food aid and other emergency provisions, the admiral lobbied hard to get this measure repealed.

In the formation of American policy, yet another factor was at work. While Washington saw an opening for itself in the new Turkish order, it saw similar opportunities in Greece. But they had to be pursued cautiously. As long as Greece was under a military regime – a regime, moreover, which in November 1922 shocked the world by executing six leading opponents for losing the Anatolian war – there was a certain awkwardness about upgrading relations between Washington and the cradle of democracy. Throughout 1923, America's senior envoy to Greece was a chargé d'affaires, not an ambassador. But in the absence of full-blown diplomatic ties, a huge aid programme could be the centrepiece of a new Greek–American relationship. Venizelos was one of the first people to see this. In autumn 1922, he told an American interviewer that the European powers were too exhausted by war and political upheaval to be of much assistance to Greece. It was on the financial and organizational gifts of the United States that his country now depended.

In early October 1922, the American administration decided on an ambitious relief operation for the refugees who had arrived in, or were *en route* to Greece. Certain conditions were laid down: the European Allies, whose reckless imperial games were in part to blame for the crisis, must contribute their share. So must the Greek government. It must be made absolutely clear that any funds expended in Greece were intended to consolidate the peace, and help to demobilize the army, rather than ease the way for new military adventures. The American government would act as co-ordinator, but most of the funds would be raised in the form of voluntary donations from the American public.

On 7 October 1922, President Warren Harding convened a meeting of the main aid organizations at the White House. Next day he expressed the hope that, 'the heart of the American people will respond generously in enabling these agencies of relief to meet the crying emergency'. A month-long appeal was launched the following month, on Thanksgiving Day. The lead role was assigned to two agencies: the American Red Cross, which had been very active in Europe during the First World War, and Near East Relief. During eight months of intensive work among refugees in Greece, the ARC used its limited personnel with remarkable efficiency. After arriving in Athens at the end of October 1922, a team of expatriates whose numbers never exceeded forty-five managed within a few weeks to set up an emergency feeding operation which provided daily rations for nearly 500,000 people – more than half the total number of refugees then in Greece. With a total expenditure of $2.6 million, the ARC's work in Greece was its biggest single foreign operation at the time and one of the biggest humanitarian missions ever undertaken. Some of its best work lay in training local staff – especially Greek women – so that when the expatriates pulled out in mid-1923, much of its mission could continue.

But the ARC had its own long-term interests to protect. It was keen that its Greek operations should not overshadow its work in other parts of the world, and it was also adamant that the Greek government should not be allowed to slip into a habit of long-term dependence. It insisted, therefore, that appeals for its Greek operation should be publicized in one place only, its monthly magazine, the *Red Cross Courier*; and from the end of March 1923, it began to issue warnings of its imminent withdrawal from Greece – despite the pleading of the Greek government that it stay for longer. Shortly after its arrival in Greece, the ARC found itself resisting the suggestion from the public welfare minister, Apostolos Doxiades, that it simply assume total responsibility for all refugee relief operations – in effect, replacing his ministry. It also rebuffed pressure from another quarter: the League of Nations, at the behest of the ambitious Fridtjof Nansen, wanted to take the humanitarian operation in Greece under its control. The ARC insisted on maintaining its independence.

The other American agency, Near East Relief, had played a huge – but in Turkish eyes, controversial – part in assisting Ottoman Christians over the previous decade. It had grown out of an organization called the Committee on Armenian Atrocities. In late 1922, NER was obliged to leave Turkey but was able to evacuate the 25,000 or so Greek and Armenian orphans in its care and rehouse them in Greece. The neoclassical Zappeion Palace in central Athens, one of the city's best-known landmarks, was among the many public buildings which were turned into orphanages. On the island of Syros, NER built an orphanage for 2500 youngsters.

Near East Relief was by this time an accomplished fund-raising institution: an agency with a powerful constituency – fuelled by sympathy for the plight of the Armenians – and not shy about blowing its own trumpet. In November 1922, its European representative, Gordon Berry, made an appeal from Athens which was intended at once to highlight the appalling plight of the newly arrived refugees, and to underline the efficient and indispensable role of NER in dealing with 'the greatest exodus in the history of mankind' – the outflow of Christians from Anatolia, which was also, at the time of writing, the 'world's greatest tragedy'. Things were especially bad, he warned, in 'old, old Salonica – in Bible times one of the important points where the teachings of Christ were pronounced by Paul and the early apostles'. The existing total of 100,000 refugees was being increased by daily arrivals of between 3–10,000 more.

Many had taken up temporary residence in warehouses on the waterfront, with just eight by ten feet of floorspace allocated to each family. A stairway leading down to the sea had been turned into a temporary latrine, creating a sanitary hazard on which 'descriptive comment fails for lack of words'. The only food the new arrivals could be sure of receiving was a daily ration of a quarter of a loaf of bread, and sometimes a few potatoes.

In Athens, Berry reported, things did not seem quite so dire on the surface. There was less obvious sign of refugees walking the street and begging for help. But he pointed out that NER was providing a vital service by operating, out of the parliament building by Constitution Square, an information service for people in search of missing family members. 'How frequent the cry of happiness and relief as a mother is joined to her child . . . One glimpse of that mother's face would repay you a thousand times for whatever gift you may ever have made,' the eager fundraiser insisted.

Knowing the sensitivity of American charity donors to the Armenian issue, the NER drew particular attention to the plight of Armenian refugees. On the road from Athens to the coastal suburb of Faliron, 2000 Armenians were building themselves simple, neat dwelling places of clay, with tiny gardens, while another 113 orphaned Armenian girls were lodged on a ship in Piraeus harbour. 'The decks leak, their beds are greasy floors, of the old freighter, blankets are scarce, food is not much in evidence even once a day, but their faces shine with the confident belief that Christians the world over are coming to their rescue.'

Into an almost uncontrollable situation, then, a dose of breezy American optimism and efficiency was introduced. But even as the relief operation got under way, the influx of refugees was accelerating steadily, descending on all Greece's main ports from several directions at once. When the first wave of refugees arrived, initially in the Aegean islands and later on the mainland, some were received well by individual benefactors who acknowledged them as ethnic kin and co-religionists in need of help. Refugees who landed in Crete, where the spirit of Greek pride was strong and the code of *filotimo* or honour set much store by hospitality, had warm words about the locals who received them. But wherever the refugees landed, there was a limit to the effectiveness of individual acts of kindness, and such transactions were hostage to all the misunderstandings and resentments that can arise between the donors and recipients of charity.

Take the case of Anna Karabetsou, who fled from the village of Nif (Nymphaion), fifteen miles east of Smyrna with her mother and teenage sisters.

The ship delivered us to Salonika. They brought us to the courtyard of the church of Saint Minas. It was full of people inside . . . because of the feast day of the elevation of the Cross the following morning. We sat out on the marble; we didn't have a blanket or anything. The clock struck midnight and a gentleman came up to us, saying: 'Haven't you anything at all?' He went and brought us two new blankets, telling us to lie on one and take the other to cover the children. He came the following day as well, bringing little jackets and children's clothes.

Then, Karabetsou recalls, there was a general handout to the refugees.

We were all given a spoon, a saucepan and a plate. We joined the queue to receive our ration. But it was very hard for us, I was crying – and when people saw me they took pity on me and led me to the front of the queue.

Karabetsou's mother then heard that her grown-up son had survived and was in Piraeus. They took a ship there but at the last moment it was barred from landing because the harbour was already full of refugees; so they were left on the island of nearby Poros instead, where they knew nobody. 'There were empty houses on Poros. They put six or seven families in each one. Then the town crier announced that all refugees must come to the sea and receive their ration of bread – so we went down.' Karabetsou was then approached by a man who invited her and her sister to his home, a proposal they took up rather cautiously.

We went with him. He had a nice house, a wife and three little daughters. They were sitting at a well-laid table and waiting for us. They had egg and lemon soup, meatballs, fish and homemade bread. Where were we supposed to start? We took a couple of spoonfuls of soup, and we couldn't keep anything down . . . and then they realized why.

Apparently the two young women were embarrassed at being fed lavishly while their fellow refugees were starving, and perhaps unable, in their malnourished state, to digest rich food. Their hosts, 'put everything they had on plates in a box for me and my sister to take away – we thanked them and went away'.

Saroula Skyfti, another woman who fled from a village in the Izmir hinterland, remembers a chilly reception on the island of Chios.

It was drizzling, and all the doors were closed to us. Perhaps the people of Chios were frightened of us, I don't know. They looked down on us from upper windows, as we tried to shelter from the rain. We worked out among ourselves that Chios wasn't a place we could stay . . . We went into a grocer to buy a few things. We took out money to pay but the grocer wouldn't take our banknotes. 'Those notes are no good here, I don't want them,' he said. So we left our things and went out.

Then, Skyfti says, they met a police officer who took pity on them: he went back into the shop, asked the owner, 'Aren't you ashamed?' – and paid for the purchases himself. But her group of refugees had a much better reception at Souda Bay in Crete.

As soon as they saw us, they cooked meat soup for us and handed it round. Anybody who had their own tin can or saucepan took a helping and some bread and brought it back to their relatives; anyone who didn't have those things just drank the soup there and then. Then they put us in a bus and brought us to Chania, every single one of us who had arrived on the ship . . . there was a committee of men and women there who shared us out and provided us with lodging wherever there was empty space. All the people from my family and village were put in a cafe with a billiard table whose owner had gone to America. We were like little children playing houses; each family took one corner and used chairs to divide it off, and one family made the billiard table a bed. A woman from the neighbourhood brought us a mop and bucket so we could clean up, and she let us wash in her own house . . .

As long as the refugees arriving from Turkey were relatively healthy, the ordinary citizens of Greece could go some way towards meeting their immediate needs. But all this changed when ships started arriving from the Black Sea, packed with sufferers from infectious disease. A pompous report in *The Times* of London, sent from Istanbul on 8 March, gives an inkling of a ghastly state of affairs.

> The question here of the newly arrived refugees from Pontus is much complicated by the prevalence of disease among those unhappy folk, which makes it difficult to arrange their accommodation. The unwillingness of the authorities to expose the earlier arrivals to fresh infections, and the inadequacy of the hospital facilities has already led to distressing cases of smallpox victims who are inadequately isolated in small and open caiques awaiting the decision of those responsible for providing shelter who are at their wits' end how to do so.

One reason for the logjam, *The Times* noted, was the fact that the Greek government had suspended the admission of new refugees; the arrival of disease-ridden ships at its own ports was causing an unmanageable crisis. To take one example, a ship arriving in Piraeus from Samsun, on the north Turkish coast, in January 1923 had carried 2000 passengers. Of these 1600 were stricken with typhus, smallpox or cholera, and two of the three doctors on board were seriously ill.

As the epidemic spread from Turkey to Greece, the initial Greek impulse of generosity, in which the schools, churches, theatres and even the opera house were turned into shelters, gave way to a more desperate mood. Some refugees squatted in factories, with or without the owners' consent. Others constructed makeshift homes out of Standard Oil cans; shanty towns became a feature of every urban area in Greece. In the often condescending accounts of outsiders, Athens took on a bizarre appearance: colourful peasant costumes and strange dialects made their appearance in the heart of the Greek capital, as the new arrivals desperately tried to make a living on the streets, whether as pedlars, shoeshine boys or simply beggars. Clothes were often improvised from sacks, and shoes out of old rubber tyres.

The Reverend W A Wigram, chaplain to the British legation in Athens, was interested by the strange forms of speech on the refugees' lips – and by the fact that they included Anatolian Christians of all kinds, including Georgians, Assyrians and Armenians as well as Greeks. 'Who would have foreseen that the war would tear Assyrians from their eyrie in the mountain by Nineveh and hurl them on the shores of Attica?' he observed in a report from Athens in February 1923. He was equally bemused by the dialects of Georgian spoken by some of the new arrivals. Among these were 'men who talk Turkish when they want to be understood of the civilized, but who among themselves use a dialect which nobody has identified but some bold theorizers have assumed to be Mingrelian . . .' In between his speculations on philology, the reverend gentleman acknowledges that a tragedy was unfolding. Prominent Greek doctors, 'whose standard of duty has hitherto not been low', were becoming reluctant to treat refugees because their more privileged patients feared being treated by someone who had been exposed to smallpox and typhus. And despite the relief agencies' best efforts, there was a place in Epirus where, following the death of two doctors, 'all victims of typhus and smallpox were herded together in one room and left to recover or die.'

The saturation of all reception facilities was a particular problem in the port of Patras, where one in four residents was already a refugee, and just before Christmas, three big freighters carrying a total of 6000 people, came into the harbour. In the royalist strongholds of the Peloponnese, such as Patras, the newcomers aroused resentment because it was anticipated, correctly, that their arrival would boost the political fortunes of Venizelos and the republicans. The bitter oral testimony of a woman from Giresun, on the Black Sea Coast, who sailed into Patras harbour in late December is a graphic illustration of this hostility.

Winter. Christmas, early morning of the 22nd. What wonderful people they were! Callous, very callous, the people of Patras. Hungry, tired and weary from the journey, we heard them welcome us: 'What do you want in our country, sons of Turks? Go and see your friend Venizelos.' They made us sleep in open sheds. They saw our babies lying on the cement and didn't even say, here's a sack to put over your baby . . .

By the end of March, the Greek government agreed to lift its restrictions on the arrival of refugees from the Black Sea, after an assurance that the deportations of Greeks would be suspended. In fact, the expulsions only slowed down, at best. The whole episode of moral blackmail, using 'typhus ships' as a weapon, brings home the suspicious atmosphere that persisted between Greece and Turkey despite the glimmering of a strategic understanding which existed between their leaders.

Whatever it felt about Turkey, the Greek government could hardly ignore advice from the western powers, on which it was desperately and increasingly dependent. On 27 March 1923, the Greek state's envoy in Istanbul told Athens of a terrible crisis in the city. The Greek community's traditional network of medical care and social welfare, once rather impressive, had been stretched to breaking point. The director of Istanbul's main Greek hospital had died of typhus and many other staff were ailing. The Greeks in Istanbul wanted Athens to help by providing funds for a new, makeshift hospital. Athens could not possibly assist, but it used this appeal to make a fresh bid for help from the League of Nations. It was only a few days later that the American government, after prompting by the American Red Cross and 'donor fatigue' at home, warned Greece that emergency assistance would stop within a few months. Some longer-term solution to the plight of Greece's refugees was urgently needed, and it could not be devised without a huge input of expertise, as well as hard cash, from abroad.

By mid-1923, some progress had been made in combating smallpox, a disease which responds well to vaccination. Typhus, which is transmitted rapidly by lice among any group of people living in crowded conditions, was still a problem among new arrivals. If the death rate from this scourge was curbed, much of the credit goes to the smallest and least well known of the three American agencies which were at work in Greece: an entirely independent, New York-based organization, formed by female doctors in 1911, called American Women's Hospitals. Its operations in Greece were directed by Esther Lovejoy, a humorous and intelligent figure whose memoir, *Certain Samaritans*, is among the best accounts by an outsider of the crisis. After witnessing the destruction of Izmir, and the evacuation two weeks later of the women and children who had survived the experience, she travelled back to New York to raise funds for relief work, sailing steerage on the grounds that every penny saved could be used to help the refugees. By the end of 1922, her colleagues were hard at work in the overcrowded hospitals of the eastern Aegean islands: local people were fascinated and awestruck by an organization where all power, including the power to write cheques, was in female hands.

By far the heaviest burden shouldered by the women doctors from America was the supervision of Macronissi, a bleak, storm-tossed and normally uninhabited islet off the coast of Attica, just seven miles long,

which the authorities designated as a quarantine station for refugees sailing towards Athens. In her memoir, Lovejoy vividly describes a visit to the
island on a stormy day in February 1923. A ship called the *Ionia* was listing between the coast and the island, unable to land. A few days earlier,
the captain had signalled: 'Four thousand refugees. No water. No food.
Smallpox and typhus fever aboard.' The following day, as the seas calmed
and the passengers were brought ashore, Lovejoy observed:

> . . . [a] tragic procession made up of women, children and the aged, and
> a small proportion of able-bodied men, struggling through the sand
> with their bundles on their back. Many of the old people were
> exhausted, and had to be helped to the camp of the 'unclean', where all
> the newcomers were obliged to remain until they were deloused and
> their meagre belongings disinfected.

The AWH team had already established three field hospitals: one for
typhus, one for smallpox, and one for non-contagious diseases, but: 'A
great many people died soon after landing, most of them from exhaustion due to lack of food and water, and other hardships incident to this
terrible migration.'

A male American aid worker who had been aboard the *Ionia* tried hard
to convince Lovejoy it was too dangerous to leave a handful of American
women on an island whose temporary inhabitants had been driven nearly
mad by the sufferings they had undergone at sea: they had seen many of
their children die, and had to endure the sight of small bodies being cast
overboard and floating round the ship. If the island was storm-bound and
water ran out, the refugees might rise up and kill their American supervisors. But these warnings were brushed aside by the senior doctor on the
island, a lady from Omaha called Olga Stasny who insisted: 'My children
are grown and married . . . I have no duties which could take precedence
over my duties here.' In the end, Stasny remained on the island, almost
continuously, for another five months. Her main Greek assistant, Dr
Pompouras, died of typhus but Stasny herself survived the experience and
was able to return to her native Nebraska.

Lovejoy's stay on the island was much briefer. Hours after watching the
refugees 'move slowly by our cauldrons, where they were given their allot-
ments of dark bread, and mush or beans . . .' she found herself eating

reluctantly at Athens' smartest hotel, the Grande Bretagne. She describes her sensations with disarming honesty: 'Fresh from Macronissi, the spell of that horrible place was on my spirit. The room seemed full of hungry children . . . There was enough jewellery displayed in that dining room to have fed the outcasts on Macronissi island for a month.' Later that evening she sent a report to the AWH board:

> Refugee conditions indescribable. People, mostly women and children, without a country, rejected of all the world; unable to speak the Greek language; herded and driven like animals from place to place; crowded into damp holes and hovels; shortage of food, fuel, water, bedding and clothing; cold, hungry and sick . . .

Lovejoy had a sharp eye for the human dimensions of the problem she was tackling, and a practical sense of the available solutions. Arriving in the Cretan port of Rethymnon, she quickly became aware of some of the bizarre consequences of the population exchange: the town was packed with Muslims who had crowded in from rural districts of the island, where their community now feared revenge killings by Christians. Rethymnon, where some Muslims held senior positions on the town council, was perceived as a relatively safe place for people of that faith to remain, pending their deportation to Turkey. As well, thousands of Christian refugees had arrived in the port from Anatolia – and in many cases, their main language was Turkish. So as part of the 'cleansing' of Greece, Turkish-speakers were sailing into Greece, and Greek-speakers were about to be expelled from Greece. At the same time, Lovejoy's testimony suggests, this use of religion, rather than language, as a litmus test did correspond to people's feelings about which distinction mattered. In Rethymnon, Christian residents were looking after their fellow Christians, including those who spoke Turkish; and Muslim residents were caring for their rural co-religionists. These acts of intra-Muslim solidarity were being negotiated in Greek, the only language anybody on Crete spoke.

In Crete, Lovejoy worked closely with a colleague, Marian Cruikshank, who shared her Oregon roots and practical attitude. Cruikshank was hailed by Cretans as a 'prophetess' after accurately predicting that an epidemic of typhus and smallpox was imminent at the barracks outside the Cretan port of Iraklion, where 3000 newly arrived refugees were packed in. At the height of this outbreak, Cruikshank saw smallpox patients crowded three or four to a bed, abandoned by terrified nurses, with dirty sheepskin coats covering their sores. Her reputation was only enhanced when the American doctor showed them how to control typhus by installing proper washing and delousing facilities.

In Rethymnon, Lovejoy and Cruikshank saw refugee children begging for scraps of meat outside a restaurant. Cruikshank exclaimed that she longed to see the politicians and diplomats who had been responsible for the population transfer swapping places with its victims. Watching the young urchins, the Oregon doctor said she wished 'these kiddies could hang around Parliament Terrace on the Thames, the Capitol Restaurant at Washington, the cafes near the Chamber of Deputies at Paris and Rome, and particularly around the lake hotels near the Ouchy Quay in Lausanne'.

Was this too harsh a judgement? Defenders of the Lausanne accord would argue that its purpose was to bring order and regulation to a population transfer that was bound to happen – and was already happening in the most brutal conditions. In any case, even as the American doctors applied their skills, energy and common sense to relieving the refugees' immediate woes, it was obvious that something more than emergency relief was needed. Sixty miles from Lausanne, at the League of Nations headquarters in Geneva, bureaucrats were already contemplating a longer-term solution to the challenge of settling the refugees and stabilizing the eastern Mediterranean.

International efforts to help the people who had been uprooted by the Anatolian war ran along two separate tracks. On the one hand, there was an initiative led by the League of Nations, with its highly regarded organization, the High Commission for Refugees, headed by Fridtjof Nansen, and with considerable input from Britain (the League's most powerful member). On the other hand, there was a unilateral contribution from the government, aid agencies and citizens of the United States. Sometimes these two tracks ran nicely in parallel; at other times, they got badly twisted. Having been the broker-in-chief of the population transfer, and one of the people who shouldered the political and moral cost of the proposal when it was first made public, Nansen wanted to ensure that he and his organization played a leading role in implementing the exchange, and in bringing about its perceived benefits; in other words, an early return to productive activity for the people involved, especially farmers. As early as September 1922, when the League first authorized Nansen to start helping the refugees of the 'Near East', the hat was passed round the League for contributions to a relief operation under the Norwegian's authority. Britain said it would provide up to £50,000 if its fellow League members would offer the same amount. The response was paltry. Ten other countries came up with a total of £19,200, which London duly matched – but the £50,000 target was never reached.

Undaunted by this, the High Commission for Refugees got going rapidly, under the direction of its energetic leader. In some impressive work, the HCR acted as a co-ordinator of assistance to the huge number of destitute Greeks, Turks and Russians who had converged from various directions on Allied-occupied Istanbul. It also engaged in a sort of pilot resettlement project where the grim logic that underpinned the Greek–Turkish exchange was first put on show.

This project focused on one sensitive part of Greece – western Thrace. With assistance from the HCR, a small proportion of the dispossessed Greek farmers of eastern Thrace, whose mass exodus in October 1922 had been observed and vividly described by Nansen and Ernest Hemingway, found new homes and smallholdings rather quickly, on land immediately to the west of the new Turkish–Greek border. In total about 10,000 refugees from eastern Thrace, as well as other places, had the relative good fortune to be settled rapidly in western Thrace – on fields which the Greek authorities seemed anxious to make available. Something more than charitable spirit, or even self-aggrandisement by the League or the HCR, was at work in this project: the Greek government was at pains to 'Hellenize' western Thrace as quickly as possible. In order to achieve this aim, it was not merely settling Greeks on its new borderland, it was also expelling Ottoman Muslims in quite large numbers – even as negotiations were going on in Lausanne for the exemption of this region from the population exchange. What the HCR's pilot resettlement in western Thrace showed, perhaps, was the grim truth that underlies any project to settle or 'plant' a piece of land for geopolitical reasons: it is easier to install new people in a territory if you throw out at least some of the existing inhabitants first.

As early as April 1923, Nansen was able to report that with the HCR's help, eleven villages in western Thrace had been settled with Greek refugees – and were on the way to self-sufficiency, thanks to the maize and tobacco crops that would, within a few months, be gathered in. The newcomers were already engaged in such profitable activities as charcoal burning, brick making, lace making, embroidery and carpet making; and 16,000 mulberry trees had been planted, laying the basis for a silk industry. Thanks to an appeal from Lady Rumbold, wife of Britain's chief representative in Istanbul, the settlers had been provided with a field hospital; and people in Britain, responding to an appeal from churches and local branches of the League of the Nations, had contributed no less than 200,000 items of clothing.

But as Nansen was well aware, his agency's efforts were little more than a drop in the ocean when set against the broader challenge of finding homes for more than a million people in Greece and avoiding a public health disaster which could blight the whole region. If the advantages of 'unmixing the people' of the Near East were to be realized and further suffering avoided, money would be needed on a far bigger scale than kindly British churchgoers could provide. The only place where the necessary funds could be raised was the international capital market; and that was out of the question unless the world's hard-nosed bankers were given some assurance that the money would be spent, as promised, on getting refugees back into productive employment – where they could earn enough to repay the loan. The Greek government, in whose ranks Nansen had close friends, also sensed these hard realities. They would have little choice but to agree to any terms their financial benefactors might care to set. In a procedure that would be repeated in dozens of countries in the late 20th century, Greece would have to undergo a form of intensive international care that did not quite amount to a colonial takeover but nonetheless involved a huge surrender of real power.

So in early 1923, even as they struggled to salvage the best possible deal from the Lausanne peace negotiations, the authorities in Athens found themselves manoeuvring between two potential financial saviours. One was the United States and the American Red Cross, whose $2.6 million emergency relief operation was already in full swing, dwarfing any other humanitarian operation in the region. The other was the League of Nations, as personified by Nansen and the other diplomats, mostly British, who wanted the newly-founded world body to realize its potential. As shiploads of refugees continued to arrive in every harbour of

Greece, it was clear that there was an urgent need to switch over from emergency relief – which could not be sustained at the current levels – to a longer-term effort to find homes, land and employment for the newcomers. But the division of the donors into two separate camps made this harder.

The American Red Cross, sensing 'donor fatigue' at home long before the term was coined, and a drain on its operations in other parts of the world, simply wanted to get out of Greece as soon as possible, though not so abruptly as to upset the State Department, with which it had always worked closely. The State Department understood the desire of the ARC to extricate itself, but it did not want to be responsible for a disaster. The Department's Near Eastern Division was headed at the time by a promising young man called Allen Dulles, a Presbyterian minister's son who thirty years later became one of the first heads of the CIA and, along with his brother John Foster Dulles, ranked among the central figures of the Cold War. Allen Dulles' handling of the Greek refugee dossier was, as one might expect, diplomatic. At his behest, the ARC was encouraged to help the Greek government (and further its own interests) by devising a refugee settlement plan which would bring a swift end to the need for emergency aid. At the same time, other countries were told, in February 1923, that America would not be party to any settlement programme unless the ARC was given a prominent role. At the end of March, the State Department made a further attempt to concentrate the minds of the other western nations by warning that the ARC would in any event terminate its emergency work among the Greek refugees in three months' time. It suggested rather pointedly that European powers who still had 'territorial and other interests in the Mediterranean area' should be making a contribution to a settlement plan; if they did so, America would help too. The reaction of the Europeans was sulky and non-committal. They suggested that America should make a more concrete proposal, and a firmer promise to lead the way, if it expected Europeans to fall in behind its proposals.

In any case, a separate initiative to stave off disaster among the Greek refugees, and get them working again, was working its way through the bureaucracy of the League of Nations, promoted mainly by Britain. On 2 February, the Greek envoy to the League of Nations, Nikolaos Politis – a man with an almost pathetic belief in Nansen's ability to pull off diplo-

matic and humanitarian miracles – made a formal application to the
League's Council for help raising a loan of £10 million. Without the moral
support of the League it would be impossible for Greece to borrow that
amount without paying punitive rates of interest. Greece was asking the
League to act as an early version of the International Monetary Fund. In
other words, as a global body that could mediate between a weak, finan-
cially strapped government and the bankers of the world by acting as
guarantor – to the financiers – of the poor country's good behaviour.

The League launched an investigation to see what revenues and assets
Greece could offer against a loan. It also named a 'Greek committee' – with
British, French and Italian representatives – to consider the financial data.
Nansen told his British deputy, Colonel James Procter, to make a study of
what, in practice, could be done with a £10 million loan and how quickly
the resettled refugees could start paying it back. Within a couple of months,
Procter delivered a report which described the enormity of Greece's problems, but also showed solid British pragmatism in its approach to solving
them. The proposed sum of money, he reckoned, was the bare minimum
needed to resettle the newcomers in Greece, who as of 1 March 1923 numbered about 1,060,000. Of these, some 860,000 were 'indigent' – in other
words, they had either arrived penniless, or whatever funds they brought
with them were now exhausted. In Athens, refugees amounted to nearly 40
per cent of the local population; in the adjacent port of Piraeus the figure
was 25 per cent, while on the island of Mytilene it was 10 per cent and in
the Aegean islands as a whole 48 per cent. Of the 860,000 destitute people,
494,000 were of farming stock, while the rest had previously been town
dwellers. The ratio of women to men was said to be 58:42 – but this figure
(including, of course, boys and old men) surely understates the desperate
paucity of able-bodied males among the refugees.

As Procter's report shows, the insistence of Nansen and others that the
refugees must be 'put to work' – preferably on the land – reflected something more than a puritanical belief in the virtues of honest labour.
Hungry, unproductive refugees were a desperate and unsustainable
burden on Greece's exchequer and balance of payments. Set them to work
on the land, and a vicious circle would be turned into a virtuous one. In
1920, the report noted, Greece's per capita consumption of cereals had
been 230 kg; with a million more mouths to feed, it would need an extra
230,000 tonnes of cereal. But if, with the refugees' help, an extra 580,000

hectares of land could be cultivated, Greece could eliminate the need for cereal imports. Greek farmers were accustomed to paying 10 per cent of their revenues in tax; if the newly settled refugees were asked to set aside that amount in loan repayments, their debt could be cleared quite rapidly. But it was essential, the report pointed out, to settle grain farmers in their new holdings by February 1924, and growers of other crops by March; otherwise another whole year would go by without a harvest. Rural resettlement, for all its huge direct and indirect benefits, was quite costly at the outset; Procter suggested that £6 million would be needed to get 100,000 families, or 500,000 people back on the land. As for urban resettlement, that could be done with a much smaller outlay: wheelwrights, ironsmiths, carpenters, brick makers, boat builders and so on could be set up in business with very modest amounts of capital. The government could also engage in public works, such as road making and the draining of marshes, that were designed to give jobs to refugees. By all these devices, another 200,000 people could be put to work at a cost of £1.5 million. On top of that, Procter believed, as much as £1.8 million would be needed to support those who were too old or infirm to support themselves – and another £3 million was required in short-term emergency relief. So all in all, about £12.3 million would be needed to handle the refugee crisis.

In early summer 1923, as the American Red Cross closed its feeding stations, the chances of raising such a sum seemed very remote. Nansen had warned in April that the refugees were 'literally faced with starvation' during the summer unless more outside help was obtained. In May, America's Allen Dulles weighed in with a proposal for an international commission, in Athens, that would co-ordinate both relief and resettlement to the tune of $500,000 in each of the next six months. But there was a precondition: Greece must give way in a long-running financial dispute between Athens and Washington. This related to America's share of the so-called Tripartite Loan, through which the United States, Britain and France tried to shore up the finances of their Greek ally in the final stages of the First World War. As part of this deal, America had offered Athens a credit line of $50 million, and the Greek authorities, somewhat over-hastily, issued a corresponding amount of drachmas. But only $15 million was paid out by the American side, and the lack of fresh funds from the United States had contributed to a plunge in the value of the drachma. What Allen Dulles wanted was for

Greece to soft-pedal its demand for the outstanding credits.

In any case, the prospects for Americans and Europeans finding common ground, in mid-1923, seemed to be receding. This was partly because rivalry between London and Washington had grown rather intense. C H Bentinck, the British chargé d'affaires in Athens, warned his masters that Greece's trade with America was overtaking its commerce with Britain. He was deeply, perhaps excessively sceptical about the motives for the American relief operation. He wrote:

> It was sometimes asked, whether this great display of charity on the part of America was entirely altruistic, or whether in return for American assistance in one of the darkest hour's of Greek history, the Greek government might not be called on to grant all sorts of commercial and economic concessions which in the circumstances they can hardly refuse.

Meanwhile Washington's enthusiasm for the League of Nations and its activities in Greece was dampened further when Bentinck boasted to Ray Atherthon, America's man in Athens, that the League's effort to raise a resettlement loan was 'virtually British' in inspiration; and when Nansen made little secret of his belief that America had shown meanness of spirit over the war-time loan. Yet another source of transatlantic friction was the fact that the American Red Cross, in the person of its Greek representative William Haskell, became dubious about the usefulness of further aid to Greece – and in particular, sceptical about Nansen's ideas on how to help the refugees. With a vehemence that embarrassed even the State Department, Haskell said the Greek government should stand on its own wobbly feet. None of this squabbling was any help to the refugees.

Even within the League, where the idea of helping Greece enjoyed general sympathy, obstacles cropped up. On 25 June, the League's financial committee reported that although Greece did have some securities that could be used to raise a resettlement loan, the total should – in view of the instability of the political conditions there – be no more than £6 million. Years later, a Greek diplomat blamed these delays on France, whose ambassador to the League had at one point denounced the whole idea of involving the world body in raising credit for the refugees. 'Address yourself to bankers, we are not financiers here!' the French envoy had exclaimed, in an outburst the Greeks never forgot. The French and Italians could offer one semi-serious argument for caution in lending to Greece, as long as the Lausanne conference was dragging on: a financial lifeline might tempt Greece into fresh military adventures and upset the region's fragile equilibrium. But on 24 July, the Lausanne Treaty, with its 141 articles was finally signed. It established the Turkish republic as an independent state, with none of the entrenched privileges for western powers that were built into the Ottoman system. In the final stages of negotiation Turkey waived its demand for financial compensation from Greece, and was given sovereignty over a small strip of Thracian land, the western hinterland of Edirne, instead. Otherwise, the terms of the population exchange, agreed six months earlier, were reaffirmed. Western Thrace, while placed under Greek sovereignty, would retain its Muslim inhabitants (or take them back, if they had been expelled); elsewhere in Greece Muslims would be deported to Turkey.

With these peace terms finally settled, it was now incumbent on the League to get on with implementing the exchange and mitigating its effects. Part of the League's role was spelled out in certain, rather unrealistic provisions of the treaty. The League was required to set up a 'Mixed Commission' of Greeks, Turks and neutrals (ie people from countries which had not fought in the First World War) with a formidable range of responsibilities. In theory at least, this panel's job was not merely to 'supervise and facilitate' the exchange, but also to 'carry out the liquidation' of property left behind by the exchangees, to value it and prepare the way for massive compensation payments.

The League also had a more urgent task: to organize the practical details of resettlement for those who were already in Greece. By September, the League's British-dominated bureaucracy had worked out in detail, and agreed with the Athens authorities, its plan for a Refugee Settlement Commission which would be vested with enormous power. The Greek government would turn over to the RSC, as its absolute property, 500,000 hectares of land. With the League's backing, Greece would raise, and turn over to the Commission, a credit whose initial amount would be somewhere between £3–6 million. The servicing of the loan would be assured by the panel of creditors which had been established in 1898 after Greece went bankrupt in the wake of a brief but disastrous war against the Ottoman empire. Although Nansen might have wished it otherwise, the RSC was explicitly forbidden from engaging in emergency aid to the sick or hungry. All its work must be concentrated on 'settling' the newcomers to Greece in homes, farms and jobs – in a way that would provide an income and allow the credit to be paid off swiftly. This provision was felt to the best way of maximizing the chances of winning over the world's sceptical financiers. In the hope of patching up transatlantic quarrels, the American relief organizations were invited to nominate the RSC's chairman. His deputy would be a nominee of the League, and the committee's two other members would be Greeks.

These arrangements looked ingenious, on paper at least. In September, as the Hellenic government licked its wounds from a diplomatic spat with Italy (which had bombarded Corfu in retaliation for the killing of a group of Italian officials in northern Greece), it had little choice but to accept the terms devised by its benefactors. To some degree, the RSC would function as a state within a state; but there would be enough Greek input into the work of the committee, which took over parts of local ministries of health and public welfare, to save Hellenic honour. Even on those terms, it was still an open question whether the RSC, operating in a country whose constitutional future was highly uncertain, and whose military rulers were not fully recognized by any western power, could win the confidence of the world's bankers. As emergency relief for the refugees in Greece dried up, the spectre of a fresh wave of avoidable deaths from exposure, exhaustion and disease among the refugees from Anatolia was still looming.

Into this confused and ominous situation, there stepped the quick-minded, powerful and well-connected figure of Henry Morgenthau. Born in 1858 to a German–Jewish family which emigrated to America when he was a child, Morgenthau had been a successful lawyer and real-estate magnate before embarking on a diplomatic career as Washington's envoy to the Ottoman empire. Like virtually all the main western envoys to that region, he developed strong preferences. In Morgenthau's case, the feelings he nurtured were scarcely concealed. His sympathy was for the Ottoman Christians, Greek and Armenian, who in his view had suffered badly at the hands of their Turkish overlords; and he worked to convince his bosses in Washington that they should share this view. As the First World War raged on, he developed an intense dislike for the young leaders of the Committee of Union and Progress who had forged Turkey's alliance with Germany against Britain, France and Russia. According to Morgenthau, one of those leaders, Talaat Pasha, had 'barely concealed' his desire to do away with the Armenian community – and had demanded to know why the ambassador, as a Jew, should be concerned about the fate of Christians. Among Turkish historians, Morgenthau is denounced as a propagandist who was indifferent to the suffering of Turks, and who exaggerated the plight of Armenians in order to rally sympathy for the Entente powers. Whatever his guiding passions, they were more complex than that. As an ambassador in wartime Constantinople, he had met some of the most accomplished and talented representatives of the Greek and Armenian communities. But despite his admiration for Venizelos and his philhellenic sympathies, and in common with most observers who knew the region well, he disapproved of the Greek landing in Smyrna in 1919, which Venizelos masterminded. Quite correctly, he sensed that Greek expansionism in Anatolia would have terrible consequences for the Ottoman Christians.

By autumn 1923, those consequences were still being felt in an agonizing way. But Morgenthau was well placed to overcome transatlantic squabbles, and also to mediate between the hot-blooded world of Greek politics on the one hand and the detached and sceptical environment of international finance on the other. In his own reminiscences of his mission to Greece, he emerges as a subtle, charming, shrewd and where necessary, ruthless figure with a keen sense of the strengths and weaknesses of his interlocutors. Like Fridtjof Nansen, he was an early example of an international 'trouble-shooter' with a personal charisma that cut across the barriers of citizenship and culture.

The fact that he was from the United States helped to assuage the fears of some Americans that their country's generosity would be exploited by scheming Europeans. The fact that he was a friend of the Constantinople Greeks made him a welcome interlocutor in Athens. And the fact that he was willing to work through the League of Nations made it plain to Europeans that he did not belong to the isolationist, America-first school of foreign policy.

Arriving in London in late October, he conferred with Montagu Norman, the chairman of the Bank of England, as well as Sir Otto Niemeyer, the Treasury's Comptroller of Finance. The Bank of England, in an act of faith, had in August put forward an initial credit of £1 million on the understanding that it would be repaid as soon as the larger refugee loan had been negotiated. In Paris he consulted Sir Arthur Salter, the 'financial wizard' of the League of Nations, and Venizelos, who urged him to speed up the population exchange – which in practical terms meant the deportation of Muslims from Macedonia to create space for the new arrivals, who needed at least 40,000 houses if they were to have any hope of shelter in the coming winter.

On arrival in Athens, where he rapidly became one of the most powerful figures in the internal affairs of Greece, Morgenthau delivered a pep talk to Greek newspaper editors.

Greece's problem is primarily a business problem and one that is familiar, in its essence, to every businessman of wide experience. It is the problem of a going concern that is temporarily embarrassed. In undertaking to reorganize such a concern and put it back on its feet, the first thing to determine is whether it has enough assets to make recovery possible. On that point, there is no question in your case. And the refugees themselves are an additional asset. They bring you fresh manpower to develop your resources of lands and materials. For example, the Turks who are being removed from Macedonia are evacuating more than 40,000 houses and farms. The refugees will cultivate these farms more efficiently, and wholly for the benefit of Greece.

The latter phrase was a revealing one. Whatever proposals the financiers, diplomats and politicians of the world were dreaming up to ease the plight of Greece and the Anatolian Christian refugees, they all rested on a single assumption. The Muslims who happened to live in Greece were not in any sense the Greek government's responsibility: they were a tolerated minority at best; undesirable aliens at worst. The sooner they could be removed, the sooner Greece could resettle its 'own' people, the displaced Orthodox Christians. In the new Balkan order, every state existed 'for' a particular ethnic group, and the contours of that group were often defined in religious terms. Too bad for anyone who was born in the 'wrong' place, or who eluded easy definition.

CHAPTER 7

Saying farewell to Salonika:
the Muslims sail away

... We, Muslims, will never accept this exchange, and we declare that
we are pleased with our Greek government.

> From an appeal to the Lausanne conference by the
> mufti of Langada, near Salonika, in January 1923

... This transfer of populations is made especially difficult by the fact
that few if any of the Turks in Greece desire to leave and most of them
will resort to every possible expedient to avoid being sent away. A thousand Turks who voluntarily emigrated from Crete to Smyrna have sent
several deputations to the Greek government asking to be allowed to
return. Groups of Turks from all parts of Greece have submitted peti-
tions for exemption. A few weeks ago, a group of Turks from Crete
came to Athens with a request that they be baptized into the Greek
church and thus be entitled to consideration as Greeks. The government however declined to permit this evasion.

> *The Times*, 5 December 1923

My father, Ahmet Bey kept a sweetshop in the Cinarli district of
Salonika, near the house of Mustafa Kemal. My best playmate there was
a Greek girl called Tarasia who died in childhood. I can still remember
going to Tarasia's funeral, watching her family kiss the icons and promising myself I would never forget her. I still think of Tarasia every time
my grandchildren bring me a doll. My mother told me we got along
well with our Greek neighbours, and they cried when we sailed away.
As for my father, he was a big strong man, but he lost his mind when

he was forced to leave his newly built house and shop in Salonika. When our ship was approaching Selimpasha on the Turkish coast, he turned to my mother and said, 'Let's go home now.'

Mukaddes Bayri, interviewed near Istanbul in 2003, aged ninety.

When Henry Morgenthau went from Switzerland to Greece to take up his new job, he travelled by train via Yugoslavia, and his first Greek stop was in Salonika. So in early November 1923 he spent several hectic days there, shuttling between refugee camps, grand civic receptions and the newly formed Refugee Settlement Commission, which was destined to do its most important work, replacing Muslim farmers with Christian ones, in the nearby fields of Greek Macedonia.

At the time of Morgenthau's arrival, Salonika had been in Greek hands for just eleven years, and was still home to an extraordinary mixture of cultures and religions. It had been the most sophisticated of Ottoman cities, and despite a terrible fire in 1917 and the effects of three wars, it retained the vibrancy of late Ottoman society. In common with Constantinople, Smyrna and (on a smaller scale) Trebizond, the Salonika of the late 19th century was a combination of smart seafront mansions, shops selling European luxuries, modern transport, old fashioned Oriental alleys and markets, frescoed churches and shady Muslim graveyards. It was here that Mustafa Kemal was born in 1880 or 1881, in a two-storey house that still stands, utterly disconnected now from its concrete surroundings. As late as 1908, it had seemed possible that Salonika's medley of races and religions might lurch towards modernity in tandem rather than separately. That was the year when Orthodox priests, rabbis and Muslim preachers rejoiced together in the streets over the liberal constitution which was ushered in by the rebellion of the 'Young Turks' – a movement in which Kemal, as a junior officer, had played a minor role. But this moment of fraternity proved to be short-lived. Within months of the uprising, various forms of Christian nationalism were fraying the empire's edges while Turkish nationalism was gripping its centre.

What made Salonika unusual was the fact that the largest single element in its population were Spanish-speaking Jews, descendants of a community which had been expelled from Spain in 1492 and found Ottoman rule more benign than any Christian regime. The fire of 1917 had destroyed a large part of the old Jewish neighbourhood, and although there was no suggestion of arson, there were suspicions that the city's new Greek masters might use the blaze as an excuse to dislodge the Jews from their central place in local life. As the city fathers prepared to greet Morgenthau, relations between the Jewish community and the Greek administration were wary, but had not broken down completely. So the international envoy found himself greeted by the Jews as a co-religionist and by the Greeks as a philhellene. On one of his Salonika days, Morgenthau proceeded from an afternoon reception at the city hall to tea at the American consulate, and thence to a reception that was jointly hosted by eight Jewish organizations. 'It is amusing,' he recalled afterwards, 'that three of the organizations were Zionists. I could not refrain in my talk from telling them how essential it was for them to be real Greek nationalists, which they are not.' Not many people, either before or since, have been so confident of the compatibility of Greek and Jewish nationalism – although historians of the latter movement say it was modelled to quite a large extent on the former.

In between hobnobbing with local dignitaries, Morgenthau paid a visit to the harbour, where he received a sharp reminder of the reason for his presence in Greece. A ship carrying refugees from the Black Sea region had just sailed in.

A more tragic sight could scarcely be imagined. I saw 7000 people crowded in a ship that would have been taxed to normal capacity with 2000. They were packed like sardines on the deck, a squirming, writhing mass of human misery. They had been at sea for four days. There had not been space to permit them to lie down to sleep; there had been no food to eat; there was not access to any toilet facilities. For those four days and nights, many had stood upon the open deck, drenched by an autumn rain, pierced by the cold night wind, and blistered by the noonday sun. They came ashore in rags, hungry, sick, covered with vermin, hollow-eyed, exhaling the horrible odour of human filth – bowed with despair. And yet these old men and children and women only a few weeks before had been living at peace, in happy homes, useful and industrious citizens, comfortably housed and clothed, and fed with the fruits of contented labour.

For literary effect, Morgenthau may have exaggerated the climatic extremes of the north Aegean, and it is unlikely that the refugees had been living in comfort quite so recently as he suggests; but the human tragedy was real enough. In any case there is no reason to doubt that this man of the world was genuinely moved by the suffering he witnessed at the outset of his commission's work to alleviate the refugees' plight. His pro-Greek instincts also inspired in him a buoyant confidence that such labours could bear fruit.

> Fortunately, I . . . had known the Greeks in Turkey for what they were: high-spirited, clever, energetic, capable – otherwise I might well have doubted that those animated heaps of filthy rags that debarked from the ship had in them enough of human resources to be salvaged. Imagination alone, unaided by such knowledge, might well have failed me.

What Morgenthau fails to mention, however, is the other human drama that was unfolding in Salonika harbour around that time. A few days after he witnessed the arrival of that boatload of human misery, consisting of destitute Christians of Anatolia, a small fleet of creaky Turkish passenger ships and freighters began taking people in the other direction. The Muslims of northern Greece were being deported to a new life in the Turkish republic. Turkey wanted to receive them, Greece wanted rid of them; nothing else was of any consequence. In most cases, the fate of these migrants was not as terrible as that of the Anatolian Christians who fled either in the heat of war, or as a result of forced marches followed by forced embarkations on ships riddled with disease; but the Muslim exodus was bad enough.

For the people it affected, mass deportation marked the culmination of a decade of rule from Athens in which they had lived with uncertainty at best, persecution at worst. This belied the Utopian prediction once made by Venizelos, as a young Cretan politician: he said that in the contest for Macedonia, Greece would eventually prevail against the Slavs by showing itself to be a more benign ruler of Muslims. In fact, the north-

wards extension of Greek territory in 1912 had widely varying consequences for the kingdom's new Muslim subjects. Many Ottoman
landowners were killed or chased away by their tenants. Humbler Muslim
peasants were harassed and bullied by policemen from Crete or the
Peloponnese, but this did not usually imply any direct threat to life or
property. In Salonika, the Muslim share of municipal property fell sharply
and it became harder for the community to maintain schools and
mosques. In 1913–14, as Greek Orthodox Christians displaced from
Thrace and western Anatolia started flooding into the city and its envi-
rons, the Salonikan Muslims faced pressure of a cruder kind – many of
the newcomers broke into their houses and shops and started squatting
there. At the same time, an exodus of Muslims from all over the southern Balkans was gathering pace. By April 1914, some 140,000 Muslims
had sailed out of Salonika harbour to seek refuge in Turkey; just 24,000
of these were fleeing Greek rule, while the remainder had been driven out
by the Serbs or Bulgarians.

During the final phase of their life in Salonika, the city's Muslims
enjoyed a rather benign atmosphere, thanks to the twists and turns of
Greek politics. In the elections of November 1920, they joined forces with
the Jews and Greek royalists to cast their ballots against Venizelos, in what
seemed, at the time, to be a vote for an end to the war in Anatolia. The
war in fact continued, but the fraternity which the successful anti-
Venizelist vote generated in Salonika did not immediately evaporate. So
just before their departure, the city's Muslims benefited from a more tolerant atmosphere, including relative freedom to publish and teach in
Turkish. But immediately after the Turkish victory in Anatolia in
September 1922, and the seizure of power in Athens by republican, pro-
Venizelos officers, the intercommunal climate in Salonika darkened once
again. The young Venizelos might have been an advocate of benign, pater-
nalistic Greek rule over Muslims; but by the end of the Turkish–Greek
war, the political movement known as Venizelism had become identified
with 'Greece for the Greeks' nationalism.

Taken as a whole, Greece's treatment of the Muslims who lived until its
sway between 1912 and 1922 was relatively decent by the standards of
Balkan conquerors, in that it stopped short of systematic cleansing or persecution; but those are not standards which anyone would want to apply
today. After the end of Turkish–Greek war, several thousand Muslims

were summarily evicted from their homes in Greek Thrace, precisely the region which was supposed to be spared from the population exchange. But elsewhere in northern Greece, as many as 300,000 Muslims, mostly herders and share croppers, were still living more or less peacefully on the eve of the deportation. That made their expulsion all the more bewildering. Relatively unsophisticated peasants, with a deep attachment to their native soil, were abruptly informed by their village elders that they were being summarily deported to another country, with only a vague promise of compensation for the property they were leaving behind. The bewilderment was particularly acute for an important category of Muslim peasants in northern Greece who were known as *Valaades*, people who spoke no language except Greek.

In a sense, the Valaades of northern Greece are the counterparts of the crypto-Christians of the Black Sea region: a community whose religious and cultural identity was ambivalent. The Valaades – so nicknamed because of their frequent use of the expression *Va Allah*, by God – consisted of rural communities who had made a relatively late and in certain respects, superficial conversion to Islam, sometimes as recently as the early 19th century. According to a social historian who has studied the Grevena region in northern Greece, some local villages adopted Islam under pressure from Ali Pasha, the legendary Albanian chieftain who dominated Epirus, impressed Lord Byron and parleyed with the European powers before falling foul of his Ottoman masters. These converts continued not only to speak Greek, but also to show respect for local Christian churches and saints, and in some cases observe Christian fasts. They took Muslim names with Hellenized diminutives: Soulios for Suleyman, Bratkos for Ibrahim and so on. Asked where their real allegiances lay, they would give teasing answers: 'I am a Turk, but of the Virgin Mary', or say things like, 'There is nothing but an onion skin between us [and the Christians].' Local Greek Orthodox Christians seemed to view the conversion of these communities with a certain understanding; they were 'cousins' who had left the fold, but were certainly not on a par with Muslim Albanians, who were resented as cruel landlords or thieving outlaws, or indeed with the 'Turks from Asia' of whom a handful had been settled in Macedonia. In some cases, the Valaades may have been crypto-Christians, observing the Christian sacraments in secret; but that status could not survive more than a generation or two without the 'crypto-priests' who played such an important role in the Black Sea region.

By the time of the population exchange, the Valaades were living at a respectful distance from their Christian cousins, but with no particular hostility. After 1912, with the advent of Greek rule, it became easier to convert back to Christianity, and a handful of Valaades did so, usually in order to marry Christian women. Once they had been baptized and anointed with holy oil or chrism, they were accepted as fully Christian, and the fact that they had once been Muslim became a source of banter, nothing worse. On the eve of the population exchange, there was another small wave of last-minute conversions to Christianity, but this was not particularly encouraged by the Greek authorities. For the majority of the Valaades, the population exchange meant exactly what it did to every other Muslim peasant in northern Greece: departure to a new and unfamiliar country which was determined to take care of them, while the country of which they were notionally citizens was equally determined to expel them. In practical terms, this meant loading all the family's moveable goods onto wagons, bringing as many farm animals as possible, and walking or riding in carts from one town to another, until the convoy reached Salonika. In some cases, part of the journey was made by truck or train, and sometimes there were prolonged stopovers in towns like Veria or Kozani.

There was one important difference between the exodus of the Christians from Turkey and that of the Muslims from Greece. For the latter, the whole exodus was supervised, in a supposedly benign spirit, by envoys from the migrants' future homeland, Turkey. The Lausanne convention had provided for a 'mixed commission' of Turks, Greeks and neutrals whose job was to oversee the population exchange, including its financial aspects. It was the Turkish members of this commission, as well as the Turkish Red Crescent, who took responsibility for the Muslims of Greece as they were being transported to Anatolia. On paper at least, the commission had the task of helping every departing Muslim family to prepare an exact inventory of the fixed property it was leaving behind; this would then form the basis of compensation claims on arrival in Turkey. In fact, it was impossible to follow such an elaborate procedure for every migrant. Each householder simply gave his village elder a rough written estimate of what he was leaving behind, and this was passed onto the commission.

In theory, helpful Turkish supervisors were supposed to assess who was capable of paying for the journey to Anatolia, and guarantee free passage to those who could not. But when the convoys of Muslims arrived in Salonika harbour, there were bitter complaints from those who had been asked to pay but obviously lacked the money. Many spent part of their modest savings on accommodation in Salonika. For those who could not afford even that, tent cities sprang up, and the Turkish Red Crescent supplied them with wood and coal to keep warm. The Red Crescent also vaccinated as many as possible of the future Turkish citizens against the various diseases that were rife in the harbour; but this did not prevent an outbreak of plague in 1924, one of the many factors which delayed the exodus. In its early stages there was panic in the harbour because the ships demanded fares in Turkish lire and nobody possessed that currency. An enterprising American eased this problem by setting up a *bureau de change*. In theory, livestock were counted as moveable assets which the exchangees were entitled to bring to Anatolia. But some of the departing Muslims were robbed of their animals, or forced to sell them at knock-down prices before they reached the harbour. In many different ways, the ideal of a 'humane' transportation to Turkey was overturned by the chaotic conditions of time.

The winter of 1923–4 was exceptionally severe, and this had harsh consequences both for arriving Orthodox Christians and for departing Muslims. Groups representing the Greek refugees called on the authorities to 'get the Turks out' as quickly as possible, and drew spiteful attention to the fact that some of the Muslims were taking gold coins, animals and other chattels with them, while Christians had been forced out of their Anatolian homes with nothing. In view of the bad weather, it might have made sense to postpone the start of the exodus until spring 1924; but because of the tense atmosphere and the widespread belief that the refugees must be 'put to work' in the fields of their respective countries as soon as possible, the first big wave of shipments began in December 1923. For many refugees this meant enduring a voyage, and a landing in Anatolia, in atrocious conditions; some ships had to bob around in heavy seas for days on end because it was impossible to put out landing craft.

The main points of departure for these Muslim migrants were the northern Greek ports of Salonika and Kavala, and the Cretan harbours of Chania and Iraklion. According to Onur Yildirim, a Turkish economist who spent seven years studying the effects of the exchange, the total number of Muslims transferred from Greece to Turkey had reached 348,000 by November 1924; of these 279,900 made the journey on ships procured by the Turkish government, while the remainder were transported overland, or in a few cases made their own arrangements.

For the small minority of northern Greek Muslims who had retained their wealth, the departure to Turkey was a relatively civilized affair. Vedia Elgun, a garrulous Istanbul lady in her eighties, recalls that her father, a wealthy man of partly Greek descent, made the journey from his native Salonika to Istanbul in stately fashion. He hired his own ship to transport his extended family and five children, of which Vedia, aged not quite two, was the youngest. The clan was sorry to leave behind its estate north of Salonika, and its extensive properties in the city itself; but at least one member of the family managed to be reclassified as a Greek citizen and remained in Salonika as a successful entrepreneur in olive oil and shipping. Other wealthy Muslim Salonikans who had left between 1912 and 1922 were not so lucky. As soon as they abandoned their property in Greece, it was sequestered by the state or seized by opportunistic locals.

In the Greek foreign ministry archives, there is a thick file of exchanges between the governments of Britain and France on the one hand, and Greece on the other, about the property rights of various wealthy Salonikan Muslims who enjoyed British or French protection. At one point in 1919, the Greek government had rashly offered to restore urban property in full, and agricultural property up to a modest fifteen hectares, to northern Greek Muslims who were willing to return and reclaim what they had abandoned. Over the following two years, the Greek ministry was peppered with demands, channelled through western embassies, to clarify and deliver on this offer, and it gave ever more ingenious reasons for declining. In view of the unwritten rules of Balkan warfare, in which the possession of land or buildings is often more than nine-tenths of the law, it would have been extraordinary if the Greek government, at a time of war with Turkey, had upheld the rights of absentee Ottoman landlords against those of land-hungry Greek refugees. But the dispossessed property owners thought it worth a try.

In any case, the great majority of northern Greek Muslims were not wealthy or influential characters who could rally western embassies in their defence. They were used to following orders, in an unquestioning way, from local religious leaders and village elders; and when they were told to move to another country, they saw no alternative but to obey and make the best of it. The human pain caused by this massive dislocation has rarely found expression, either in the literature or the official history of Turkey or Greece. In Greek nationalist versions of history, the very existence of Muslims in Greece – let alone the fact that many spoke Greek and were deeply attached to their native soil – is often excised. In Turkey, meanwhile, it is acknowledged that new citizens arrived from the Balkans in the early days of the republic; but the manner of their departure, and the sort of lives they led before their exodus does not receive much attention. In the Turkish case, one reason for this silence is the fact that the removal of Muslims from Greece to Anatolia took place with the assent and co-operation of the Ankara government, and of its leader, Mustafa Kemal. So to lament the deportation – either the manner of its execution, or the need for it to happen at all – is to risk questioning the republic's foundation story.

In both Greece and Turkey, there are some honourable exceptions to this silence. The memoirs of a village schoolteacher in the Grevena region of Greece include a vivid description of the puzzlement he felt as a child over the departure of his Muslim playmates.

I was twelve years old. I remember seeing a crowd of people proceeding slowly and purposefully [from the outskirts of Grevena] towards Kozani, some on foot and some mounted. I saw the older ones dabbing their eyes with handkerchiefs, while the younger ones seemed to be marching in a more optimistic spirit, imagining the Utopian conditions of their new homeland. There was a family friend of ours among them, and my heart went out to him. I felt an impulse to go up to him and say 'May the hour be a good one for you', but something, I can't say what, held me back. I can still picture the heads of each of one of them as they left. Some turned back and waved their red fezzes at the Christians who had gathered to see them off . . . The next Saturday, I went back to my home village and my little brother told me how the Turks from our little settlement had left too. Our aunt had lifted him up on her shoulders and shown him the great mass of people who were heading down the road towards the town of Kivoton. My brother never forgot the scene. His aunt said to him: 'Yes, little boy, look hard at them because you will remember them . . .' My brother said: 'Do you mean Karis, and Fexos, and Liamas and Mazas are all going to leave?' 'Yes, child, not a single one will remain,' said our aunt, watching the twists and turns of the receding crowd with a certain sadness in her eyes . . .

Another striking account, from a Greek point of view, of the Muslim exodus, is offered by Michalis Papaconstantinou, a former Greek foreign minister, in an autobiographical novel based on his childhood in the town of Kozani where his family were prominent citizens. In the opening scenes, the boy narrator describes his grandmother, a tiny, strong-willed and religious lady, preparing busily for a divine liturgy which the local priest was going to celebrate at her behest. Only at the last moment does she disclose to the priest the reasons why she has requested these special prayers: both for the Christian refugees who were pouring into the region from Anatolia, and also 'for the others, for the ones who are leaving'. Initially the priest objects: 'For the Turks? But they are anti-Christ!' For a moment, the pious woman hesitates: 'You mean it's not right?' But then the priest, impressed by the lady's sincerity, changes his mind. 'God is for everybody – for the Christians, and for the anti-Christ ones as well . . .'

Such stories – implying that the departing Muslims were human beings whose feelings should be respected, even if their departure was inevitable – stand out in a Greek context because they are so rare. But in Turkey, too, it is only in the last few years that elderly people who began their lives in Greece, or their children, have felt able to mourn the lives that were left behind and articulate the pain of departure.

On half a dozen recent occasions, parties of Turkish citizens, mostly in their eighties and nineties, have made pilgrimages to places in Greece where they were born; to the lands from which they or their families were expelled in 1923 or 1924. These journeys, mostly to remote areas on Greece's northern edge, stirred up intense and often conflicting emotions in everybody who took part. The returnees were generally welcomed by local people. In the words of Sefer Guvenc, a founder of the Lausanne Treaty Foundation which organizes these excursions: 'There is no other place in the world where I could take coachloads of Turks and receive loud, persistent invitations from ordinary people, complete strangers, who want to take the visitors into their homes and ply them with coffee and sweetmeats.' In a quieter way, the travellers have been greeted warmly by the Greek families who had taken over their ancestral villages and farms. In many cases, these families consisted of Christian refugees from Anatolia or their progeny; so quite a few spoke Turkish, at least in the older generation. Wherever possible, the visitors from Anatolia would be guided to the homes and burial places of their parents. Sometimes they would gather up soil from their forebears' graves and bring it back to Turkey.

If these return trips to Greece are bitter-sweet and confusing, it is not only because of the profound emotions that any adult can experience when transported – by an encounter with a place or person, a snatch of music or a smell – to the 'other country' of childhood. It is also because the people involved have lived the great majority of their lives as loyal and contented subjects of an all-embracing Turkish state; a state which promised (and in some ways, delivered) even more benefits, and demanded even more exclusive loyalty in return, than most western states do. They have been taught, for example, that the Turkish republic, founded by Mustafa Kemal Ataturk, is the ultimate guarantor of their welfare and security; and they in return must be faithful to that republic, its language, culture and ideals – without differentiating themselves too sharply from other citizens of the republic. For those who have imbibed such beliefs, it can be confusing to be reminded of the fact that they were born under a different flag, and in some cases speaking another language; and to confront the fact that life under that flag was not always unbearable. It is equally arresting to be confronted with the fact that the governments of Turkey, Greece and every other country in the world assented to and, in a way insisted on, their removal from the land of their birth.

One person who has wrestled with these dilemmas, both as a public servant and as an individual, is Turhan Tayan, a former cabinet minister who paid a visit to the home town of his parents in northern Greece, a place known as Kivotos in Greek and Krifce in Turkish. This town was almost exclusively inhabited by Valaades – Greek-speaking Muslims – although the Ottoman authorities also planted a few Anatolian Turks there because of suspicions about the town's loyalty.

As Tayan disclosed afterwards, he made the trip in memory of his mother and father, a long-lived pair who were born at the start of the 20th century and died at its close. His parents (presumably Valaades) had spoken better Greek than Turkish when they were deported as young adults, in 1924. But because of the tense political atmosphere, it was never possible for them to go back to their birthplace. Only with a relative thaw in Turkish–Greek relations had been it possible for their son to make the pilgrimage.

> My parents had a big house with a courtyard, horses and servants, but now, as I discovered, there are only a few stones where their house once stood. I had a solemn feeling when I saw the place and I gathered up some earth. My father had wanted to see this place so much, and I went out of respect for my forebears. Our graves had been destroyed, so I simply prayed for everyone who had died there before the population exchange . . . But the decision to take people back to their own lands and states was a realistic one, if you think how conditions were back then. It had become hard for Muslim Turks to live in northern Greece, and likewise it was impossible for the Greeks of Turkey to go on living with Turks; we have to accept this. And it was a great success for our young republic to find the necessary transportation to bring [the Muslims] to Turkey and accommodate them . . .

This belief – that for all its difficulties and shortcomings, the management of the Muslim exodus was a triumph for the 'young Turkish republic' – is very widespread in Turkey, and not only among politicians. In one sense, it reflects something real: given that the new Turkish state was barely capable of administering Anatolia at the time, it is indeed remarkable that it oversaw the exodus from Greece in such a way that most of the exchangees survived the experience, however little they enjoyed it. But for many migrants, the ideological pressure to believe in the achievements of the 'young republic' probably made it harder to express the pain and the trauma of deportation, or to speak in a balanced way about the lives their families left behind.

The challenges of existence as a Muslim in newly Greek Macedonia are well described by Isa Erol, a highly intelligent octagenarian who has lived most of his later life in Silivri, a coastal town in European Turkey which has been swallowed up by greater Istanbul. He was born in 1920 in the vil-

lage of Labanovo (known in Greek as Simandro) near Grevena and was
deported to Turkey with his parents when he was not quite five years old.
His first language, and the language his parents spoke among themselves,
was Greek, though he has largely forgotten it now. Although his own
memories of Greece are fleeting at most, he has spent a lifetime puzzling
over the reminiscences of his parents and their generation – and over the
origins of Greek Macedonia's Muslim population.

*Our village was mixed – Greek Orthodox and Muslim – but we all spoke
Greek. My mother came from a somewhat larger town – Naslic, known today
as Neapolis – and that's why she spoke Turkish as well; but for my father and
most other people in the village, Greek was the only language they knew.
When our region was at peace, my father used to have very good relations
with his Christian Greek neighbours. He was an expert at processing tobacco;
and he would go round all the villages of our region – Christian, Muslim and
mixed – and offer his services. In those days when there were not so many
cigarette packets, but every man carried a tobacco pouch, his skills were
always in demand . . .*

*We had a solid, two-storey house built from stone and enough land,
livestock and fruit trees to provide for most of our own needs. The only things
we had to buy from the local town were salt, sugar, margarine, candles and
fuel for our lamps. I can still remember gathering in large gas-lit houses on
winter nights to hear our elders tell stories – it was the only entertainment we
had in those days. The older boys in our village went to an Islamic school and
learned to read in the old script. Altogether it wasn't a bad quality of life we
had . . . But during the Balkan wars, irregular fighters of various stripes,
what we call çeteler in Turkish, started roaming through our villages and
many people were captured or killed. My uncle was among those who died.
But even then, our relations with our immediate neighbours were not
affected. Whenever we heard that Greek troops or irregulars were about to
raid our village, we Muslims would take refuge in some larger town – like
Kastoria – and we would ask our Greek neighbours to protect our properties,
if possible, during our absence. It also worked the other way round. Whenever
the Turkish army was preparing an attack on one of the Greek settlements to
the south of us, the local villagers would move somewhere – like our village –
where they felt safer. And they would ask their Muslim neighbours to guard
their possessions . . .*

This account, based on the memories of Isa Erol's family and others in their community, may be a little romanticized – but it provides a healthy counterpoint to at least two ideologically inspired myths about Christian–Muslim relations in Greek Macedonia on the eve of the population exchange. The nationalist version – as propagated in both Greece and Turkey, with only slight variations – is that these relations were so poisonously hostile that neither community could find security except in physical separation from one another. The liberal anti-nationalist myth often suggests that relations were perfectly warm and harmonious and could have remained so if the population exchange had not been imposed as an artificial exercise in segregation. In fact, the truth lies somewhere in the middle. As anyone who is familiar with rural society in the Balkans or the Caucasus can testify, things are never that simple. Warm and cordial business relationships, and personal friendships, can transcend the intercommunal division in surprising ways; but that does not abolish the division – or alter the fact that in the event of a general conflagration, almost everybody tends to seek security behind the walls of his or her own community, and life becomes uncomfortable for those who try to occupy the middle ground.

Like almost everybody who was directly affected the population exchange, Isa Erol asks himself why it all happened, and what the story implies for the identity and cultural origins of people like himself. 'Recently, I have been looking in the library and studying the story of the Ottoman conquest of the Balkans. It's clear that right from the beginning, groups of people were being moved from Turkey and settled in the Balkan region,' he reckons. Behind these delvings into local and regional history is the belief – and perhaps the wish to believe – that most Macedonian Muslims came from the Turkish heartland; in other words, they were not local Balkan Christians who converted to the faith of their conquerors. At best, that is partially true. The impressive medieval mosques in the ex-Ottoman lands of the Balkans are a reminder that from the early days of the Sultan's conquest, Turkish Muslims were certainly living in large numbers in the southeastern edge of Europe. But it is also true that over the next five centuries, Balkan Christians – of various ethnic and linguistic backgrounds – were converting to Islam. So no Macedonian Muslim family can be sure that it did not have Christian ancestors.

Why should that be an issue at all? It might well be asked. Perhaps because in its purest form, Turkish patriotism is so all-encompassing that it seeks to play down all other sources of identity. Behind the Turkish republican slogan – 'Happy is he who calls himself a Turk' – lies the belief, and indeed the historical fact, that people of many different origins (Arab, Albanian or Bosnian, for example) were welcomed as equal Turkish citizens as long they were prepared to learn Turkey's language and abide by its laws. But the slogan's other implication is that once the desired state of happiness – Turkishness – has been attained, past lives are expunged or become irrelevant, just as they do in the French Foreign Legion or certain monastic orders. If you are indeed happy to call yourself a Turk, it should not be necessary to imagine yourself (or even your ancestors) as anything else. So for Turkish citizens who were born in Greek Macedonia, it was not always easy to accept the fact that an important part of their cultural origins might lie outside the Turkish world. Nor was it easy for the rest of Turkish society to accept that there might, in the past, have been some other claim on their fellow citizens' loyalty. An important feature of the Turkish republican world view, in its early unreconstructed form, was that nation and state were very nearly identical or co-extensive. While it was conceded that there might be a few Turks outside the borders of Turkey, it was believed that 'Turkishness' was something mainly defined and imposed within the republic's borders. At its most rigorous, this nationalist spirit creates a certain awkwardness about the fact that the Muslims from Greek Macedonia had ever lived outside Turkish territory; so it is hardly surprising that people who were born under the Greek flag find themselves wrestling hard with questions of identity.

Only in the very recent past has it become easily possible for Turks who were born in Greece to share with others their inner struggles. Isa Erol insisted, on the eve of a return visit to his birthplace in 2003 that he did not miss his old village because 'Turkey is my homeland now.' Almost every Muslim survivor of the population exchange would say the same – and it would not be a dishonest statement, in the sense that Turkey has provided them with safety, and adequate material circumstances for most of their lives. But on returning from his village, where he was welcomed by a Greek family from deep in central Turkey, Erol confided to a journalist that his feelings had changed:

I found the place where my house stood, but it wasn't there any more, there were just green fields. The new residents of the area – Greeks from Karaman in central Turkey – had built a new house just beside ours and they welcomed me in. I got very emotional when I stepped on the piece of land where I was born. My homeland is Turkey, but I wish the population exchange had not taken place, I wish we still lived there. After seeing my village, all my feelings had changed. Turkey is my homeland, but in these [Greek] places a good life could have been lived. But there is nothing that can be done about it any more . . .

The Karaman Greek family and Isa Erol were at least partly familiar to one another, because in late 1923 a group of Karaman Greeks, part of the vast wave of refugees that was pouring in from Anatolia, were billeted on the village – and Muslims were required to share their homes and property with the new arrivals. So the people who received him on his return visit were presumably close relatives (of the second or third generation) of the Christian refugees who had 'lodged' with Isa Erol's family. As he describes that period: 'If you had six fields, three were given to the Greeks – and if you had two calves, you had to give one to the Greeks . . .' Among migrants in both directions, this is a familiar story.

Surprisingly enough, this interlude of co-existence – which occurred in hundreds of villages all over northern Greece – is remembered rather fondly by many of the people involved. Indeed, it could be said that between late 1923 and the end of 1924, the villages of Greek Macedonia witnessed one of the most bizarre episodes in the entire history of war and peace, love and hatred, suspicion and trust between people who consider themselves Greeks, and people who regard themselves as Turks. For periods ranging between a few months and a whole year, houses, household property and farms had to be shared between two communities, Christians who had just arrived from the battle zones of Anatolia, and Muslims waiting to be deported to Turkey. There is plenty of objective evidence that this phase of shared existence was painful, costly and uncomfortable for both sides. The Muslims found that parts of their homes, farms and even places of worship were being requisitioned, and they could not object. The Christians had arrived in a state of destitution, deeply shocked at the loss of a relatively prosperous life in Anatolia and longing to live in normal conditions again. Yet in the reminiscences of many people, this phase of living with the 'other side' in cramped circumstances is often remembered with fondness.

The fact that so many villages saw a period of involuntary symbiosis between incoming Christians and outgoing Muslims reflects a double delay in the execution of the exchange. On one hand, the Greek Refugee Settlement Commission could not, in its first year or so of life, function as smoothly as was intended. It had neither the money nor the spare land to make permanent arrangements for the destitute people in its care. At the same time, the population exchange was somewhat complicated by the Turkish government's insistence, for reasons of nationalist pride, on handling the mass transfer of Muslims from Greece to its own territory with little outside help. In particular, time was taken up by a vigorous debate within Turkey's new ruling class over what sort of ships – foreign or Turkish – should be used to make the transfer. Not surprisingly the latter course was chosen, although it might have been more rational to use vessels from other countries.

As a result, the mass deportation of Muslim peasants from Greece – which was supposed to provide the main, though not the sole, source of land for the Christian refugees – did not really get into full swing until the spring of 1924. But the destitute Christians who were clogging the Salonika seafront could not, from the authorities' point of view, be allowed to wait that long. As a temporary arrangement, some were billeted on Muslim homes, farms and villages all over northern Greece. That is why the last thing the Muslims of Greece experienced before their deportation was a period of living cheek by jowl with Christian families from Anatolia.

Countless migrants retain memories of friendships, especially between women, that were struck up in these unpromising circumstances. In many cases, the newcomers from Anatolia would offer their 'hosts' friendly tips on where in Turkey their temporary neighbours should try to settle. Sometimes, the newly arriving Christians would half-seriously 'invite' their Muslim hosts to visit or even occupy their old houses – and look for treasure hidden in the garden.

Another feature of these relationships was a sort of formalized banter about politics, in which the Muslims would proclaim their faith in Mustafa Kemal, creator of the new Turkish republic where they were now destined to live. For the Christians, Mustafa Kemal epitomized their com-

munity's defeat and the circumstances which had forced them to leave
Anatolia. But this banter about Kemal was more than casual chit-chat.
Among the departing Muslims, the word had gone out that Mustafa
Kemal was a great and charismatic leader who would henceforth take care
of them and protect them from any arbitrary violence, from Greeks or
anybody else. In a world of fear and confusion, they had finally found a
protector. Faith in Kemal's wisdom clearly played a huge part in recon-
ciling the Muslims of Greece to their deportation. If he decreed it, it must
be the right thing to happen. Among the incoming Christians, word
seems to have gone out that they should not be too harsh in challenging
the faith of their temporary Muslim friends (except at the level of friendly
joshing) in the greatness of their leader. On both sides, people took seriously the belief that Kemal stood ready to invade Greece, and avenge any
mistreatment of the Muslims who were soon to be his subjects.

In some places, interactions between soon-to-depart Muslims and
newly arrived Anatolian Christians were complicated by language difficulties. The nature of these difficulties was paradoxical, like so much else
about the population exchange. There were future citizens of Greece who
spoke nothing but Turkish, and future citizens of Turkey who only spoke
Greek. In some of the villages round Grevena, the main language of the
local cafe changed from Greek to Turkish, as Greek-speaking Muslims left
and Turcophone Christians arrived. But most of the time, these temporary, enforced Christian–Muslim friendships in the villages of northern
Greece were facilitated by the fact that everybody involved spoke decent
Turkish.

One such relationship is recalled by Ramazan Ezer, born in the village
of Sevindik, north of Salonika, in 1917. Interviewed in mid-2004, in a
coastal suburb of Istanbul, where he and many other refugees settled, he
vividly remembered being deported, with his family, at the age of six – as
well as the events prior to his deportation:

*Before we left, about fifty or sixty households in our village were partially
taken over by incoming Rum [Greek Orthodox subjects of the Ottoman
empire] refugees. The Rum family who lived with us spoke even better
Turkish than we did. They took two rooms, and we – my parents, my
grandmother, my sister and I – were left with two rooms, so there was enough
space for everybody. The Rum grandmother got along very well with my*

Muslim grandmother, who had lost her husband to the Bulgarians. The Rum
grandmother used to urge us to settle if possible in Hayrebolu [a town on the
coast of eastern Thrace] where she and her family had lived comfortably. At
least for that short time, the Rum granny had no difficulty with us – but she
did worry about some of the other Christian refugees who were settling
nearby; some of them spoke Russian but not Turkish. These must have been
Pontic Greeks who had spent a generation in Russia. Compared with those
Pontians, the lady from Hayrebolu found it easier to talk to us. But I can also
remember hearing one of the Rum ladies saying wistfully: 'Your Mustafa
Kemal is a warrior with a sword in each hand, and a sword on each leg . . .'
To a six year old it seemed an odd thing to say, and at the age of eighty-six I
can still hear her words resounding in my head.

From his own memories and those of his parents, Ramazan retains a host
of other images of living in Greece, leaving under duress and resettling in
Turkey. During the family's final years in Greece, relations between their
district's main communities – Christians who were either Greek or
Bulgarian, and Ottoman Muslims – had neither been idyllic nor unremit-
tingly hostile. Often their tone was affected by events far beyond the ken
of ordinary farmers and cattle dealers such as his father. He recalls one
episode, when the Anatolian war was turning in favour of the Turks, in
which:

. . . the Greek police took about fifty men from our community, tied them up
with a rope, and led them to a river, where they were threatened with death
unless they gave up any guns they had. Then they separated one man, and
told the others he had been killed – although they hadn't really killed him.
Anyway our men – including my father – insisted they didn't have any guns,
and when they were asked if their neighbours had any guns, they refused to
answer – so they were beaten severely and we had to put strips of meat on
their backs to heal the wounds.

In general, Ramazan Ezer's family – and others in his village – had much
worse memories of the Bulgarians than of the Greeks. Everyone in his village could recount the story of a nearby Muslim settlement in which
Bulgarian fighters had taken all the men to a mosque, and all the women
to a stable – and then burned both groups alive. After 1918, when the

Ottoman empire was defeated, Bulgarian fighters took the chance to storm his village. Most of the Muslim men fled in the nick of time – but those who stayed, such as his maternal grandfather, were killed. 'There were no Greeks in our village, but there were some in the nearest town, and most of the time we had no problems with them,' Ramazan Ezer recalls.

Another story that loomed in the collective memory of Ramazan Ezer's village concerned a battle between Greeks and Bulgarians – some time in the twilight Ottoman years – in which: 'The Greeks fired cannons against the Bulgarians, but could not hit them – so a Turkish soldier asked if he could use the cannons, and he was more successful.'

His father was a trader in livestock; they tried to bring their donkey, at least, to Anatolia but it was stolen by gangsters – apparently Muslim Circassians who had fought on the Greek side in the Turkish–Greek war – when the family stopped at an inn on its way to Salonika. The robbers also took most of his father's money. So the family had an anxious ten-day wait in Salonika harbour, eking out their last remaining pennies, as they waited for a ship to take them to Turkey. He has no particular complaints about the voyage, although in some ways his family were lucky; one of the ships that plied the route his family took, from Salonika to the coast south of Istanbul, sank shortly after delivering a shipload of exchangees.

The arguments inside Turkey over transport for the refugees have been well documented by Onur Yildirim, who is fair-minded in his analysis of the effects of the exchange on Christians and Muslims like. Initially, the government conducted an international tender for the transfer, and shipping companies from many countries, including Greece, put in bids. The lowest bidder was Lloyd Tristino of Italy. But a Turkish politician, Mustafa Necati, managed to convince the Grand National Assembly in Ankara that assigning the job to foreigners was at odds with the national interest, and the initial decision was overturned. Two weeks later Necati was given the new job as head of a resettlement ministry, and at his behest the job of bringing 'home' the new citizens of Turkey was assigned to the state-owned Turkish Maritime Company and the Navigation Administration, another public agency. As Yildirim points out, this decision flew in the face of common sense; most of the TMC's seventeen boats were much older and much less seaworthy than those of Lloyd Tristino. But there was a way to correct this, while simultaneously boosting the national cause;

it was decided that the government would pay 600,000 liras for the TMC to buy new ships. A caustic commentary on the subject, quoted by Yildirim, notes that the foreign bidders would have sweetened their offers even further – for example by slashing their normal freight rates and promising to use Turkish coal – if the government had been interested; but clearly it was not.

The row over shipping highlights a broader truth about the population exchange. In Greece, the government fully acknowledged – and perhaps exaggerated – its own inability to cope with the vast human tragedy, and formidable economic challenge which it faced in October 1922. In Turkey, the spirit of economic and political nationalism was so strong that it could trump the considerations of common sense or humanitarianism. Turkey was truly determined to be an independent country, however much hardship this might impose on ordinary people.

In its own heavy-handed way, the newly established Turkish state did take responsibility for its new citizens, almost from the moment they set out from their villages in Greece. The migrants' voyages to Anatolia were not the nightmare journeys endured by the desperate, disease-ridden Greek families, mostly without breadwinners, who were pushed out to sea from Turkish ports in early 1923. But they were certainly not pleasure trips. Rusty, crudely furnished steamships were crammed far beyond their capacity for a voyage that could last between three and ten days. Only the sick, the elderly and children could be sure of a cabin. Most people simply had to camp on the decks and corridors. There was some effort to provide milk and hot food for the sick and vulnerable, but most passengers were expected to see to their own sustenance. But for those who were determined to see the population exchange as a heroic undertaking, these difficulties merely provided fresh material. In the breathless words of an Izmir newspaper, *Turk Sesi*:

> Winter snow . . . towering waves and all the other forces of nature were unable to stop the population effort . . . [but] the recent harsh weather has made us forfeit just a few days in the struggle to deliver our immigrant brothers into the merciful hands of Anatolia . . .

CHAPTER 8

Adapting to Anatolia

Iskender Özsoy is a journalist of the old school, with a goatee beard and perfect, self-effacing manners. He has lived all his life in Tuzla, a pleasant coastal suburb on the Sea of Marmara, southeast of Istanbul. There are only half a dozen families in the town who can trace their presence in the area as far back as the mid-19th century and beyond, and he takes a quiet pride in belonging to that group. Delving even further in the past, he can identify Ottoman forebears who fought in battles around Ankara in the 15th century.

This keen sense of history has made him a valuable chronicler of the social and economic changes which have overtaken his town during the past century. Tuzla's shifting demography is a microcosm of western Anatolia. From the late 19th century onwards, Muslim refugees from the fraying edges of the Ottoman empire, in the Balkans and the Caucasus, began turning up on the Marmara coast and in most cases blended quite rapidly into the existing Muslim–Turkish population. But until 1922, the dominant ethnic group in Tuzla was a Greek Orthodox community of fishermen, farmers and small traders. They all fled after the Turkish–Greek war in 1922, sending the local economy into a prolonged decline. Then, in the second half of 1924, those Christians were partially replaced by Muslim 'exchangees' from Greece. Two ships brought load after load of people from Salonika to Tuzla, which became one of the main entry points for migrants from Greek Macedonia, in part because an old naval hospital (now part of Istanbul Technical University) had been converted into a giant quarantine station. The newcomers were made to pass through a *hamam* or steam bath, and their clothing was disinfected. Many complained afterwards that children and elderly people became ill after being forced to don clothes that were still damp. Some of the people who sailed into Tuzla were then dispatched northwards and lodged in a yoghurt factory in the town of Mimarsinan before being settled in various parts of eastern Thrace, on the European side of Istanbul; but several thousand were told to stay at or near their point of arrival, and were given houses and land which had previously belonged to the Greek Orthodox families of Tuzla.

Only in recent years has Özsoy become fascinated by the social evolution of his home town. Now in his fifties, he spent the first quarter-century of his career as a conscientious newspaper journalist, editing pages and designing layouts – and as he puts it, enabling other people to tell stories which did not, in the end, affect him very much. Then he began to realize that an important chapter of Turkish and Aegean history had been unfolding under his nose in the very neighbourhood where he had always lived; the process by which Greek-born residents of Tuzla, gradually and not without pain, turned into ordinary Turks.

Most of the people who settled in Tuzla were arable farmers from the Kilkis region, north of Salonika. They had little idea about fishing or olive growing, the main economic activities of their new homeland. Instinctively, they were shy of living on the coast, and they insisted where possible on taking houses a few blocks, at least, from the seafront. But the newcomers' biggest trial was the initially hostile attitude of the Turkish locals. In the 1930s, there was a state of *de facto* segregation in the town. Newcomers and longer-established residents went to different mosques, used a different water pump and avoided social relations. Reality was still a long way from the idyllic state of affairs that was imagined by romantic Turkish nationalists: one in which all citizens of the republic were bound together by common loyalty to the newly created state, and by common adherence to the new ideal of Turkishness. Most of the migrants who came to Tuzla used Turkish as their main language, and followed the standard form of Sunni Islam, so they had no obvious linguistic or religious difference with the existing population. But in the absence of big contrasts, petty ones are often exaggerated. This is what Sigmund Freud meant when he spoke of the 'narcissism of small differences'. The older residents would ask the immigrants why they drank soup instead of tea for breakfast; and 'locals' also learned to pick out

newcomers by focusing on aspects of their appearance. Some of the immigrants descended from the Yuruks, an ethnic group which in centuries past
had been nomads, scattered across Anatolia and the Balkans, who mixed
Islam with an elaborate folk religion. Mustafa Kemal claimed to have some
Yuruk blood. People of Yuruk origin often have high cheekbones and a
ruddy complexion, and Yuruk men sport curling, carefully tended moustaches; so on the streets of Tuzla, these features become a token of non-local
origin.

At bottom, however, the quarrel between newcomers and locals was
simply a squabble between two nervous and introverted groups of people
over a finite amount of economic assets. The older residents did not care
to worship with their new neighbours, saying there was no room in the
main mosque, so the exchangees created a makeshift mosque out of a
church. (As Özsoy recalls, this building later became a wedding salon,
then a cinema, and then it was pulled down; of the six churches that functioned in Tuzla before the population exchange, none is still standing.
Indeed there are only three public buildings of any kind which date from
the 19th century, and are still intact: a hamam, a wine cellar and a
mosque.)

Very gradually, the town's social divisions eased, in part thanks to a
schooling system, and a political discourse that laid great emphasis on
equality of rights and obligations among all citizens of the Turkish republic. Only in the 1950s did intermarriage between immigrants of Greek
origin and 'locals' start to become common. As late as the 1970s, when
Özsoy himself married, the social distinction was still palpable. He came
from old Tuzla stock, while his bride descended from recent incomers;
such unions still caused a certain *frisson* among the extended families on
both sides. But long before he married Özsoy was also aware of certain
relationships whose intensity was sharpened by the very fact that they
transcended the intercommunal divide.

*I knew of two men – one of them an uncle of mine, and the other a cousin of
my wife – who had both been born in Tuzla in 1932. As teenagers, they
became close friends and declared themselves to be blood-brothers, despite the
fact that one was a 'local' and the other belonged to a refugee family from
Greece. The friendship survived into adulthood. My uncle died twenty years
ago, but my wife's cousin still remembers his blood-brother with tears in his*

eyes, and I have always considered my uncle's friend as a kind of surrogate uncle of my own.

By the early 21st century, the distinctions among Tuzla's residents have been blurred even further, though there are still certain districts of the town with a noticeably high density of Greek-born families. In the life of the town as a whole, families which came from Greece have recently established a certain dominance, after decades of living as underdogs. They have long since overcome their aversion to living near the sea and acquired some desirable waterfront properties. In some ways, the fact that many people had parents or grandparents who were born in Greece has become little more than a minor curiosity of local history.

Yet Özsoy has developed a passion for garnering reminiscences from elderly Turkish citizens, in Tuzla and many other places, who can still remember a childhood in Greece, the voyage to Anatolia, and the difficulties of adaptation to a new homeland. What concerns Özsoy is the psychological wounds which the Tuzla exchangees have suffered from the denial, or partial suppression, of their families' collective memories. Until recently, at least, there was pressure to play down everything that connected them with their places of origin – just as their Orthodox Christian counterparts, adapting to life as refugees in Greece, were often forced to play down or deny their connections with Anatolia, including their knowledge of Turkish.

When Özsoy began his researches, the Greek-born residents of his home town were reluctant, at first, to share their most intimate memories, but gradually some impressive stories began to emerge. For example, one neighbour, Ali Eren, could recall his early life in a big stone house in Sevendik, north of Salonika, which he had left at the age of five. His father had been a prosperous farmer and tax collector in Macedonia, but he had to settle for a more modest living as a baker when the family relocated, more or less comfortably, in Tuzla. Ali Eren could clearly remember the immigrant community choosing an imam to lead prayers in their newly converted church-turned-mosque, which was very near his family's home. Also in his neighbourhood, and obviously connected with the church, there was a sacred spring or *ayiazma*; this is a Greek word, which has also passed into Turkish, for a source of water which Orthodox Christians have identified as holy. (All over Turkey there are places where

an *ayiazma*, a water source once revered by Greek Orthodox people, now
attracts simple and pious Muslims. This is one of the many points at
which Greek and Turkish folk religion converge.) For Ali Eren, a poignant
incident occurred twenty-five years ago, when a party of visitors from
Greece came to his family home in Tuzla. Initially their main concern was
to collect water from the *ayiazma*. But then a Greek woman introduced
herself and shyly explained that she had been born in the house where Ali
Eren now lived. It had belonged to her father, who was the local priest.
After some hesitation, she accepted the offer of a tour of her childhood
home.

As we approached one door, the lady began to cry. She said her father, the
priest, would never have allowed her into that room. And she thanked me,
saying she wished me well in her father's house . . . And I became
sentimental, too, because our family had also left a great deal behind in
Greece.

Ever since the population exchange, and in particular since the passions
engendered by war have died down with the passage of time, there have
been many such encounters between families and individuals from different sides of the Aegean. Until quite recently, such incidents – moments
of profound connection between human beings on different 'sides' with
a common experience of loss – could not easily find public expression. A
desire to help people articulate these feelings, before the last generation
that remembers the exchange dies out, is one of the main motives for
Özsoy's oral history work. Moving beyond his home town, he has gathered dozens of stories from elderly, Greek-born people, mostly in the
Istanbul region. In some cases, the reasons for the newcomers' difficulties
on arrival in Turkey seem more obvious than they did in Tuzla. Some
migrants had to cope with language problems, others with a difference in
religious practices.

A few miles from Tuzla, in the coastal town of Darica, Özsoy has discovered a Greek-born community where the strains of integration, at least
for a couple of decades, were keenly felt. Most of the families there orig-
inated in Crete, and just like the Cretans who settled in Ayvalik, they have
retained to this day a strong attachment both to the Greek language and
to the landscape of their home island. With every successive generation,

memories of the community's Cretan origins and the desire to preserve them tend to grow a little weaker. But in recent years, links with Crete have been reinforced by visits in both directions and also, very discreetly, by reunions among extended families that straddle the religious divide.

The matriarch of one such clan holds forth in the family's noisy cafe in the middle of Darica. Fatma Gultekin is in her nineties, a careworn but impressive figure with a long, dark headscarf framing an aquiline face. She has eleven great-grandchildren and at least one great-great-grandchild. It seems unlikely that any of them will ever learn the Greek language, which was the only tongue of her early childhood in a village near Siteia in Crete. But her descendants are never allowed to forget where the family came from.

Of course we miss Crete, it was our homeland, people always miss the place they left. My father had an orchard, growing olives and all kinds of fruit, so many fruit trees you could hardly get in there. It was a wonderful place with plenty of water, it used to come cascading down the rocks towards our land . . .

Perhaps by a slip of the tongue, the Turkish word she uses for Crete is *vatan*, a rather formal term which normally refers to the country whose passport you hold. Most Greek-born citizens of Turkey would say the Turkish republic was their *vatan*; in other words, the state or fatherland to which their lives and destinies were now committed. When referring to their place of origin in Greece, they would use a somewhat folksier word, like *memleket*: my home patch, the place that nurtured me. But for Fatma, Crete seems to loom even larger than that.

At the same time, she stresses that she is a proud and loyal citizen of the Turkish state, who believes in the unfailing rightness of the decisions of its founder, Mustafa Kemal Ataturk.

Ataturk brought us here to separate us from the Greeks. We just came here with our beds and our bed covering, that's all. Ataturk told us, you don't have to take much with you, he would provide us with property. And indeed when we arrived here, the authorities did give us a house, which we repaired, and a few acres of farmland. It was Ataturk who sent a ship to fetch us from Crete, and when we heard about it we just left our villages and went down to the

*port and sailed away. Before that, we had been afraid of the Greeks. I don't
know what exactly they did, but I know they were doing bad things. They
were burning and killing people, not in the city but in the countryside. So we
broke free from Greece, and we slept in peace here.*

*It was a hard voyage because our ship had an accident, near Canakkale on
the Turkish coast. It took us eleven days altogether to get to Darica. But we
slept better here, even though the local people weren't very keen to accept us.
They called us half infidels, they didn't like the fact that we spoke Greek, and
our older people couldn't learn Turkish. Then gradually they got used to us.
At first we Cretans would only marry among ourselves, but over time we
started to intermarry with the local Turkish people. And bit by bit our
relations got better . . .*

In old age, Fatma is more comfortable in Turkish than her mother
tongue, but she has a friend and neighbour, a fellow Cretan with a towering forehead and jutting chin, who sighs with relief whenever he is given
the chance to relapse into the language of his boyhood. Hüseyin Çetin
speaks Cretan Greek with a glorious, rough-edged eloquence, instantly
recalling the language that you expect to hear from any rheumy-eyed old
man, nursing his ouzo and beads, in any village cafe in any corner of the
Greek-speaking world. What he most wants to discuss is not his early
memories, or his current life in Turkey, but a brief return trip to his home
village, and the reunions with childhood friends, that he enjoyed four
years earlier. 'If you ever go to my home village, will you please, please tell
them I'm sorry I didn't thank them enough? Will you tell them I'm sorry
I haven't been back?' he tells a visiting Greek-speaker, in between accounts
of every conversation, every glimmer of mutual recognition that he experienced during his fleeting trip home. Every word he heard from
contemporaries in the village cafe is lovingly rehearsed: 'Don't tell me you
are . . . Suleyman's boy? Weren't your fields just . . . *there?*' In the evening
of life, Hüseyin's spirit has returned to his native island.

These are the sort of stories which Iskender Özsoy began gathering in
the immediate vicinity of his home, and then further afield; tales of dislocation, nostalgia and in most cases successful integration, albeit at a
high personal cost. His keenest regret is that he did not start collecting
such reminiscences sooner. In the towns and villages of eastern Thrace,
Özsoy has found a remarkably high concentration of Valaades (people

who grew up in Greek-speaking communities in the mountains of northern Greece). Their attachment to their native tongue seems less fierce than
that of the Cretans, and in quite a few cases they have virtually forgotten
it in later life. What they remember, though, is the social exclusion they
experienced on arrival in Turkey because of their unfamiliar speech. Not
so much because Greek was an 'enemy language', more because their
reluctant neighbours would have objected to any characteristic that made
the newcomers different from other Turkish citizens. The local Thracians'
derogatory nickname for the newcomers was *patrioti* or *sympatrioti*. That
was because, in their perfectly standard colloquial Greek, Muslims from
northern Greece would often hail one another, on meeting in the street,
with some greeting like, '*Kalimera, sympatrioti!*', ('Good morning, fellow
countryman!').

Among many of the elderly exchangees who now live in villages near
Catalca, on the European side of Istanbul, nostalgia for their childhood
in the Greek mountains, a region known for its pure bracing air, is repeat-
edly expressed through a vivid image, presented to visitors as though it
were literally true: 'We came from a place where the air is so clean that you
can hang the carcass of a sheep from a tree for days or even weeks on end,
and it still won't rot. But in this place, the air is so damp that you can't
even keep a piece of meat in the fridge . . .' Behind this extravagant image
lies the reality that many of the people who moved from the Greek highlands to the flat sunflower fields of Thrace found the change of climate
was bad for their health. There were no terrible epidemics, but anecdotal
evidence suggests that mortality rates among these newcomers to Turkey
were higher than average.

For some of these Muslims from northern Greece, there was another,
painful source of friction between the world of their childhood and their
adopted Turkish home. In the old country, their families had been
Bektashis, practitioners of a secretive, mystical form of Islam that empha-
sizes transcendental experience and the cult of holiness by wise
individuals, who were given some honorific title such as *sheikh* (teacher),
or the more homely sounding *dede* (elder). As with Christian saints, the
sanctifying influence of these individuals was believed to endure after
their death; and holiness was ascribed not only to their bodies but also to
'secondary relics' such as clothing and personal effects. While the
Bektashis regarded their faith as perfectly consistent with the teachings of

Mohammed, more orthodox Muslims viewed them with suspicion. At the level of popular religious practice, there was considerable overlap between the customs, beliefs and sanctuaries of the Bektashis and those of simple Orthodox Christians. This commonality between the 'folk religion' of Christians and Muslims in the Ottoman world was explored in a classic work of ethnography by the British scholar, F W Hasluck, published posthumously in 1929 but based on research conducted many years earlier. As Hasluck notes, the Bektashi order was especially strong in Albania, where it may have claimed the allegiance of an outright majority of notional Muslims, and also around the Greek–Albanian border – the very region from where many of the 'exchangees' now living in Turkey originally came. It is hardly surprising, therefore, that some of the elderly Turkish citizens interviewed by Özsoy have vivid recollections of their families' attachment to Bektashi practices in the northern Greek highlands.

One of his interviewees, Hüseyin Gunay, had memories of regularly walking over the mountains with his parents for three hours from his home village of Plazhomista (now Stavrodromi) to visit a remote *tekke* (shrine) where a famous sage lived. He described the shrine as a place where 'animals were slaughtered' and ordinary people brought their problems in the hope of receiving some wise advice. When his village moved *en masse* to Anatolia because of the population exchange, they brought the contents of this tekke. Its guardian had apparently died – but they still attributed holiness to a cap, prayer rug and other personal belongings from the shrine. But in Turkey, it proved impossible to maintain the cult, and these sacred objects were scattered.

These reminiscences, gathered by Iskender Özsoy in the early 21st century, dovetail neatly with Hasluck's research, undertaken eighty years earlier. The British scholar found that among the Greek-speaking Muslim communities of the Anaselitza region of northern Greece, who were seen as quite recent converts to Islam (having switched faith in the previous 150 years), the Bektashi order had a huge following. Hasluck says the area had two Bektashi shrines, both linked with a Muslim saint, Emineh Baba, who appeared to have been a real historical figure, executed in the late 16th century for echoing the controversial views of an early Sufi mystic and martyr who had spoken heretically of achieving union with God. The Bektashis of northern Greece held that on the eve of his execution,

Emineh appeared in a vision to his sister and vanished only when compelled to eat food. As Hasluck observes, there were echoes in this story of the Gospel accounts of Christ's appearances after the Resurrection. The shrine described to Öszoy was almost certainly one located high in the Pindus mountains, at place called Odra; this tekke was occupied – according to Hasluck – by 'an abbot and two or three dervishes' and stood near a mysterious cave whose creation Muslims ascribed to Emineh, while Christians linked the cavern with one of their own early saints, Minas.

Another of Özsoy's elderly interviewees, Murteza Yonet remembered that there was a Bektashi shrine right in the middle of his northern Greek village.

I remember kissing the hand of the dede *– the wise man – who guarded the shrine and receiving pocket money. It was a* tekke *where there were no songs, but serious conversations . . . The old man used to say, 'Patience, my son.' Then he died, and during the population exchange, we took his bones to Turkey, but we don't know what happened to them there. We carried on these [Bektashi] practices for a while after coming to Turkey, but then they died out.*

This account also corresponds neatly with the findings of Hasluck, who describes a tekke in an ordinary village house, occupied by an abbot who claimed to be a direct descendant of the Muslim saint, Emineh.

In extreme old age, Özsoy's interlocutors apparently felt they had nothing to lose by describing religious practices which were intimately associated with the earliest years of their childhood, and abandoned with reluctance by their families on arrival in Turkey. This was not because the Bektashi order was absent in the new country: its holiest shrine, the mausoleum of its founder, Haci Bektash, was located in the heart of Anatolia. But in the early years of the Turkish republic, officialdom strongly disapproved of mystical and semi-secret forms of Islam, and of spiritual brotherhoods which formed a counterpoint to officially sponsored forms of religion. In a landmark speech in the town of Kastamonu in spring 1925, Mustafa Kemal had condemned the practices of mystical fraternities like the Bektashis – 'worshipping at dead men's shrines' – with great vehemence. In the new Turkey, such primitive traditions were to be eschewed – along with the wearing of the fez, once a universal token of

Muslim Turkish identity but now rejected in favour of European forms of headgear.

During the 1920s, as Greek-speaking Muslims tried to settle down in European Turkey, they found themselves in an atmosphere where almost any departure from the norm – be it linguistic, spiritual or sartorial – could be held against them; and this apparently made it impossible to maintain their beloved Bektashi practices in the face of pressure from standard Sunni Islam. Rather tellingly, the locals – observing that the newcomers were not frequent attenders at the ordinary local mosque – used to denounce them as 'Ali Pasha Muslims' – as though Ali Pasha, the great Albanian chieftain of the early 19th century, was responsible for their religious laxity. There could have been a grain of truth in this. Ali Pasha was more of a warlord than a mystic, but the Bektashis had certainly flourished in his fiefdom.

Whether they were linguistic, religious or purely psychological, the difficulties experienced by the exchangees from Greece can hardly be understood without reference to the revolutionary changes that were sweeping over the whole of Turkey. The Greek-speakers, or the Bektashis, were by no means the only people in the country who were being taught to conceive their collective identity in a new way. The entire nation was being redefined, reeducated and reordered as its masters undertook a 'revolution from above' that was relatively peaceful by the standards of modernizing projects in the 20th century but left little room for dissent. It was not just the immigrants from Greece who found this process bewildering; their tormentors – the people who denounced them as 'sympatrioti' or 'Ali Pasha Muslims' were also in the throes of wrenching change as the old Ottoman theocracy was dismantled, the Latin alphabet was introduced, and the very word 'Turk' was given a new meaning.

With a handful of exceptions, the refugees from Greece were not active players in the new Turkey's political game, but they were certainly significant pawns, as arguments raged over how well they had been treated. On paper, it should easily have been possible to find ample land and housing for the 400,000 or so newcomers who arrived in 1924, even when the war damage to Turkey's housing stock is taken into account. At least 2 million Christians – Greeks and Armenians – had been deported or killed over the previous decade; they had been richer than the average Anatolian and many of their farms, shops and homes were ready and waiting to be transferred to new hands. But in practice, the absorption of the Muslim migrants from Greece was often an ill-managed shambles. Sometimes the problems were an almost unavoidable consequence of Turkey's battered and chaotic state after more than a decade of war; sometimes they were perfectly avoidable.

On the face of things, there was no lack of institutions, or impressive sounding plans, that were intended to regulate the influx of Muslims from Greece. In theory, every family was supposed to receive housing and land that bore some relation to what it had forfeited in Greece. Initially, however, all the authorities could promise was property worth 17.5 per cent (or as of 1924, 20 per cent) of the amount left behind. There was a vague promise that further handouts would follow as soon as Greece and Turkey had settled all their mutual claims.

Meanwhile the politician Mustafa Necati, who had successfully insisted that only Turkish ships would be used for the deportation, tried to turn his newly established agency, the Ministry for Exchange, Reconstruction and Resettlement, into an effective bureaucracy. At its height, the ministry had a network of local offices in Anatolia and wide-ranging powers. In theory, this network was supposed to find appropriate settlement areas for every immigrant family, helped by a supposedly fail-safe system. The newcomers were divided into three groups – tobacco growers, arable farmers, and growers of olives and grapes. But these categories turned out to be absurdly broad; within each group, there were wealthy landlords as well as peasants and share croppers. An 'olive grower' could be anything from a farmer to a merchant in olive-based soap. Worst of all, there was no provision for the large numbers of migrants whose skills and lifestyles were urban rather than rural.

In practice, the procedure by which newcomers from Greece were directed to towns and regions in Turkey was quite arbitrary. There was room for some negotiation between the authorities and groups of migrants, but the exchangees were in a weak position unless they had brought enough money to make their own arrangements if necessary. Newcomers were dispatched, almost at random, to all the places where Greeks had once lived: the west coast, the Black Sea coast and also to places deep in the heart of Anatolia where there had been significant pockets of Christian life. In practice, the western regions – especially in Thrace and the Aegean ports – were the most popular. In April 1924, there was a demonstration in Istanbul by a group of 450 migrants, newly arrived from Drama in northern Greece, who were being sent, against their will, to Samsun on the Black Sea coast, where many of Drama's present day residents originate. As gendarmes looked on, they demanded to be sent instead to nearby Thrace; women were put in the front line of the protest to stop the police intervening. In the end, the authorities got their way. The migrants were convinced they had no choice but to settle in the Black Sea port. Once they arrived in their destination, poor migrants had very little scope for improving their lot; if they made any trouble, the government could simply suspend their modest welfare payments.

It was only after migrants reached their area of settlement that some attempt was made to provide them with land in rough accordance with their skills, and with houses, often forfeited by Greeks. If they were town dwellers who had been assigned to a mainly rural area – or vice-versa – it was often too late to correct the mistake. For example, a group of farmers, complete with their livestock, was assigned to the urban centre of Kayseri in central Turkey. They were given homes and commercial premises, where they duly installed their beasts, but no fields. Nor was the matching of agricultural skills and farms very successful; tobacco growers found themselves landed with vines, fruit farmers with wheat fields.

The real difficulties often began after a notional allocation had been made: in many cases, the houses which migrants were promised had already been grabbed by another family, or were in irreparably bad condition. In Izmir in particular, most of the housing left behind by Greeks and Armenians, and still intact, had already been snapped up by at least three categories of people: victims of the September 1922 fire; people from the inland towns which had been burned by the retreating Greek army; and unscrupulous local politicians who grabbed whatever they could.

Generally, the new migrants from Greek Macedonia and Crete found themselves in acute competition with previous waves of refugees (from the Balkans and the Caucasus, for example) who insisted they were every bit as entitled as the settlers from Greece to any state handouts. In the end, as Onur Yildirim points out, it was locally powerful politicians who intervened to adjudicate in competitions for property. The same politicians, as well as corrupt civil servants, were often guilty of seizing choice properties for themselves, their families and their cronies. In October 1923, for example, it was reported from Izmir that some of the best ex-Christian properties in the city had been grabbed by local bigwigs, who parcelled them out among members of their family. Far from being used to shelter those in greatest need, some of these houses were simply rented out for profits which rose steadily as the housing market grew tighter.

There was nothing much that ordinary peasant families from Crete and Greek Macedonia, hoping for a decent place to settle in a town like Tuzla or Darica, could do about these abuses. But the general air of scandal which marred the whole enterprise of refugee settlement in Turkey did have consequences for the newly formed republic; and perversely, the consequences included political doom for those who protested on these refugees' behalf. Things came to a head in late 1924, as the final shiploads of migrants from Greece were arriving and the cracks within Turkey's newly established elite were beginning to show. While the personal authority of Mustafa Kemal was beyond question, there was intense competition among his lieutenants, pitting a hardline nationalist majority – those who wanted to proceed swiftly with setting up an authoritarian, secular state – against a cautious minority, who in some cases were unhappy about the speed with which the old Ottoman institutions, including the Caliphate, had been abolished.

At a debate in the national assembly in November 1924, the cautious camp led by Hüseyin Rauf Orbay, a naval officer and veteran of the nationalist struggle, made a harsh verbal assault on the hardline majority. The moderates stressed in particular the corruption which had surrounded the reception of newcomers from Greece; it had caused the refugees unnecessary hardship and lined the pockets of people who were already rich and powerful. The nationalist principle of 'doing it our way' and rejecting all forms of foreign help or supervision with the resettlement of refugees (in sharp contrast to what was happening in Greece) had turned out to be a smokescreen for cronyism and sharp practice at the refugees' expense; at any rate, so the moderates alleged. If they singled out the issue of resettlement, it was presumably because this was the most obvious and egregious way in which the ideals of the republic – a Turkish state that would serve and protect all Turks – were being violated.

But far from rattling or shaming the government, the allegations simply served as an opportunity to turn the tables on the moderates and force them out of the ruling party. Ismet Pasha, the protagonist of the Lausanne conference as well as the Turkish–Greek war, treated the moderates' assault as evidence of disloyalty, rather than as a constructive call for change. He called for a vote of confidence and won it handsomely. The thirty-two deputies who backed Hüseyin Rauf duly left the ruling People's Party and went into open opposition under a new banner, the Progressive Republican Party. This movement's manifesto, while conforming to the general line of secular nationalism, favoured policies that many would regard as common sense: decentralization rather than concentration of power in Ankara, a cautious openness to foreign loans, a clearer separation of powers. Various other groups of discontents climbed on the opposition bandwagon – including religious conservatives from the east, and people in the west, including refugees from Greece, who had seen government corruption at first hand. But in a way that any historian of Soviet Russia could easily recognize, the emergence of a potentially attractive opposition was taken by the ruling faction as a cue to dispense with opposition altogether. It could now be argued with greater force that if a multi-party system meant slowing the revolution down, it was a luxury that Turkey could not afford.

Fresh opportunities to turn the screws on the moderate opposition, this time in a decisive way, emerged over the next two years. In February 1925, there was a rebellion by Kurdish tribes on the east. This had nothing to do with official corruption in western Turkey, but it created a climate where a general crackdown on all opposition seemed imperative. A 'Law on the Maintenance of Order' was passed which made it easy for the government to ban newspapers and opposition groups. The entire independent press of Istanbul – including those newspapers which had criticized cronyism – was shut down, and all the city's leading journalists were arrested. In June 1925, the new opposition party was closed down too. A year later, when Mustafa Kemal was about to arrive in Izmir, it was announced that a plot to assassinate him had been foiled. In a wave of arrests, almost all the parliamentarians who had once formed the small opposition group were rounded up, and sixteen of the accused were sentenced to death. Hüseyin Rauf, who was abroad at the time, received a ten-year jail term *in absentia*. Although he was eventually rehabilitated and served as ambassador to London, the movement he founded – and his attempt to hold the government to account for tolerating corruption – had been ruthlessly crushed.

Those are the political circumstances in which today's elderly, Greek-born citizens of Turkey reached consciousness. If they seem deferential to authority, and passionately defensive of the man who founded their republic and 'evacuated' them from Greece, it helps to remember the atmosphere in which they grew up.

While they were used as instruments in Turkey's political game, the great majority of the 400,000 newcomers from Greece blended gradually into Turkish society; they were busy struggling to survive, rather than shaping their new homeland. If the population exchange left a decisive mark on the early Turkish republic, it was more because of the departure of its Christian population, than because of the addition of 400,000 Muslims. The exodus of Christians, confirmed and virtually completed by the Lausanne treaty, transformed both the demography and the economy of Turkey. Between 1913 and 1923, the proportion of non-Muslims in Anatolia fell from 20 per cent to 2 per cent. This reflected the death or expulsion of all but a handful of the two main Christian communities, the Greeks and Armenians. The remaining Christians consisted of the 120,000 Greeks who were permitted to stay in Istanbul and about 65,000 Armenians: a total of less than 200,000 compared with about 3 million before the decade of war. The country was also deprived of the great majority of its entrepreneurs, merchants, middlemen and even skilled labourers. In all of these callings, Greeks and Armenians had played a dominant role.

At the time when shiploads of Muslims from Greece were arriving in Turkish harbours, its economy was in a parlous state and it was by no means clear how the gaps left by the Christian exodus would be filled. A minority of the newcomers from Greece – those who had been professional people or merchants in cities like Yannina or Salonika – seemed well placed to reinforce the ranks of Turkey's Muslim bourgeoisie, which was still embryonic. To some extent, this promise was fulfilled. To this day, there are upper middle-class dynasties in Istanbul who are proud of their roots in Greece. Some of these families emerged from the prosperous world of late Ottoman Mytilene; others once belonged to an influential group in Ottoman Salonika, known as *dönme*. They descend from the Jewish followers of a 17th century religious leader, Sabbatai Zevi, who proclaimed himself Messiah but eventually embraced a form of Islam. The word 'dönme' has derogatory overtones in Turkish – in other contexts, it can mean a turncoat or even a transsexual – and ordinary Sunni

Muslims regarded the Salonika dönmes with suspicion, seeing their religious practices as something intermediate between Judaism and Islam. But for the purposes of the Greek–Turkish population exchange, the dönmes were classified as Muslim and they were duly deported from Greece – thus avoiding the fate of their Jewish kin who remained in Salonika and were annihilated by the Nazis. In their new home in Istanbul, the dönmes from northern Greece have continued to play a prominent role in business and professional life.

Amid the Greek-born residents of Turkey whose lives Iskender Özsoy has studied, there are some dignified old ladies whose families belonged to the elite of Ottoman society. They can still recall the elegant *fin de regime* atmosphere of their homes in Greece. In small drops at least, they brought their refinement and high culture, and in certain cases their professional skills, to Turkey. One such lady, Raziye Ogus, spent the first decade of her life in a comfortable mansion in the lakeside town of Yannina, which became part of Greece in 1912, the year after she was born. Her father was a successful lawyer, with plenty of Greek as well as Albanian friends. Her home life was formal, punctuated by family prayers – Muslim prayers, of course – but the language of the household was more Greek than Turkish. When the family arrived as 'exchangees' in the town of Pendik near Istanbul, their Turkish was poor; she had been attending the Greek school in Yannina, following all the lessons except Christian instruction and prayer, from which she and her sisters would discreetly withdraw. 'After we arrived in Turkey, we had to communicate in sign language. When we went to the shop to look for matches, we had to draw a picture . . . it was hard to learn Turkish at first, but we loved our Turkish school,' insists Raziye, who is now a dutiful citizen of the republic, but in her early nineties retains the refined bone structure and delicate manners of a noblewoman.

Vedia Elgun, another grand lady from northern Greece, recalls that her father – accustomed to life as a gentleman of leisure – found Turkey a very difficult place to earn his daily bread. But in due course, the family managed to move to Giresun, on the Black Sea Coast, where her father ran a hazelnut farm and they were given a large, formerly Greek mansion with an impressive rose garden. Her father was an acquaintance of Mustafa Kemal – a fellow Salonikan, born in much humbler circumstances – and took pride in that connection. For middle-class ladies like Mrs Elgun and her son Ahmet, a multilingual import agent, it comes naturally to take advantage of life's opportunities, and seek advancement, in whatever country they find themselves. These qualities have been Turkey's gain.

But among the 400,000 or so Greek-born Muslims who came to Turkey at the same time as the infant Vedia and her family, this was very much the exception. Most of them were humble, deferential souls who instinctively saw themselves as victims rather actors in the march of history. Indeed, the great majority of Turkey's new, Greek-born citizens were bystanders in the contest over the country's economic future which was unfolding during the 1920s and 1930s, in the wake of the Christian exodus.

The main players in that struggle were the nascent Muslim bourgeoisie (still a pale shadow of its Christian counterpart, but gradually growing); the new class of politicians and bureaucrats; and foreign investors. In the Turkish republic's prickly, xenophobic climate, the role of the latter was a sensitive issue. As well as ridding the nation of its Christian minority – long seen as a Trojan horse for foreign capital – one of Turkey's main aims in Lausanne had been to end the economic privileges enjoyed by foreigners who had 'turned the Turks into strangers in their own land', as many people complained. In this aim they were partially successful: the 'capitulations' under which the foreign companies and their representatives had enjoyed legal as well as tax privileges were duly abolished. But the western powers had also scored some economic points at Lausanne. They successfully insisted that Turkey could not raise import tariffs for at least six years. The net result was to create a climate, for the remainder of the 1920s, in which foreign companies and the emerging Turkish business class were both satisfied. In different ways, both could happily gobble up the pigeon pie left by the Christian exodus.

Foreign companies operating in Turkey were sometimes irked by pressure from the authorities to dismiss their non-Muslim technical staff (often Greeks and Armenians) and replace them with Muslim Turks; it was not always possible to find people with the necessary skills. But thanks to the import regime laid down at Lausanne, foreign companies were able to maintain or boost their exports to a Turkey that produced relatively little for itself. There was also some new investment in manufacturing, with foreign funds playing a bigger role than Turkish capital. In this area too, the disappearance of some important competitors – the business empires once controlled by Ottoman Greeks and Armenians – was a windfall for Turks and westerners alike.

But the country's whole climate changed after the world economic crash of 1929, which dealt a devastating blow to its fragile bourgeois and merchant class. The following year, more than 1000 firms in Istanbul and Izmir went bankrupt. This opened the way for an entirely new phase in Turkey's history: one in which the state bureaucracy took the upper hand and put into action an intensive, almost Soviet-style programme of industrialization, designed to shelter the country from the vicissitudes of the world economy. Some new industries were fully state-owned. In other cases, they were notionally private but relied for their existence on ties with the bureaucracy. Closely linked to the new campaign for state control of the economy was a further tightening of political control. The one-party state was consolidated, and promotion of Turkish nationalist ideology was intensified. The political force which might have mitigated these developments – the moderates led by Hüseyin Rauf, who had first raised their voices in defence of the refugees from Greece – had long since been eliminated. By the end of the 1930s, Turkey was an authoritarian, partially industrialized state, in which power was firmly vested in the hands of the political elite and its corporate friends. This cosy relationship was made much easier by the fact that both sides – the politicians and the state-sponsored businessmen – were Muslim Turks. The old domination of business by Greeks and Armenians was a fading memory.

During the Second World War, there was another, murky chapter in the story of Turkey's adaptation to life with a sharply reduced number of Christians. While Turkey remained neutral, the world conflict destabilized its economy and threw off course the project of carefully managed industrialization and external trade. As many Turks saw their living standards plunge, there was resentment of the 'profiteers' who were alleged to be taking advantage of shortages and bureaucratic snarl-ups; and many of the perceived 'profiteers' belonged to Turkey's remaining ethnic minorities – those Greeks and Armenians who had managed to go on living in Istanbul, the dönmes from Salonika, and the Jews. It was in this climate that in November 1942, a harsh new wealth tax was introduced. It was levied to a disproportionate extent against the non-Muslim minorities, who were forced to pay a rate ten times higher than Muslims, and denied the chance to stagger their payments over time. In many cases, this forced businessmen from the minority groups to sell their firms and assets to Muslims; and those who could not pay at all were either expelled or condemned to forced labour. After two years the tax was abolished, partly under British and American pressure.

Well before this episode, the concentration of political and economic power had already made it easier for the republic's masters to propagate a new understanding of Turkishness, to which all citizens were expected to subscribe. This ideology linked the origins of the Turkish nation to the ancient inhabitants of Anatolia, such as the Hittites, and also to the legendary founders of the Turkish race in Central Asia. Wherever Turks had once lived, it was stressed that the current locus of the Turkish nation was Anatolia, the borders of the Turkish republic. In contrast with the nationalist doctrines that were being promoted elsewhere in Europe at the time, the Turkish republic's official philosophy had no aspiration to expand the country's borders. But it was clearly expected that anyone who now lived within the existing borders – however they had arrived, and whatever language they may once have spoken, be it Greek, Albanian, Serbo-Croat or anything else – should henceforth speak Turkish and adhere to the Turkish national ideal. The people affected by this climate included the Greeks and Jews of Istanbul. Under a campaign called 'Citizen, Speak Turkish!' they risked being fined if they used any other tongue in public. Also affected, perhaps in an even more draconian way, were the Muslim Greek-speakers who had come from Crete or Greek Macedonia.

The new nationalist mood did not imply any particular hostility to the Balkan countries, such as Greece, from which so many of Turkey's inhabitants had been expelled under varying degrees of duress. On the contrary, at a time when Turkey's foreign policy called for good relations with the Balkans, it was felt that people should avoid nursing an excessive sense of grievance over lost Balkan lands or the past sufferings of Balkan Muslims, in Greece and elsewhere. So to a large extent, the entire past lives of those Ottoman Muslims who came from the Balkans (both their sufferings, and any positive memories they had of the place) were air-brushed away. They were all Turks now, and that was all that really mattered.

This, then, was the sort of atmosphere in which the children of Greek-speaking families from Macedonia, Mytilene and Crete learned to be good Turkish citizens. If family memories of Greece, and the Greek language were nurtured at all, this was something which happened behind firmly closed doors. It is little wonder that elderly, Greek-born people feel shy – but also, at times, pathetically grateful – when, in the final years of their life, an author or journalist comes along and invites them to open those doors.

CHAPTER 9

The pursuit of clarity

On the seventh anniversary of the proclamation of the Turkish republic, a military parade took place in Ankara under the benign, fatherly gaze of the state founder, Mustafa Kemal, and a distinguished foreign visitor. The honoured guest was Eleftherios Venizelos, who had returned from self-exile in Paris two years earlier to win a handsome election victory and resume the leadership of Greece. In the evening of his political career, Venizelos was not especially successful in handling the country's domestic affairs, but his flair for diplomacy remained intact. His meeting with Kemal in October 1930 is a remarkable instance in modern European history of an exuberant reconciliation between two nations and their leaders at a time when memories of bitter conflict were very much alive.

From the moment of his arrival in Turkey, Venizelos was hosted with a mixture of public fanfare and personal warmth by Kemal and his prime minister General Ismet. The general, later known as Ismet Inönü after the battlefield where he beat the Greek army twice, was well known to Venizelos as a tough sparring partner in the Lausanne negotiations. But on meeting again in Istanbul, the two prime ministers exchanged compliments that were handsome even by the standards of diplomatic *politesse*. At a gala dinner, they agreed that Turkey and Greece were not merely in harmony over all regional questions; they were well placed to act together as agents of peace and stability in the Mediterranean. Moving on to Ankara, where some important diplomatic business was concluded, Venizelos had a discussion with Kemal about the possibility of a partnership or federation between the two countries, an idea which his host seemed to take quite seriously. The streets of Ankara were decked out with

Greek flags. Venizelos was the star guest at a ball in the capital organized by Turkish Hearth, a nationalist movement that was striving to promote new theories about the country's history and identity. Venizelos joked to Ismet that his treatment, cordial as it was, did not quite match up to the warm welcome which had been accorded in Greece a few weeks earlier to a Turkish sports team; it had been cheered more loudly than any other team when it took part in the Balkan Games. Ismet, apparently in the same bantering spirit, retorted that the Greeks were a more effervescent people than the Turks.

The jocular tone of these exchanges seems astonishing, given that barely eight years had passed since Turkey's defeat of Greece in a war which had brought monumental suffering to both sides. The wounds from that conflict were far from healed. Despite the efforts of refugee set-tlement agencies in both countries, thousands of uprooted families were still struggling to find adequate shelter and make a decent living. In both countries, an entire generation had been blighted by the loss of a high proportion of able-bodied men. Nor had the atmosphere in the Aegean been calm since the conclusion in Lausanne of a peace treaty that was supposed to settle all outstanding matters between Turkey and her neigh-bours. Indeed there had been several moments, over the previous few years, when renewed conflict seemed possible.

But it would be a mistake to infer that there was something illogical or inconsistent about the striking display of friendship between Kemal and Venizelos. At their meeting in Ankara, the two leaders were attempting to bring to its logical conclusion an enterprise they had begun in Switzerland: the establishment of stable, neighbourly relations by remov-ing all grounds for ambiguity or misunderstanding, whatever the human cost might be. The aim was to erect well-defined boundaries, both liter-ally and metaphorically, between the two nations. At Lausanne, both countries had accepted the need to divide up, in a clear and irrevocable way, every square inch of territory, every economic asset and above all, every person and family whose status and identity might otherwise have been in doubt. Once this had been achieved, each country could get on with the business of constructing unitary states where a single language, religion and ethnic consciousness prevailed. At any rate, that was the theory, and it was a theory to which Kemal and Venizelos were deeply committed.

To the extent that Turkey and Greece continued, even after 1923, to have quarrels, it was mostly because the parcelling-out process had not quite been completed. In particular, there was tension over the treatment and status of those groups which had been left out of the population transfer: the Greeks, and their Patriarch, who were allowed to stay in Istanbul; and the Muslims who remained in Greek Thrace. By comparison, the ultimate fate of those who did undergo exchange was not much of an issue in Turkish–Greek relations. In the domestic affairs of both countries, especially Greece, the absorption of new arrivals was certainly a big issue, but it was of relatively little importance for foreign policy. Once the two-way expulsion was complete, each state disowned all further interest in the fate of its erstwhile citizens. The Greek state was indifferent to the welfare of the Greek-speaking Muslims from Crete or Epirus, once they had been packed off to Turkey. The republic of Turkey was similarly unmoved by the welfare of Turkish-speaking Christians who had previously lived in Cappadocia or near the Black Sea, and were now struggling to adapt to life in Greece. Population groups of the 'wrong' religion could not be regarded as ethnic kin, whatever language they used. On that matter, there was a deep mutual understanding between the Turkish and Greek states, from the moment the Lausanne agreement was signed.

With respect to the 'exchanged' peoples, the biggest unresolved problem was the shape of the financial settlement that was supposed, under the Lausanne accord, to take place between the two states once it had been worked out which nation had suffered the greater economic loss. But in these discussions, the desirability of a divorce was not questioned; it was simply proving difficult to agree on the precise terms of the settlement. A far bigger source of Turkish–Greek tension, during the post-Lausanne years, lay in the 'non-exchangees': the fact that the treaty, by exempting certain groups from expulsion and guaranteeing their cultural and educational rights, had given each state not merely a right but almost a duty to intervene in the other's affairs. The government of Athens had an obligation to maintain an interest in the welfare of the Greeks of Istanbul, and their spiritual leader, the Patriarch. The authorities in Ankara kept a wary eye on the Muslims in Greek Thrace – not just to see how they were being treated, but also to see how they were reacting to the revolutionary changes in the Turkish motherland.

So for the two architects of the Lausanne accord, Kemal and Venizelos, it made perfect sense, seven years on, to look for ways of neutralizing the various sources of tension which the treaty had failed to bring to an end. Both leaders could see storm clouds gathering in Europe. Both leaders wanted to press on with the construction of fully-fledged modern states, with a clearly defined identity to which all, or virtually all citizens could subscribe; and neither wanted to be distracted from that important business by smouldering diplomatic disputes. In each country, the incorporation and assimilation of newcomers, and their transformation into loyal and useful citizens, had already made some progress, but the process was still fragile, and at times controversial. With so much domestic business piling up, it made sense for Turkey and Greece to draw a line under their outstanding differences.

In Turkey, internal arguments over the welfare of newcomers from Greece and other parts of the Balkans had, by 1930, to a large extent been silenced by an increasingly authoritarian state which was imposing revolutionary change on all its citizens, whatever their territorial or linguistic roots. The Greek scene was more complex and fluid. To anyone viewing the situation from inside Greece, the statement that by 1930, some progress had been made towards the acceptance of the new arrivals from Anatolia – both economically, psychologically and culturally – might have seemed a surprising one. Because the political preference of the refugees was overwhelmingly for the liberal, pro-Venizelos camp (at least until their hero made his historic trip to Ankara, which disappointed some of them), the newcomers' role in Greek politics was often the subject of bitter arguments. Among those who still sympathized with the dynasty which had been formally dethroned in spring 1924, it seemed that the refugees had been used rather cynically by the liberal republican elite to entrench its power and banish forever a royal house which was still very popular in parts of 'Old Greece' like the Peloponnese.

But that was only one side of the story: intensely as they resented the 'refugee factor' in politics, the royalists did not in the end question the refugees' right to call themselves Greek or to participate in Greek politics. Over time, the royalists reluctantly came round to the view that they, too, must make an effort to win the refugees' votes and address their demands. In any case, any assessment of the success or failure of Greece's state building and resettlement efforts in the 1920s depends on whose perspective is being considered: that of bureaucrats (whether local or international) and politicians, or of the refugees themselves. By the 1930s, thousands of newly expelled families were still living in grinding poverty, and in mourning for their ancestral lands. But from officialdom's point of view, the worst had been avoided – an uncontrollable humanitarian and medical crisis, upsetting the whole region – and some headway had been made in turning newcomers from consumers of aid into producers of wealth.

In October 1928, shortly after regaining power, Venizelos had given a strikingly upbeat claim about the progress Greece was making in absorbing the destitute Orthodox Christians of Anatolia.

> The refugee population, which during the first years constituted a liability for the country and for which great sacrifices are imposed, even today, has started to become an asset. And if one takes into consideration the wonderful human material of which this population is formed, we may be certain that Greece, with her present population, faces the future with full confidence.

Cynics would retort that the new arrivals in Greece, whatever their economic impact, were certainly a political asset for Venizelos. Yet he was not completely wrong to say that some quite rapid strides had been made towards harnessing the refugees' talents and energy, and helping them to better their own lot. A French professor, observing northern Greece in 1930 through distinctly rose-tinted spectacles, offered an even more optimistic commentary on the state of the countryside in places where Anatolian Christian farmers had been settled in place of Muslim ones.

> Those miserable Turkish hamlets, nothing but hovels of mud and straw lying in the midst of uncultivated plain or of unhealthy marshes, are now replaced by large cheerful villages . . . All around one sees sheaves of maize, fields of tobacco, kitchen gardens, orchards and vines. What a miracle!

These romanticized accounts obviously describe Greek resettlement at its best. They take no account of thousands of newly planted refugees who, on being told they would have no clear title to the land they had been given unless they started paying for it, simply sold up and moved into town, where some drifted into the underclass. An assessment at the opposite extreme is provided by the bitter words of a refugee newspaper, *I Mikrasiatiki*, published in the town of Halkida in February 1931.

> About 500 refugee families arrived in Halkida, and 300 of them were installed as farmers in a housing development erected by the Refugee Settlement Commission which was already on the verge of collapse. However, because these newcomers had no aptitude for agriculture, and also because malaria was beginning to decimate their numbers, they abandoned the houses they had received and returned to Halkida – with the exception of forty families who stayed and took up residence in the rotten and insanitary shacks [around] a Turkish cemetery . . .

The newspaper in question, whose political agenda included stiff opposition to the terms of the Turkish–Greek settlement in 1930, was obviously intent on accentuating the negative, and it had no difficulty in finding material to support its case.

But the Frenchman's description is not completely false either. In some places, where skilled and land-hungry farmers were provided with ploughs, seeds, animals and buildings, the results were indeed quite spectacular. Quite a lot of the credit for this goes to the discreet and efficient work of the resettlement agency which had been set in motion by Henry Morgenthau, using his international connections to lobby for Greece on the world capital markets, and his political savvy to make some carefully calculated interventions in the country's domestic scene.

By the time of its dissolution in December 1930, the Refugee Settlement Commission founded by Morgenthau had installed 570,000 refugees – about half the total number – on smallholdings in northern Greece. It had built over 50,000 new houses for these farmers, and refurbished a similar quantity of homes abandoned by recently expelled Muslims. Thanks to the combined efforts of the RSC and the Athens government, these newly settled farmers had received about 145,000 horses and cattle, and 100,000 sheep and goats. In urban areas where refugees lived, the RSC had by 1929 constructed over 27,000 houses, and the Greek state a comparable number. That was an impressive administrative achievement, though it did not cancel out the pain caused to ordinary people by the population transfer. At a time when Venizelos and his Turkish hosts were exchanging flowery compliments over lavish gala dinners, at least 30,000 refugee families were still living in primitive tin huts on the outskirts of Salonika and Athens. Meanwhile the Cretan Muslims, though adequately sheltered in their new Anatolian homes, were a long way from matching the living standards they had once enjoyed on their beloved island.

In both countries, hopes of economic recovery suffered a body blow with the world crash of 1929, which severely depressed the world prices for their most important exports, from tobacco to rugs. But at the time of their exuberant meeting, both Kemal and Venizelos felt they had good reason to take a certain cautious pride in their social and economic achievements – while remaining acutely conscious that these achievements were precarious and needed sheltering from any diplomatic storms.

In neither country, moreover, was it possible to exclude the risk of domestic storms. Refugees in Greece were an increasingly vocal lobby, and the urban ones in particular were capable of making their anger felt on the streets. The whole effort to absorb the refugees in Greece has often been criticized for its 'agricultural bias' – and for the fact that in seven years of intensive work, it laid out only £2 million on urban housing projects compared with £10.5 million on rural settlement.

It is certainly true that there were social, political and strategic reasons for concentrating the absorption effort on the fields of northern Greece. The towns and cities of Greece were already overcrowded, insanitary and at risk of becoming hotbeds of political unrest. There was no easy way of finding employment for urban refugees without antagonizing the existing population. The rural areas of the north, by contrast, were under-exploited even before the Muslims were expelled. After the exodus, the government saw a strategic imperative to populate these empty fields as quickly as possible with farmers who – regardless of what language they used, or what unfamiliar customs they had brought from Turkey – felt and wanted to be Greek. From the authorities' point of view, Christians from the heart of Anatolia, even if they spoke nothing but Turkish, were a valuable bulwark against any fresh designs on northern Greece by the Slavs. The sooner they could be established on the fields of Greek Macedonia the better. As for the American-led RSC, it had no remit to dabble in geopolitics or strategy, and its mission was carefully limited to the housing and productive employment of the newcomers. But from this viewpoint also, intensive settlement on the underused lands of Greek Macedonia made sense, especially when the agency was dealing with entire communities from distant parts of Anatolia who had kept their social structure intact and simply wanted another place to reestablish their little world.

Although the RSC came into existence in November 1923, the £10 million credit that it needed to begin intensive work was not floated on the world bond market till the second half of 1924, and despite the moral support offered by the League of Nations, the rate of interest was relatively high. Morgenthau needed all his financial and diplomatic skill to reassure sceptical bankers in London and New York that the abolition of the Greek monarchy in spring 1924 was a responsible move (which he had discreetly encouraged) and would not lead to instability. Once the agency's financial basis had been assured, he returned to New York; but the RSC retained its rule that the board must consist of an American, a Briton and two Greeks.

While the individual board members changed quite frequently, the agency had a powerful *esprit de corps*. From the very start, the organization trod a careful – and on the whole, very skilful – course between the turbulent realities of Greek politics and the demands of the outside world, including the League of Nations and the country's creditors, for financial prudence.

Inevitably, there were tensions in the agency's relations with successive Greek governments, given that it was exercising something close to sovereign power on Greek soil. In early 1925, the RSC faced rent strikes, squatting and open rebellion in the refugee settlements of Piraeus, and it was dismayed when the government pointedly refused to order the police to act in its support. A noisy lobby of urban refugees was pressing the government to proceed swiftly with the sale of properties (not just houses but schools, mosques and other communal buildings) which the recently expelled Muslims had left behind, in order to raise money for a 'compensation fund' from which urban newcomers, in particular, would benefit. Yielding to this demand would have led to a crisis in relations with the RSC, which was expecting to use some of these buildings to house refugees, and which had used the 'security' represented by formerly Muslim farms and houses to raise international capital.

But during its six years of operation, the RSC had enjoyed some periods of very amicable co-operation with the Greek government, and only one phase of acute crisis, during the regime of General Theodore Pangalos, who took power in June 1925 and was overthrown in August 1926. In a climate of populism and xenophobia, in which quarrels were picked with both Turkey and Bulgaria, the Pangalos regime arrested a popular and respected Greek agronomist, Ioannis Karamanos, who worked for the RSC in Salonika and was held in high esteem by the refugees who were struggling to establish themselves on the lands nearby. Karamanos and two of his associates were arrested on some unconvincing malpractice charges and hauled before a military court which had the power to impose the death penalty. The RSC responded coolly but firmly. It offered unwavering moral support to its beleaguered employees, and continued to pay their salaries, while warning the Greek government that its standing at the League of Nations was in peril. At one point, the position of the two Greek board members of the RSC became untenable and they resigned, leaving the board without a quorum. Here too, the agency reacted with Anglo-Saxon phlegm. It quietly rehired the board members as 'advisors' and proceeded as best it could with resettlement work.

By June 1926, despite the stormy political climate, some 623,000 refugees had been provided with homes and become economically self-supporting, but the RSC reckoned it would need another £5 million to accommodate the remainder of the newcomers, some of whom were still living in desperate circumstances. The country's international standing began to improve again after the overthrow of the Pangalos regime by another soldier-politician, General Ioannis Kondylis, in August 1926, and negotiations began for a fresh loan. After more than a year of haggling between the Greek government, the League of Nations and the banks of London and New York, a credit of £7.5 million (with a net yield of £6.6 million) was put at the disposal of the RSC in order to complete its resettlement work. This allowed the agency to engage in a final burst of urban construction before it dissolved itself, and turned over all its remaining functions to the Greek government in 1930.

By this stage, some of the nightmares which haunted Greece in the immediate aftermath of its military disaster in Anatolia had been firmly banished: the possibility of a complete social breakdown, mass starvation or civil war. The successes that refugee settlement did achieve have to be measured against those very real dangers. Yet the claim that the newcomers were already proving to be an economic asset to Greece, rather than a drain on its resources, has to be qualified. The output of the main agricultural products of northern Greece, cereals and tobacco, climbed impressively, as one would expect at a time of intensive land reclamation, drainage and resettlement. National wheat production, for example, rose from 246,000 tons in 1922 to 450,000 tons in 1928. Tobacco exports were worth £6.8 million in 1923 and £10.8 million four years later. But as arable land was used more intensively, stock breeders suffered. The old, underutilized Ottoman estates had at least provided cheap grazing for shepherds who were accustomed to driving their sheep and goats long distances over northern Greece in search of pasture. Under the new order, grazing land became scarce and more expensive. But even as it set up model farms and dispensaries and handed out advice on fertilizers and crop rotation, the RSC showed some sensitivity to the culture of rural Greece. In each village it made a series of land distributions, carefully calibrated by size and soil quality, using a formula that was intended to make every family a stakeholder and minimize jealousies. The result was that the average family ended up with a series of small plots in different places. This did not make for efficiency but it was perceived as fair.

In the towns, some impressive new industries, especially carpet-weaving and silk-making, sprang into existence, using skills which had been imported wholesale from Anatolia and the willing hands of women refugees who were desperate to feed their families. By the late 1920s, there were bitter complaints from Turkey that its export of carpets (for which the main customers were in the United States) had been crowded out by Greek competition. In any case, demand for these carpets, which were machine-made but exotic and Oriental enough to appeal to American consumers, plunged after the 1929 crash – and the newly established Greek industry went into rapid decline.

All this created a sobering background for the reconciliation between Venizelos and Kemal, who soon afterwards received his better-known sobriquet of Ataturk, father of the Turks. Neither politician had any detailed grasp of economics, but both were concerned to protect their domestic projects from external shocks, whether financial, diplomatic or military. Kemal in particular could also see that Europe as a whole was far from stable. By analogy with his own country's experience, he sensed that Germany would not tolerate the peace terms which had been imposed after 1918. This factor kept alive the old spectre of war by proxy in southeastern Europe, with every major power egging on and manipulating its protégés. A particular worry, for Turkey and Greece alike, was the fact that Bulgaria remained an 'unsatisfied' power, intensely frustrated by the loss after the First World War of its access to the Aegean Sea. Another worry was that Italy, under Benito Mussolini, was dreaming of reestablishing influence in Anatolia and the southern Balkans.

This created a strong incentive for Turkey and Greece to tidy up loose ends, and reduce the risk that the status of the non-exchanged, in particular, would lead to further flare-ups. In early 1925, there had been a real risk of fresh war after the Turkish authorities ordered the expulsion of a newly elected Patriarch, Constantine, on the grounds that he had not lived in Istanbul since 1918 and therefore could not be exempted from the population transfer. The Greeks insisted that the prelate had the right to remain because of Ismet's reluctant promise, made at Lausanne in January 1923, to keep the institution of the Patriarchate in Istanbul. The 'mixed commission' of Greeks, Turks and neutrals – supposed to settle any disputes over the population exchange – gave a first indication of its ineffectiveness by issuing a tortuous and indecisive statement on the question of Patriarch Constantine, which failed to avert his expulsion. When the exiled Patriarch arrived in Salonika he was greeted by thousands of people, many of them fellow refugees from Anatolia. The bombastic General Pangalos led calls by the Greek military for a fresh recourse to war. He said the government would meet the same fate as the six royalist leaders, executed for treason in October 1922, unless it stood up for Greece's interests. The Turkish press suggested simplifying the whole question of exceptions to the population exchange by expelling all remaining Greeks from Istanbul and accepting the expulsion of the Muslims in Greek Thrace.

By May 1925, that crisis was almost defused. The Greek religious leaders agreed to nominate a different Patriarch while the Turks (partly at the behest of Ismet Pasha who was reappointed prime minister in March) stepped back from threats to expel all the remaining Greek Orthodox bishops from Istanbul. In June, Greek and Turkish officials signed an accord in Ankara that was supposed to regulate all outstanding questions about the interpretation of the population exchange, and its exceptions. It was agreed that all those who had been wrongly expelled – Istanbul Greeks and Thracian Muslims – could go back to their homes and occupy or sell their property, or at least receive compensation. The accord denied full satisfaction to one important category of people: the tens of thousands of Istanbul Greeks, including some owners of prime real estate in the heart of the city, who had fled the country without passports in the immediate aftermath of the Turkish military victory in autumn 1922. However, these people were at least given the notional right to sell off their property, through agents, within four years.

Well intentioned as it was, the Ankara agreement was never implemented. This was partly because a lobby of Athens-based Istanbul Greeks prevailed on the League of Nations not to recognize it, on the grounds that it strayed from the letter of the Lausanne treaty. The main reason was that General Pangalos took power a few weeks after the deal was made, and Turkish–Greek relations immediately took a sharp turn for the worse. The general was a reckless opportunist, who had the idea that he could obtain some leverage for Greece from Britain's ongoing quarrels with Turkey over the oilfields of northern Iraq. This tactic failed, and Turkey retaliated both by moving troops closer to the border with Greece, and by making further seizures of property which had belonged to Istanbul Greeks. In March 1926, the Turkish parliament decreed that property in Istanbul which had been 'abandoned' by Greek Orthodox owners fleeing to Greece should pass to the full ownership of the refugees who were occupying them.

Only after Pangalos fell, in August 1926, did things start to improve. By the following summer, a new attempt to settle the most difficult property issues between the two countries, and in particular to guarantee at least partially the rights of Istanbul Greeks, had been ratified by both governments. This latest accord was on terms somewhat more favourable to Turkey than the previous one. It laid down a procedure for each government to purchase, at market rates, the property of people who had been expelled, and it called on Greece to pay £500,000 to settle outstanding balances. But in practice, this agreement also proved difficult to implement, in part of because of internal political strains in both countries. For example, the League of Nations had identified 119 properties in western Thrace which had been wrongly taken from their Muslim owners and should now have been restored to them; but the Greek government held back from abiding by this decision because of pressure from its own land-hungry refugees from Anatolia. The Turkish government duly retaliated by seizing more Greek property in Istanbul.

The hard fact was that it was very difficult to put into practice any regime which depended on goodwill and decency being shown either by Athens or Ankara to minorities which were associated, by religion or national consciousness, with the 'other' side. From the viewpoint of domestic politics, there was no advantage to a Greek government in showing kindness to the Thracian Muslims, and there was a widespread desire in Turkey to complete the virtual expulsion of the Ottoman Christians by getting rid of the remaining Istanbul Greeks. In 1928, the Turkish government threatened to expel up to 20,000 Istanbul Greeks on the grounds that although they had lived in the city before 1918 (a crucial criterion for the right to remain) they could not conclusively prove that they intended, all along, to stay put. The Turkish authorities also seized ninety properties belonging to the Zariphis family of Greek bankers, who had enjoyed enormous wealth in late Ottoman times. This was an effort to put pressure on Greece to pay its promised £500,000. There were renewed suggestions on the Turkish side that only a draconian solution would work. Either the compulsory population exchange should be completed (in other words, Greek Thrace and Istanbul should be cleansed of Muslims and Greek Orthodox Christians respectively, like everywhere else) or else a lowish maximum number of Greeks should be allowed to stay in Istanbul and all the rest expelled. Greece, for its part, warned that a mass expulsion of Istanbul Greeks would lead to war.

Venizelos, returning to power in 1928, saw the danger of a fresh crisis, and also the futility of further nitpicking negotiations about the terms of the exchange. Discussions had run into the ground, both over the terms of the ultimate financial settlement between the two countries, and over the fate of the Istanbul Greeks. With regard to the former, the Greek government felt sure that the assets lost by its new citizens – the Christian farmers, shopkeepers, traders and skilled craftsmen who had once dominated commercial life in many parts of Anatolia – must be of greater value than the wealth forfeited by Muslims expelled from Greece. Turkey refused to accept this: after all, the property once owned by Ottoman

Muslims included some prime urban real estate in places like Salonika, Yannina, Mytilene and Chania. Five years of negotiations had failed to bring the two sides the slightest bit closer.

To the newly reelected Venizelos, it seemed obvious that no good would come of continuing to haggle over lost property. A clean break must be made and Greece, as the defeated power, must be willing to make some large concessions in order to pave the way for this. In the medium term, he calculated, the improved atmosphere would work to the advantage of Greece, and of the Greeks who remained in Istanbul.

The result of this change of policy was an agreement signed in Ankara in June 1930, which initially caused dismay in Greece because the terms seemed scandalously beneficial to the Turkish side. Greece agreed to pay Turkey a total of £425,000 to cover all outstanding claims, both from those who did undergo expulsion, and those who were exempted, or should have been exempted, from the transfer. Through clenched teeth, the Greek side agreed that the 'lost assets' of exchanged Muslims had exceeded those of the exchanged Christians by £125,000. On top of that, it paid £150,000 to compensate Muslims who had been wrongly deprived of their assets in Greek Thrace – and another £150,000 to help the Turkish government provide restitution to ethnic Greeks who lived in Istanbul but had lost property outside the city. This was a bitter pill for Greece to swallow, but as a senior Greek diplomat observed: '. . . greater courage was required on the part of the leader of the defeated nation'.

This was not an easy idea for any Greek politician to sell. Only a leader with the broad shoulders of Venizelos could have convinced most of his compatriots that conceding so much to the Turkish position was on balance, the right thing. As it was, there were plenty of objectors. The initial reaction among some refugees who had previously regarded Venizelos with adulation was to complain of betrayal. The newspaper *I Mikrasiatiki* had some caustic things to say about the negotiating skills of the government and in particular over the economic agreements which Venizelos had struck. While Greece continued to be the sole customer for many Turkish exports ranging from coal to poultry, the government had failed to secure any rights for Greek seamen to fish in Turkish waters or offer cabotage services between Turkish ports. This was a poor show for a country which had managed to 'secure honourable terms at Lausanne, thanks to the rapid regroupment of our army [in Thrace]'. The fact that some people in Greece thought, in all seriousness, that their country was in a position to dictate peace terms after its August 1922 catastrophe gives an idea of the feverish and often wildly irrational emotions that Venizelos had to dampen.

The most obvious reason for the refugees' disappointment was the fact that the accord dashed their hopes of getting adequate compensation for lost assets in Anatolia. They had been promised that the gradual sale of sequestered Muslim assets would bring the state enough revenue to offer the refugees in Greece a decent share, at least, of the wealth they had forfeited. With the state promising to pay out large sums to Turkey, this looked much less likely. But there was also a more fundamental, and more subtle reason why some refugees were deeply troubled by the 1930 settlement. By drawing a line under the whole question of minorities and their property, it seemed to close off all remaining hope that a resurgent Athens would some day reclaim the lost homes and lands of its ethnic kin, and allow Greeks to return *en masse* to Anatolia. As the political history of many exiled communities can demonstrate, dreams are the hardest thing of all to give up.

Venizelos, for his part, vigorously defended the principle of making tactical concessions to Ankara in order to improve the atmosphere in the region and hence to allow both countries to face their domestic challenges. This was not just a matter of bowing to bitter expediency, but an opportunity for an entirely new sort of partnership between Greeks and Turks. In a revealing speech to the Greek parliament, he argued that an ethnically homogenous, or rapidly homogenizing Greece could get along very well with a homogenous, or homogenizing Turkey; and he implied that the Greeks should show some understanding for Turkey's desire to cleanse its population because Greece was, after all, engaged in something quite similar.

The idea that there might be something positively virtuous about the state which had just been established in Ankara was a difficult one for his compatriots to grasp. For most people in Greece, the new Turkish state, which had driven more than a million of their kin out of their ancestral homeland, presented an even more frightening and hostile spectacle than the old Ottoman empire, under which many Greeks had lived more or less contented and prosperous lives. But Venizelos made a bold attempt to put the opposite case: Greeks who had fought to liberate themselves from the

'Ottoman yoke' could become friends with a new Turkey which was also
doing battle, in its own way, with the Sultans' backward-looking legacy.

> Turkey herself – new Turkey – is the greatest enemy of the idea of the
> Ottoman Empire. New Turkey does not wish to hear anything about an
> Ottoman Empire. She proceeds with the development of a homoge-
> nous Turkish national state. But we also, since the catastrophe of Asia
> Minor, and since almost all our nationals from Turkey have come over
> to Greek territory, are occupied with a similar task.

In other words, both Turkey and Greece were struggling to throw off the
heritage of a multi-ethnic, traditional society and build a modern, mono-
ethnic state instead.

In some ways, the view offered by Venizelos – that a rigorously mono-
ethnic and nationalistic Turkey was not necessarily threatening to
Greece – proved quite accurate. Through the remainder of the 1930s, an
increasingly authoritarian Turkish state devoted much of its energy to
convincing its own citizens to accept an entirely different understanding
of what it meant to be a Turk. This new ideology, promoted through the
education system and the media, was pro-western in its admiration for
the technological and educational achievements of the advanced nations,
while it looked eastwards, to Central Asia, to find the origins of the Turks.
In this system, Greece was neither good nor bad; it scarcely figured at all.

So as Venizelos had predicted, the new Turkish attitude to Greece was
respectful but detached. Turkey offered arm's-length friendship to Greece
on condition that it be allowed to proceed with the steady 'Turkification'
of everything and almost everyone that remained within its own borders.
But what did this imply for the Istanbul Greeks who despite their many
travails were still a relatively prosperous and vigorous community, numbering about 125,000 in the early 1930s? Their very survival seemed to
defy the notion that a 'clean break' between the two nations was the only
way to settle, and ultimately improve their relations. The general warm-
ing up of the Turkish–Greek atmosphere did make life somewhat easier
for the Greek community on the shores of the Bosphorus. Several thousand former residents of the city, including many of those who had fled
the city without passports in the panic of 1922–3, were allowed to return,
this time as Greek citizens with residence permits.

To a limited extent, the old relationship between Greek entrepreneurial and trading skills, and Turkish resources and labour, was reestablished. But it was a precarious business, because a broader government-sponsored drive to 'Turkify' every aspect of national life – the economy, the education system, the language of daily intercourse – was in full swing. This was not conducted with any particular animus against the Greek minority, but inevitably the Greeks were affected. In 1932, for example, a law made it harder for non-Turkish citizens to be employed. This threw thousands of Greek passport holders out of work. Nor did the Greek government feel inclined to protest. At that stage, it considered the broader Turkish–Greek relationship too important to compromise by complaining over individual cases.

Another burden on the Orthodox Christians of Istanbul, who had always taken pride in running and financing their own educational, religious and charitable institutions, was the increasingly tough regulation of the city's Greek schools. For almost every ethnic Greek teacher the schools employed, they were obliged to hire and pay for a Turkish one as well. So a significant share of the community's collective wealth was devoted to paying these Turkish teachers and making sure that the city's young Greeks were fully proficient in the language, history and ideology of the place where they lived.

A handful of ethnic Greeks began to participate in the country's political life. But these concessions were fragile; they took place against a background of official determination to enforce Turkey's language, newly purified of foreign words, and its newly adopted script, in every corner of the republic.

The compact of 'mutual reinforcement' between Turkish nationalism and Greek nationalism, particularly evident during the 1930s, was also put into practice in another place where Greeks and Turks co-existed, namely Greek Thrace. For the first few years after the proclamation of the Turkish republic, the Greek authorities had positively encouraged the Muslim community in Thrace to organize and conceive itself as Ottoman and Islamic, rather than Turkish in the modern, secular sense. While it would have greatly preferred not to have any Muslim citizens at all, the post-Lausanne Greek state initially thought it would be less threatening to harbour an old-fashioned, clerically minded Islamic community than one in which modern Turkish nationalist ideology prevailed. This stance was highly provocative to Turkey. It meant that traditionally inclined Muslim clerics, who would have faced severe persecution by the new Turkish state, were able to find a secure refuge in Greece. The Greek government justified its position by noting that the Lausanne agreement referred to a 'Muslim' minority rather than a Turkish one. But Venizelos, in the spirit of his new understanding with Ankara, decreed an abrupt change in this policy. As a result, at least one old-fashioned Muslim religious leader was expelled from Greece, and the advocates of the new Kemalist notion of Turkishness were allowed to gain influence among the Thracian Muslims; they embraced Kemal's linguistic reforms and started to think of themselves as Turks.

As long as intergovernment relations between Athens and Ankara remained cordial, the existence of a pocket of Turkish nationalism on Greek soil was not perceived as threatening to Greek interests. But ever since 1930, Greek policy has wavered on the highly sensitive question: should the minority (or at least certain groups within the minority) be allowed to use the label 'Turkish' or should it be designated simply as 'Muslim'? Since the mid-1980s, the Athens government has reversed the concession to Turkish nationalism that was made by Venizelos. It has withdrawn the right of public associations in Thrace to use the word 'Turkish' in their names. In 1987, the Greek government decreed the closure of the three main organizations among the Thracian Muslims which had the word 'Turkish' in their title. This led to an upsurge in intercommunal tension, with large, angry demonstrations by the local Muslims and attacks by Greek Orthodox locals on Muslim property. As of 2005, the status and definition of the Thracian Muslims remains a contentious and potentially explosive issue in Turkish–Greek relations, even though many other long-standing grievances voiced by the Thracian minority have been successfully addressed.

When George Papandreou, a moderate who became Greek foreign minister in 1999, aired the possibility of allowing the Thracian Muslims to call themselves Turks if they chose to, he was sharply rebuked by Greek nationalists. Sooner or later, it seems likely that European institutions will settle the matter in a spirit which in most parts of Europe would be regarded as common sense: people may define their ethnicity in any way they choose. Even that will not prevent Greeks and Turks arguing about who the Thracian Muslims, excluded from the population exchange, 'really' are. The line in Ankara is that they are all, or virtually all, Turks, while the Greek position insists that they are a community united only by religion, with a great variety of linguistic and ethnic affiliation. It is argued that up to 30 per cent of them grow up speaking Pomak, a language akin to Bulgarian, while as many as 10 per cent may be Roma or gypsies. As for the remainder, Greek officials are grudgingly prepared to describe them as '*Tourkoyenis*' (of Turkish descent or origin) but not as '*Tourkoi*' (Turks).

In the background of all Greek discussion about the Thracian Muslims is the widely held belief that their very existence in Greece is undesirable and in a sense, unfair. The agreement struck in Lausanne in January 1923 was that the Muslims of western Thrace should be allowed to stay in Greece as a kind of tradeoff for allowing the Greeks to remain in Istanbul. Now that the Greek community in that city has dwindled to fewer than 2000 – so the argument goes – why should Greece tolerate the existence of over 100,000 Muslims on its soil? Even among liberal-minded Greeks, it is not unusual to come across the view that the Athens government should have 'taken the opportunity' to expel all its remaining Muslims during the Cyprus crisis of 1974.

Should it be concluded, therefore, that the deal between Ataturk and Venizelos – to accept, respect and reinforce each other's nationalist projects – has broken down completely? In fact, this is far from being true. The persisting influence of the 'spirit of Lausanne', as refined and reinforced by the two states' leaders in 1930, is of crucial importance in understanding the current situation on both sides of the Aegean. Even in situations where Greek and Turkish officialdom appear to be at loggerheads, the Lausanne treaty provides a framework for their arguments – and ensures that on certain key issues, the status quo remains unchallenged. Indeed it is often in the middle of angry disputes that the abiding importance of the 'Lausanne consensus' – of which the population exchange forms the centrepiece – becomes most obvious.

At the heart of the Lausanne consensus, and the Ataturk–Venizelos understanding, is the idea that in order to manage their relations, Turkey and Greece must eliminate all areas of ambivalence, all grey areas. As far as possible, every inch of land, every penny of wealth and every individual must be allocated neatly between the two countries, and only between those two countries. That compact has remained remarkably durable, and it does not lose its importance in situations where the precise details of its application are a matter of bitter contention.

To understand this, it may help to consider the situation which can still be faced by an individual who does risk falling into a grey area between the two governments, despite their best efforts to prevent this. It is a hypothetical case, but a composite drawn from many different real-life stories. Let us call him Kenan, and imagine that he was born around 1970 in a village near the town of Xanthi, one of the two main population centres of Greek Thrace. Like most Muslims in his community, he grew up speaking Pomak, so he can understand Bulgarian. He cannot read or write Pomak because that language has no standard written form. At his primary school, one of several hundred 'minority schools' which the Greek government provides under the terms of the Lausanne treaty, he was taught both Greek and Turkish very badly. This made it very difficult for him to receive any secondary education: his Greek was not good enough to attend a state high school, and his family could not afford to send him to either of the two Turkish-oriented private schools in the region. The only chance of getting a secondary education was to go to Turkey, board with cousins there, and attend a state school. So he completed his schooling, and eventually his university education in Istanbul. By staying so long in Turkey, he risked forfeiting his Greek citizenship; so he returned to Greece and did his military service in the Greek army – where Muslim soldiers usually get the dirtiest jobs, just as ethnic Greeks do in the Turkish army. Returning to his native Thrace, he found the politics of his home village were in ferment. There was one faction, encouraged by the Greek government, which was strongly urging the Pomaks to maintain their Slavic form of speech and distance themselves from their Turkish-speaking co-religionists. Then there was another faction, discreetly fostered by the Ankara government, which took the opposite view: even though Turkish was not their mother tongue, all Pomaks must insist on the right to style themselves as Turks and only Turks.

So Kenan has, all his life, found himself in the middle of a tug of war between two governments. He carries the passport of Greece, and some of his fellow citizens want him to be as loyal and active a member of Greek society as possible. Whatever they think he should be, the Greeks are adamant that he must not call himself Turkish in any public way. If he does so, by joining or starting an association which includes the word

Turkish, he may risk prosecution. At the same time, there are voices, official and semi-official voices, coming from Turkey which insist not merely on his right but on his obligation to call himself Turkish. To style himself any other way would be an act of betrayal.

But in fact the opposition between Athens and Ankara is not total. Underlying the Turkish–Greek bickering over who Kenan is, and what description he may use, there is one principle on which all Turkish and all Greek governments have stood shoulder to shoulder for the past eighty years. Wherever Kenan is finally assigned by political or bureaucratic fiat, he himself is the last person who should have any say over the matter. His own preferences, linguistic background or cultural inclinations are of no consequence. His personal and professional future may be either Turkish or Greek, but it is not anything else; and above all, it is for Turkey and Greece to fight over, not for Kenan to decide. The terms of the intergovernmental squabbles that rage perpetually over Kenan's head are crude and hypocritical. One side claims that all Ottoman Muslims are 'really' Turks, whose forebears crossed the Bosphorus in the 14th century. The other maintains that the Pomaks are 'really' the descendants of ancient Greeks, closely associated with Alexander the Great, who carelessly changed both their language and their religion. Both sides share the common assumption that an individual or a group can have a 'real' or objective ethnic identity without being consciously aware of it – and that this may be obvious to outsiders. As for Kenan himself, he keeps his thoughts about who he 'really' is to himself. If he has any clear ideas on the subject, he knows better than to share them with bureaucrats who treat him like a pawn in a diplomatic game and loathe the thought that he could ever have a say in determining his own status.

The impulse of the Lausanne negotiators, and of Ataturk and Venizelos seven years later, to put a stop to all ambiguity over territory and over the fate of individuals, was perhaps not an ignoble one. Governments tend to cultivate diplomatic ambiguity when they have unspoken but irresponsible aspirations, such as territorial claims which they are keen to pursue but dare not formulate openly. When they seek clarity, hard and fast rules, that is often an indicator that they genuinely want peace. The fact that some people are still caught up in a kind of no man's land between Greece and Turkey may simply be proof that the negotiators did not pursue clarity as hard as they should. There are perfectly good reasons why bureaucrats, census takers and above all military recruiting officers are obliged to make neat and clear distinctions. They have to devise categories, sometimes arbitrary ones, into which everybody in their purview can be placed. The trouble is that the lived experience of individuals and families, especially in regions with a rich and complex mixture of national and religious traditions, is never simple. In order to fit into one or the other category devised by the bureaucrats or politicians, people have to sacrifice something of their real selves, or at least to play up one side of their cultural identity and play down another.

Quite often, people yield more or less willingly to this process of categorization from above; especially in chaotic post-war conditions where, within reason, people will submit willingly to almost any government that offers them shelter, a passport and freedom from persecution. The harshness of this categorization only becomes obvious when cases arise that do not belong neatly in any of the available drawers. When people's fate is clear, they usually accept it. But that does not make the process any less harsh, or change the fact that nationalist theory is one thing, and the real life of ordinary, confused people quite another.

CHAPTER 10

The price of success

Like every other region that gained new inhabitants and lost old ones as a result of the Lausanne treaty, the highlands of northern Greece are still full of arresting signs of the population exchange and its lasting effects. For example, in Megalo Sirini, a village near Grevena, it is possible to walk into a prosperous household where an aged grandmother in black speaks the Turkish of her rural Anatolian birthplace, her middle-aged daughters alternate between that language and Greek, while their student offspring use their well-learned English to surf the Internet and follow the latest London fashions in dress and music.

This is one of a dozen places in the western half of Greek Macedonia where during the mid-1920s, the language of daily intercourse, as well as the prevailing religion, altered in a bizarre way as a result of the population exchange. The faith changed, of course, from Muslim to Christian, while the language switched from Greek to Turkish. So powerful was the impact of Turkish speech on these districts that sometimes it was the local Greeks, not the newcomers, who had to find ways of adapting. In Megalo Sirini, there was a mayor of local stock who had to learn Turkish to communicate with his fellow villagers; and the police found themselves unable to work without an informal network of Turkish–Greek interpreters. Half bitterly and half humorously, families of refugee origin recall how difficult things were for them after their arrival in this area. It was not just the language problem: in comparison with their own close-knit community, the newcomers found the existing Greek residents – the *dopioi* (locals) – standoffish and unfriendly, towards one another as well as to outsiders. An elderly woman from the Black Sea region described the contrast in graphic terms: 'We Pontians always felt that whenever somebody in the village died, each one of us should help with the funeral, whether the bereaved family were locals or refugees – but as for the locals, they would not even help each other at times of grief.' More seriously, the refugee families remember a time when they were subjected to abuse and even physical violence by locals as they went to cultivate their fields. Out of fear as well as community spirit, they would go out to the harvest in large, defensible groups.

But in the end, these reminiscences do not tell the main story in the social history of this part of Greece during the 20th century. Nor has the distinction between 'refugee' and 'local' been the area's sole or even principal cause of violence. Like almost everywhere else in the Balkans, this corner of the world has been tragically affected by broader world conflicts, both ideological and geopolitical. Between 1941 and 1944, it was occupied by German troops; then in the late 1940s, it was close to the epicentre of a civil war pitting a communist army, formed in part out of the anti-Nazi resistance, against government forces, backed first by Britain and later by America. Of the hundred or so villages which the communists claimed to control in early 1947, many were near Grevena. During the inconclusive fighting of the summer of 1947, it was one of the first medium-sized towns which the communists tried to capture. Over the next eighteen months there was bitter fighting to the north of the town, as American arms and expertise helped to drive the leftists from their mountain fastness. In the aftermath of the communist defeat, supporters of the political left complained that they faced police harassment and discrimination because of their association with the cold war enemy. During the right-wing military dictatorship of 1967–74, there was a fresh wave of repression as leftists (and politicians of many other stripes) were rounded up, imprisoned and exiled. It was often alleged that during these mass arrests, the colonels relied on the same lists of leftist suspects as had been used during the Greek dictatorship of General Metaxas in the late 1930s; during the German occupation; and then during and immediately after the civil war of 1947–9.

What these complaints suggest is that Greece has undergone a continuous ideological struggle between left and right – often involving the same individuals and families – which started in the late 1930s or even earlier, and was still raging in the 1980s when the centre-left finally gained political power and began turning the tables on its opponents. This black and white view of modern Greek history is certainly an oversimplification. But especially in rural areas of Greece, where memories are long and every family knows and watches every other, the left–right divide has been a powerful and enduring factor in local life. Anybody who set out now to write a broad social history of the Grevena region over the past century would probably pay more attention to the left–right dispute than to the distinction between locals and new arrivals from Anatolia which emerged during the late 1920s – although it is not entirely possible to separate the two. The same would apply to most other areas affected by the Lausanne treaty. If people in such regions are now willing to share anecdotes, in an almost humorous spirit, about the early difficulties between say, Turkish or Pontic speakers from the Black Sea and their Greek neighbours, that is partly because the more recent wounds left by ideological conflict are still too raw and painful to discuss. In comparison, the refugee–local feuds of the 1930s seem almost innocent.

Moreover, the trauma caused by ideological divisions is exceptionally deep because members of the same household, or group of friends, can easily end up on different sides. There are thousands of families all over northern Greece where one member served with the government forces in the civil war while another fought on the communist side. In societies where blood ties are far more important than loyalty to the state or to business partners, it is hard to overstate the pain and confusion that this situation causes. Partly for that reason, a historian or sociologist who went round villages in Greece, delving into people's memories of the civil war or even of the dictatorship which fell in 1974, would find people much less willing to talk about that topic than they are to offer anecdotes about the influx of refugees from Anatolia. That is not merely because the ideological struggles pitting left against right are much more recent; it is also because a conflict or political feud that splits families and friends is more shameful and unpleasant to discuss than any other kind. Any outsider with a modicum of sensitivity who visits the Greek countryside will quickly become aware that questions like, 'What did you do in the civil war?' or 'What did you do during the dictatorship?' are best left unasked.

At the same time, the most striking feature of rural Greek society is not the way that old sources of conflict (whether they concern regional origin, or language, or ideology) still persist; it is the fact that to quite a large extent, they have been overcome. It is true that in places like Grevena, people are still very conscious of which families are 'locals' and which came from 'Asia Minor'. It is even more true that the old left–right feud continues to affect local politics and personal relations. Yet social life is not dominated, as it used to be, by the fact that many people retain very sharp, if seldom articulated, memories of how their neighbours behaved during the civil war or the dictatorship. In a Balkan peninsula where many other forms of intercommunal conflict have survived modernization and persisted into the 21st century, the internal feuds of Greek society have gradually lost their salience. This partial healing, moreover, has taken place without much help from political leaders, who have often done as much to exploit and sharpen age-old grievances as they have to calm them down. Whatever has happened, the process seems to have been at least partially spontaneous, something welling upwards from the base of society, rather than explicitly guided by elites.

In a perverse way, the very fact that families were divided by ideology has proved a blessing as well as a curse. It ensured that even when ideological conflict was at its most intense, people did not demonize their foes quite as wholeheartedly as they would in a case where every adversary was deemed to be 'alien' and therefore undeserving of any sympathy or leniency. Along with memories of the terrible murders, abductions and acts of revenge committed during the 1940s, people in rural areas of northern Greece can often remember cases where individuals, guided by local or family loyalty, acted to mitigate the sharpness of war whenever they had the power to do so. There are stories of right-wing army officers or priests who moved quietly to protect, tip off or shelter leftists who happened to be their kinsmen, god-children or simply childhood friends. Where a police officer or bishop could save lives in his village by arranging a local truce, he would do so.

This persistence of ties which cut across political lines (and hence soften the edges of ideological division) was nicely brought home by an incident in the 1980s involving two elderly public figures from the same part of northern Greece. At an opening session of parliament, Archbishop Seraphim, the simple and deeply conservative head of the Greek church, held up a cross which most deputies meekly queued up to kiss in accordance with the Orthodox Christian rite. When Harilaos Florakis, the head of the pro-Soviet communist party, hesitated to make this gesture, the archbishop was heard to encourage him in a loud whisper, saying, '*Ela, Harilae*', (Come on, Harilaos) – in a familiar tone that suggested an old and intimate friendship.

Among Greeks of virtually all ideological persuasions, such incidents cause wry, knowing amusement rather than surprise or disapproval. After a century in which Greek leftists and Greek rightists have killed, abducted and tortured one another, people are reassured by the fact that personal bonds should persist across the widest of ideological chasms.

Indeed, even when Greece's ideological wars were at their bloodiest, each camp at some subliminal level acknowledged that the other side's ranks were filled by fellow members of the Greek family, whether in the literal or metaphorical sense. The worst insult that each side could hurl at the other was that of 'treachery' – collusion with non-Greeks. During the civil war, for example, the propaganda of the communists stressed the government's collaboration with British and American 'imperialists', while that of the government stressed the fact that in certain parts of northern Greece, there were communist units dominated by people who regarded themselves as Slavs and aspired to the creation of a Slav Macedonian state. The implication of this propaganda message was that to be a Greek communist was a grave, but ultimately forgivable, error – but to proclaim oneself a Slav, who challenged not only the ideology of the Greek state but its very identity, was something infinitely worse.

This distinction proved to be an enduring one. In the 1980s, a socialist government in Athens, in what it presented as a long overdue effort to heal the wounds of the civil war, invited veterans of the communist army and their families to leave their places of exile in the Soviet bloc and return to Greece. However the law providing for this return made it clear that the invitation applied only to people 'of Greek race' – so veterans who regarded themselves as Slav Macedonians need not apply. The Greek communist party protested mildly over this ethnic criterion but it could not do so very loudly for fear of being branded treacherous, anti-national and disloyal to the broader Hellenic community. As many Greeks see things, the fighting that has taken place 'within the family' of the Hellenic nation is on the one hand exceptionally painful to recall, precisely because all domestic violence goes against the natural order of things; but it is also something that can, over time, be forgiven and overcome because the power of the 'family' to dissolve and mitigate all internal grievances never entirely fades.

What is truly remarkable is that for this purpose, the refugees from Anatolia – however strange they initially seemed by virtue of their speech, customs, cuisine, appearance and so on – were accepted, over time, as part of the Greek 'family'. In other words, as part of the pool or universe of people within which conflict ought ultimately to be settled and grievances forgiven. People did, in due course, absorb and internalize the ideological message of the post-Lausanne state; the message that: '. . . you must accept the Anatolian Christian newcomers as fellow Greeks and compatriots, even if they seem strange, and you must accept the inevitability of your Muslim neighbours' departure, even if they seem familiar'.

Among old people around Grevena, there is an intriguing difference between the reminiscences of people in their nineties, who dimly remember their Muslim neighbours, and those who are slightly younger – whose perception of the population exchange reflects state ideology more than lived experience. Take this pair of reminiscences from a brother and sister. First, Eleftheria P, a Greek lady from Grevena, northern Greece, born *circa* 1910:

I can still recall the time before the Muslims left our town in 1924. They spoke Greek and did the same jobs as us; they were small traders or shopkeepers, or else breeders of sheep and goats. I remember the day they went away. Some kissed the earth, some took bowls of soil with them. They were decent types; their menfolk used to attend our funerals, and we would exchange presents of food on each other's feast days. They used to say politely that they would accept any food we gave them as long as it wasn't pork. They were regular people and they cried as they left us . . .

Second, Athanasios P, brother of Eleftheria P, born *circa* 1915:

The refugees who came to live among us seemed quite strange to us at first. They spoke Turkish, or a dialect of Greek we couldn't understand, and their food and clothing and manners were different. We were mountain shepherds; they kept calves and made yoghurt. They made kitchen gardens and grew tomatoes and peppers and all kinds of vegetables, and they taught us new things about cooking. But in the end, they were Greeks like us; it was our obligation to help them and we accepted one another. After a generation or more, we locals began to intermarry with the refugees. But as for the Muslims who left, that was a different story. They were Turks, and it was inevitible that they should go away.

To many people who know modern Greek history, it may seem peculiar to be stressing the degree to which, in areas affected by the Lausanne treaty, 'locals' and 'refugees' alike ultimately formed part of a network, a social world within which conflict could be managed and resolved. This argument sounds contrarian because much has been written, quite correctly, about the way in which the 'refugee versus local' distinction actually fuelled Greece's internal ideological battles, and helped to create the disunity in a nation which had previously enjoyed a degree of ideological consensus.

All that is true as far as it goes, but it is not the main point. It is certainly true that for about a decade or so after the population exchange, Greek politics resembled a sort of undeclared civil war, pitting liberal republicans who supported Venizelos against people on the political right who hankered for the return of the monarchy. The fact that the refugees were nearly unanimous in backing Venizelos caused bitter resentment among the conservatives. They accused the Venizelist camp of playing cynically on the vulnerability of the semi-destitute newcomers, of changing electoral boundaries and of failing to represent the interests of the nation as a whole. Among some monarchists, this translated into a generalized dislike of the refugees and of everything about them that seemed odd, from their dress to their speech.

The Venizelists retorted by making a nastier allegation: while the liberal-voting newcomers were, despite appearances, true Hellenes who had a right to make their voice heard, the monarchists were doing something really treacherous by relying on the votes of small non-Greek minorities; the Jews, Albanians and Bulgarians which were still part of the electorate despite the homogenizing effect of the population exchange. This sinister argument could claim some basis in reality by whipping up the memory of the elections of 1915 and 1920 when Jewish, Muslim and other minority voters did cast their ballots for the royalist side, in the hope of averting further conflict between Greece and the Ottoman empire.

At a time when the Greek nation-state (like nation-states all over

Europe) was becoming steadily more exclusive in its ethos, the Venizelists' argument proved to be a much more effective one. The liberals were successfully able to insist, in 1930, that Jewish voters in Salonika be placed on a separate electoral roll (so as to minimize their influence over national politics) on grounds it was unacceptable to allow an 'alien as arbiter' in the affairs of the nation.

The monarchists, meanwhile, could not really sustain the argument that the Anatolian Christian refugees were outsiders with no right to a say in the nation's future – even after the Venizelist coups of 1933 and 1935, in which some refugees acted as a private army or claque. Over time, the monarchists began making at least token attempts to include refugees on their electoral lists and address their grievances. After 1936, when the royalist general Ioannis Metaxas seized power and imposed a dictatorship, he became oddly popular with many refugees – partly because the quasi-fascist regime's efforts to recast the consciousness of all citizens into a simple nationalist mould implied a kind of equality among everyone who was prepared to accept the ideals of Hellenism.

A parallel can be made (despite the huge differences) with the Kemalist project in Turkey, whose effort to refashion the consciousness of every single citizen also had a sort of equalizing effect. In an authoritarian, modernizing republic, any loyal citizen who *wants* to conform to the national ideal, and is prepared to make the necessary adaptations, can expect some protection in return from the state.

For General Metaxas, the Turkish-speaking refugees in northern Greece were a welcome bulwark against Slavic influence. Not because of what the newcomers 'were' objectively, but because of what they desired to be: Greek and nothing but Greek. Likewise for the Kemalist state, newcomers from Crete who spoke nothing but Greek were more useful citizens than non-Muslims who spoke nothing but Turkish – as long as the newcomers *wanted* to be Turkish, or were at least open to persuasion that no other status was desirable. As long as they subscribed to the national ideal, and were prepared to fight for it, they could be assured of protection from the snobbishness or hostility of their fellow citizens whose roots in Anatolia went deeper. In the Greek case, all citizens were on an equal footing as long as they accepted the Metaxas regime's aspiration to create a 'third Greek civilization'.

Perhaps the biggest political effect on Greece of the population exchange was the fact that a significant minority of newcomers, especially slum dwellers and members of the small working class, threw in their lot with the communist party of Greece, the KKE. The move leftwards was especially noticeable after the Turkish–Greek agreement of 1930, which shook the faith of urban refugees in Venizelos and dashed their hopes of getting decent compensation for the properties they had lost in Anatolia. Until 1935, the KKE's appeal was limited because its support for a 'greater Macedonia' dominated by the Slavs was so obviously at variance with Greek interests. But when that policy was abandoned, the appeal of the communist movement grew. The Metaxas dictatorship forced it underground, where it developed survival skills that helped it to dominate the resistance to the Axis occupation of Greece.

If the Greek communists were tough and resilient, it was partly because many of their leaders had already been hardened by the experience of losing homes and property in Turkey and making new lives in the grinding poverty of refugee quarters in Piraeus or Salonika. Both the main leaders of the communist camp in the 1946–9 civil war – the party leader, Nikos Zahariades and the military commander Markos Vafiades – were of refugee stock. In his memoires, 'General Markos' gives a vivid account of his early life in Anatolia and discloses that at the time of Lausanne, he considered staying on in Turkey by dint of marrying a Turkish neighbour's daughter. Given the strong Anatolian connections of the Greek communists, it would be understandable, perhaps, if people on the Greek right had blamed the whole communist movement on the 'alien' influence of newcomers from Turkey who should never have come to Greece in the first place – and if as a consequence, they had demonized all refugees.

But in fact, such a crude line of argument has generally been avoided, especially since 1945. The Second World War and the Axis occupation should not simply be seen as a cause of bitter division among Greek citizens, old and new. The Greek army's campaign against the Italians in Albania, in which 'refugees' and 'locals' fought side by side, was an important bonding experience for the post-Lausanne state. To this day, Pontic Greeks often will insist that they won the right to be respected as full-blooded Hellenes by virtue of their sacrifices in that campaign. In any case, by no means all the Anatolian refugees moved leftwards on arrival in Greece; some went in the opposite direction. In the complex ethnic and ideological patchwork of northern Greece, many of the Turkish-speaking refugees from the Black Sea region moved to the political right, to what they regarded as the 'nationalist' or 'patriotic' position which was strongly anti-communist – and therefore willing to co-operate with the German occupiers against the communist-led resistance. When the Germans sponsored informal armed groups to counter the communists, they found willing recruits in the Turkish-speaking refugees, whose style of warfare drew heavily on the traditions of the irregular armed bands formed by Christians in the Black Sea region before 1922. So the effect of the refugees on Greece's internal political balance was far from simple, and in the end there was no significant group which questioned their status as Greeks, or their right to participate in Greek affairs.

So any overall analysis of the population exchange has to wrestle with a truth which is awkward from a liberal, modern point of view: in its own perverse terms, the population exchange 'worked' – in the sense that it ultimately, after many difficulties, contributed to the forging of a more or less homogenous Greek nation-state whose citizens recognized each other's right to exist. Moreover, the calculation that informed the Lausanne project on both sides of the Aegean – that a common religion would make possible the creation of a common national consciousness – seems to have been borne out. The forging of the modern Greek nation-state, and also the forging of the modern Turkish nation-state, was greatly facilitated by the existence of a common religion, which made inter-marriage possible and helped to overcome other sources of difference, such as language and local origin.

In many parts of Greece and Turkey, as this book has shown, there is clear evidence of the painful way in which the population exchange has distorted people's lives and self understanding. Both among the Greek-born citizens of Turkey, and the citizens of Greece who regard 'Asia Minor' as their homeland, it is easily possible to detect an unresolved struggle to hold together the national identity which people are now expected to pro-claim, and the lived experience of their own families. In this region of ancient settlement and civilization, there is often an unhappy mismatch between where people live now, and the places to which they feel the deep-est attachment; and that mismatch is reflected in the physical environment. Monuments and places of worship seem to be in the wrong place, or to be used for the wrong purpose. In contrast with European cities like

Bologna or Salamanca, where the past and present seem to blend quite seamlessly, the Aegean landscape is full of odd, unhappy disjunction; places where people have lived, prayed and done business for centuries feel as soulless and ill-designed as a strip development on an American turnpike. That is partly the result, of course, of ill-managed and corrupt forms of economic development; but the legacy of an artificial exercise in social and ethnic remodelling has also played a part.

But evidence to support an argument in *favour* of the triumphant achievement of Lausanne's stated goals, is also abundant. As an exercise in reconstructing people's consciousness, both the population exchange and the nation-building drives which followed, in both Turkey and Greece, have by many indicators achieved their stated purpose. If the aim was to make a reasonably neat division of a certain geographical space, of a collection of assets, and of a diverse population, then that aim has in quite large measure been realized. Compared with any major country in western Europe, Greece and Turkey are now fairly homogenous countries. The vast majority of Greek citizens speak Greek, adhere at least nominally to Orthodox Christianity and consider themselves Greek. The great majority of Turkish citizens speak Turkish, adhere to Sunni Islam and consider themselves Turks. For all the intensity of their domestic arguments, the people of each country do have a strong sense of their own nation's uniformity and singularity. Most Turkish citizens do accept one another as fellow members of the same national community, and they make a strong distinction between their own nation and everybody else. The same is true of Greece.

If the two countries are 'imagined communities' – to use one of the classic descriptions of the modern nation-state – they are powerfully imagined ones. Taking the Greek case, from Alexandroupolis in the far northeast to the southwestern corner of the Peloponnese, there is a uniformity of popular culture as well as language. You will find people will be discussing roughly the same football teams, listening to the same music, speaking the same language. The accents will be different, but the vocabulary and grammar, and above all the subject matter, will be broadly the same. In *most* parts of Turkey, the impression is similar. Across an extraordinary diversity of landscape, of levels of economic development, and of human and physical environment, there is in the end a relative uniformity of language, sentiment and everyday culture.

Still, to describe either Greece or Turkey as a 'successfully' homogenized society is controversial and risky, and in both cases the argument can only be made with caution. On the Turkish side, one major qualification is needed. Among a population of 70 million, there remains one significant group which has refused to allow its identity to be submerged in the Turkish whole, and that is the Kurdish minority, which may number as many as 10 million.

The history of relations between Turks and Kurds under the Turkish republic has been a bloody and a tragic one, and that tragedy began as an immediate result of the Lausanne regime and its aspiration to replace religious forms of authority with secular, nationalist ones. The tribal leaders of the Kurds had accepted Ottoman Turkish authority so long as it was a Muslim realm whose ruler was a caliph as well as a sultan; but when the new masters of Anatolia defined themselves in secular, ethnic terms as Turks, that consent was withdrawn. The result was a Kurdish uprising in Turkey's southeast in the spring of 1925, which ended with the execution of the rebel leaders and the internal deportation of large numbers of Kurds. Eighty years on, the Kurds have yet to be fully incorporated by a Turkish republic which for many years sought to deny their existence. During the 1990s there was a conflict in southeastern Turkey between Marxist Kurdish guerrillas and government forces that cost tens of thousands of lives.

But ghastly as it has been, the conflict in Turkey's border regions has not prevented, and in some ways has accelerated, the consolidation of a broadly accepted sense of Turkishness in the rest of Anatolia. In part because of the Kurdish challenge, the methods used by the authorities to inculcate a feeling of Turkishness have been authoritarian and periodically brutal; but these days at least, recourse to such methods is not very often necessary. In most of Turkey, and among the vast majority of Turks, there is by now a deep acceptance of the national ideal, and indeed of the notion that doubters of that ideal should be dealt with firmly. Whatever goes on in their inner world, whatever sentiments they may harbour for places and ways of life on the other side of the Aegean, Turkish citizens who originate from Greece do not generally dissent from that national ideal. The old folk of Ayvalik or Tuzla may yearn for their native soil in Crete or Greek Macedonia, but a lifetime under the Turkish flag has made them as loyal to the memory of Ataturk as most of their compatriots, if not more so.

To say this is not to justify the population exchange, or to accept that it is ever morally permissible, in a society that aspires to be civilized, for a state authority to knock on a family's door and demand that it leave for another country on the sole ground that it follows the 'wrong' religion. But it is a hard fact of modern Greek and Turkish history that this huge and ruthless project in social and ethnic engineering was more successful than otherwise from the point of the view of the states which implemented it – and indeed colluded to implement it.

It might be argued that the 'success' of Lausanne points to nothing more than the ability of 20th century governments, coaxing a premodern, peasant population into the contemporary world through mass education and political propaganda, to inculcate almost any message about identity, as long as the effort is ruthless enough and people are given no alternative. Whatever they 'really' were, the Christian peasants of Cappadocia or the Pontus, newly arrived in Greece, adhered over time to a standard model of Greekness because they had no other choice. Greece claimed their loyalty, and was prepared to offer them succour; no other state authority made a similar demand, or a similar offer. In that situation, adhering to the Greek ideal was the only available strategy for survival. It might have been possible to remould their consciousness in many different ways. Yet there are some limits to the force of this point. State ideology can refashion people's ideas about themselves in a great variety of ways, but its ability to do so is not infinite. The task of remoulding is much easier if the group of people who are being moulded do not stand on opposite sides of the crucial religious divide.

In the Turkish case, particular care and circumspection is needed in making a case for the 'success' of the Lausanne convention, and for the utility (from the two states' viewpoint) of choosing religion as a criterion for determining people's fate. On the face of things, one of the declared aims of the Kemalist revolution was to 'fight religion' and put an end to the reactionary, self-serving, obscurantist authority of the clerical elites. If Ataturk really had followed this line with the ruthlessness of a Bolshevik – in other words, if he had genuinely intended to create a new sort of community and proclaim a new focus of meaning, truth and loyalty which rendered irrelevant all previous ones – then it would hardly have mattered what religious beliefs people had held before this great experiment began. Just as the Leninists aspired to create a 'new kind of human being' or *homo sovieticus*, a new Turkish consciousness might in theory have been fashioned among people who had previously been Christians, Jews, Zoroastrians, atheists or anything else.

In practice, the foundation of the Turkish republic was not quite so radical. It took a pre-existing community, or at least one part of the pre-existing community, the Ottoman Muslims, and gave them a new way of thinking about themselves; henceforth they were Turks, or Turkish Muslims. The self-understanding of the community was redirected, but the boundaries of the community did not change. In other words, a community of Muslims was told that being Muslim was no longer the sole, or the most significant thing they had in common. Yet however much they accepted the new doctrine, they did not cease to be a group of Muslims, and to feel – at least unconsciously – the ties of confessional solidarity. That very fact gave the Turkish nationalist project a much better chance of succeeding.

It is worth reflecting on the social tensions that seethed in Anatolia immediately after the Lausanne agreement and the population exchange. It was difficult enough for Anatolian Turks to accept Muslims from the Balkans – Greek speakers, Albanian speakers, Slavic speakers, or whatever – as fellow citizens of the republic; but it would have been harder still for a deeply religious society to accept large numbers of non-Muslims as fellow citizens of a modern state with absolutely identical rights and obligations. Because the 'raw material' out of which the Turkish republic was constructed happened to be overwhelmingly Muslim, the nation-building effort (even if it claimed to be a non-religious or even an anti-religious enterprise) could go *with* the grain of religious loyalty rather than against it. It could draw on the powerful sense of fellowship which Muslims (or any other community linked by an elaborate set of beliefs) feel for one another. Moreover, given the turbulent conditions in which secular Turkish nationalism was born, the republic's masters could count both on a positive sense of Islamic solidarity, and also on the negative feelings which Turkish Muslims had come to feel towards non-Muslims in general, and the Christian minorities in particular, since the Balkan wars of 1912–13. For a Kemalist elite that was galvanizing citizens of the new republic to build a new way of life, the old interreligious jealousies and suspicions were a more promising rhetorical device than some of the more outlandish theories of Turkish nationalism. Many an

Anatolian Muslim peasant must have been bewildered by the new secular nationalist theories, asserting ancestral links with nomads in Central Asia, or with Hittites who lived 4000 years ago, as his main source of pride and self-worth. But the idea that the nation was finally being 'liberated' from the economic power of the Ottoman Christians – who were not just traitors to the empire, but usurers, cheats and exploiters of simple, decent Muslims – was much easier to swallow. Economic grievances were neatly fused with ethnic and religious suspicions to generate some of the passion needed to drive forward Turkey's modernizing revolution.

There is at least one other way which relative uniformity of faith, reinforced by the population exchange, helped Turkey's political nationalists to wrest real power from the old clerical elites. As long as a society remains deeply and irreducibly pious, internal conflict between rival faiths (or rival versions of the same faith) can serve to boost the power of religious elites, and make it harder for secular authority to assert itself. 'You need me to lead the fight against the infidels,' the clerical leaders can always say. As an exasperated secularist might put things, whenever there is an ongoing, unresolved conflict between Shi'ites who hate Sunnis, or Christians who loathe Muslims, the mullahs and priests will not go away. The Turkey which Mustafa Kemal shaped was not wholly free of internal conflict between rival versions of Islam, but it was uniform enough to make it possible for the authorities to impose a single, one-size-fits-all form of Sunni Islam as the prevailing faith, and then to fuse that faith in a relatively seamless way with the tenets of Turkish nationalism.

So religious uniformity can, in a perverse way, make easier a transition to non-religious governance. Yet as the history of the Turkish republic shows, it is not really possible for the governance of a society which is overwhelmingly aligned with a single faith to remain entirely secular. Religion somehow seeps upwards and 'sanctifies' the state. The fact that many people aspire to be taught about Islam, whether at primary school or in higher education, forces the state to become involved in managing religious instruction. The fact that many people want new places of worship forces the government to regulate the building of mosques, and so on. For the keen secularists who governed the Turkey of the 1930s, it would be deeply disappointing to learn that their country's public life in 2005 is in many ways more preoccupied by religion than it was seventy years ago. A political party with Islamist roots enjoys a handsome parliamentary majority and its leader, Recep Tayyip Erdogan, has won popular acclaim for defending the right to be a pious Muslim. If Turkey were genuinely secular, it would not be the case that holders of sensitive state jobs – policemen, judges, diplomats – are, in practice, always Muslims. Perhaps this failure reflects the fact that there is a limit to how successfully you can build secularism in a country of one religion, if that religion is devoutly professed. Yet in a multi-religious country, building secularism may be often harder still – unless religion is in any case losing salience (as was the case in modern, republican France), or the secularizing regime is exceptionally ruthless (as was the case in Soviet Russia).

Yet another calculus comes into play in a nation like modern Greece where religious affiliation, while still relatively strong, is gradually losing ground to modern belief systems. In the Greek case, it may be that religious elites, rather than secular ones, have been the biggest beneficiaries of a population exchange which helped to make sure that the country remained over 95 per cent Orthodox Christian. If, in accordance with the predictions of the young Venizelos, Greece really had turned into a country that embraced religious diversity and included many Muslims, then the Orthodox Christian clergy might have lost their battle to insist that adherence to their faith should be a necessary, if not a sufficient, condition of 'Greekness'. As things turned out, the insistence of the clergy that 'only an Orthodox Christian can be a Greek' has remained an indispensable source of strength for a church which might otherwise have lost its power over a modernizing society.

Ever since the proclamation of the modern Greek kingdom in 1831, the religious elites have often had to move deftly and energetically to retain a place near the apex of the new Hellenic state. Among the creators of independent Greece, there were some robust anti-clericalists who were exasperated by the collusion of the Orthodox Patriarchate with the Ottoman authorities to maintain the status quo and to stamp out scientific rationalism and other modern ideas. A century later, Venizelos and his fellow liberals were modernizers in matters of faith. The most prominent 'Venizelist' among the Greek Orthodox clergy, Archbishop (and later Patriarch) Meletios Metaxakis, was a radical reformer whose legacy is still regarded with intense suspicion by conservatives in the eastern Christian world. If Greece had remained a multi-religious country, as it became after the acquisition of Macedonia and Epirus in 1912, it is possible that its governance might, over time, have been secularized. But in a country that was 95 per cent Greek Orthodox, thanks in large measure to a religion-based population exchange, the hierarchs of the faith were well placed to maintain their role as junior partners, at least, in the enterprise of statehood. They have in a sense returned the favour: both at a public and a private level, the rites, sacraments and bonding influence of the Greek church have played a powerful role in shaping, dignifying and holding together the modern Hellenic state. Orthodoxy, entrenched by many articles of the Greek constitution, 'sacralizes' the state by lending dignity to public ceremonies, from the opening of parliamentary sessions to the laying of foundation stones for hotels. At a more private level, the calendar of the Orthodox church, including the inspiring ceremonies which are associated with Easter and Epiphany, forms part of the texture of modern Greek life and a common reference point for all citizens. These rites play a very clear role in mitigating social conflict, as many observers of Greece have pointed out. In a country where families and factions are intensely preoccupied, for most of the year, by competition over economic assets, or ideology, there are certain ceremonies which help the community to remember what its members have in common, and its obligation to stand together against external threats. There is no secular rite which plays this role so effectively as common participation in the Paschal feast, or in the 'blessing of the waters' – the colourful, start-of-the-year ritual which culminates in an exuberant contest among young swimmers to recover a cross which has been cast into a lake, river or sea.

In Greece as in Turkey, the state is deeply involved in religious education, and hence in assuring that virtually all pupils are taught the predominant religion in a way that reinforces loyalty to the nation. This gives patriotism a religious edge, and it also limits the power of religion to be a force in its own right. While the net result may be similar, the background is different. In Turkey, the political elite feels that it must regulate religious education in order to keep it under a modicum of control and make sure that it does not clash with the other imperative of loyalty to the nation. In Greece, where the primacy of loyalty to the secular state seems more assured, the clerical elite has nonetheless managed to persuade successive political masters that religion is still worth supporting as a way of consolidating the nation. In both countries, the role of the state as a religious educator is firmly established, and this consensus is obviously helped by the fact that in each country, almost everybody adheres at least nominally to the same faith.

But however 'successful' the Lausanne regime has been at turning Turkey and Greece into coherent, national communities – underpinned by unity of language, unity of faith and relative unity of national senti-ment – there are good reasons for doubting the stability of that success in the 21st century. Indeed there was something inherently unstable about the Lausanne bargain: an arrangement under which two nations agree to live perpetually in a state of 'ritual opposition' to one another, with reli-gion playing a role in reinforcing that opposition. The main reason for this is that 'ritual opposition' presents a perpetual danger of reversion to real conflict – and this danger is probably exacerbated when the perpet-ually ritualized 'other' adheres to a different religion.

In any case, the terms of the 'ritual opposition' enshrined by the Lausanne treaty have to be defined carefully. Under the post-1923 order, the elites of Greece and Turkey (or their more farsighted members) expected to settle down as more or less self-contained and satisfied powers who could live as good neighbours and partners, thanks to the 'good fences' which they had erected between their territory, resources and populations. In order to maintain this state of affairs, both countries agreed to suppress or play down certain parts of their recent history. Turkey agreed to excise the history of the Ottoman empire as a Balkan power, and Greece to some extent played down the collective memory of its citizens who had formerly lived in Anatolia. In a sense, both nations agreed to pretend that they had always lived in the places marked out by their current national borders, and nowhere else. At the same time, each of these self-contained and well-defined states used the memory of vic-tory against the other as an essential source of collective self esteem. The masters of the Turkish republic never ceased to remind citizens that their new state, and hence Turkey's access to the modern world, was carved out on the battlefield, out of a hard-won victory against the Greek invader. For the modern Hellenic state, the most glorious chapters in the collective memory were the uprising against the Ottoman empire in 1821, and the wars of 1912–13 which wrested the north of present day Greece from Ottoman control. The celebration of past victories does not, of course, lead automatically to present day hostility: the fact that

America celebrates its uprising against the British crown does not make it hostile to modern Britain. But it can have that effect.

Quite possibly, the 'formal opposition' of Greece and Turkey, enshrined by the Lausanne order, might have subsided into something purely ceremonial and ritualistic if it were really true that all potential areas for Greek–Turkish dispute had been resolved in 1923. In fact this was not the case, as the flare-up of the Cypriot question from the mid-1950s onwards was to prove so tragically. The very fact that the fate of one significant piece of territory – Cyprus – was not settled by Lausanne (because the island was a British colony) proved enough to reignite Greek–Turkish disputes on a whole series of other fronts, from the mid-1950s onwards. Greece and Turkey found themselves at war by proxy during the bloody events of summer 1974, when a coup on the island by Greek and Greek-Cypriot ultra-rightists triggered a Turkish invasion. This led to a *de facto* population exchange between the Turkish-controlled north and Greek-administered south which reproduced in microcosm the forced migration of the 1920s. The main difference, perhaps, between the population exchange on Cyprus, and the much larger one of fifty years earlier, was the fact that the latter was accepted by both sides as legitimate, whereas the expulsion of Greek-Cypriots from the northern third of the island remains an open sore, legally and diplomatically. In part because the Cyprus problem remains open, the broader Greek–Turkish conflict has proved maddeningly intractable, despite a concerted effort begun in 1999 by both governments to improve relations, after a period of very high tension in which armed conflict seemed conceivable. Six years on, the political atmosphere between the two countries has considerably improved, but neither on the Cyprus question nor on any other outstanding points of difference has there been any real convergence.

Assuming that interstate conflict can be avoided, are there any other reasons why the 'success' of 20th century nationalism in forging coherent Turkish and Greek nation-states, which acknowledge and in some ways reinforce one another, should not continue? In fact, there are plenty of reasons. One simple point is that in an age of easy travel and mass communication, the half truths and oversimplifications of nationalist (or religious-nationalist) ideology are harder to sustain. For example, it is now much easier for extended families, straddling the Greek–Turkish border and even the Christian–Muslim divide, to reforge old ties which go against the nationalist grain: ties which should not, according to a nationalist doctrine which treats every nation as hermetically sealed, have any right to exist at all.

There is one particularly striking example of ties recently 'rediscovered', which promise to be subversive of Greek and Turkish ideology alike. That is the kinship between extended families from the Black Sea region who were divided during the chaotic and tragic sequence of mountain warfare, deportation and forced marches during the decade which preceded the population exchange. In part because of these half-suppressed blood ties, the Pontic Greek community (a significant lobby in Athenian affairs) is rather conflicted in its attitude to Turkey. On one hand, it urges politicians in Athens to take the hardest possible line in its dealings with the Turkish authorities, and to insist, however unrealistically, that Turkish politicians acknowledge the 'genocide' perpetrated by the Kemalist forces against the Black Sea Greeks in 1921. At the same time, many Pontic Greeks are fascinated by the landscape, culture and population of Turkey, if only because they feel a connection with all three that cannot simply be sacrificed to state ideology.

So even if the Lausanne ideology succeeds in every other way, it will not be able to neutralize the influence of the bonds felt by Black Sea Greeks and Black Sea Turks who happen to be first cousins. In any Greek–Turkish settlement based merely on 'separation' and good fences, those Black Sea bonds will continue to be an awkward, destabilizing influence. Indeed, the Black Sea Greeks are among the few people in either country who have challenged the logic of the population exchange and its ongoing consequences. From their point of view, the Pontic-speaking Muslims of Turkey should be given the right, at least, to resettle in Greece, regardless of their religion. In fact it is far from clear how many would want to, as many Pontic-speakers in Turkey are staunch Turkish nationalists. But in pressing their demands, the Pontic lobbyists in Greece have correctly sensed where the real opposition lies: with Greek Orthodox clergy who feel their authority would be challenged by anything or anyone who demonstrates that it is possible to be Greek without also being Orthodox.

In a sense, though, the challenge posed to the population-exchange regime from the noisy Black Sea lobbyists is only a detail, or a symptom of something broader. It is no longer possible for Greece and Turkey to remain hermetically sealed and neatly divided from one another, for the simple reason that in the 21st century, it is no longer possible for either country to remain hermetically sealed from anywhere else. For all the hard work that each country has done to inculcate a simple nationalist ideology, both are now faced in acute form with the pressures of a multicultural Europe, and a globalized economy. These factors are transforming both the daily experience of ordinary people and the policy options of the Greek and Turkish governments as they look for a place in the new geopolitical order.

All over the region, the effects of multiculturalism on places which have been carefully 'cleansed' are painfully evident. Among the communities of proud and patriotic Greeks in the regions of Drama or Grevena which have been so patiently constructed over the past eighty years, it is now common to find that half the wage earners have gone to work in Germany, while many buildings have become holiday homes for north Europeans, in which Albanian or Ukrainian labourers are busily engaged in repairs. Or take the district of Kokkinia, part of the port of Piraeus, where a classic work of urban social anthropology was written in the early 1970s by Renee Hirschon, the pioneer of 'population exchange' studies. At that time, the suburb remained intensely conscious of its 'Asia Minor' roots, although half a century had passed since it was built to accommodate newcomers from Anatolia. In its matchmaking practices, its rites of passage, its elaborate sense of family obligations, the community retained many features of its Anatolian heritage. Despite their relative poverty, the people of Kokkinia saw themselves as heirs to a sophisticated urban culture which set them apart from the peasants of mainland Greece who had recently moved into the city. In this comparison, neither side was perceived as un-Hellenic, but the Kokkinia people saw themselves as better Greeks than their non-refugee neighbours. Thirty years on, the neighbourhood still bears clear traces of its 'refugee' past. These characteristics are a peculiar mixture; they include a strong communist vote, and a relatively high incidence of church going. But among today's worshippers at the vast and beautifully frescoed Orthodox church that dominates one of Kokkinia's central squares, the main concern is not the contrast between different shades of Greekness, it is the recent arrival in the district of an entirely new wave of refugees who are not even trying to be Greek: people from the Middle East and the Indian sub-continent, as well as Albania and other ex-communist countries. 'Now we are going to become a minority again,' is a recurrent cry among these parishioners, whose collective memory tells them that to live as a minority means to be at perpetual risk of annihilation.

Over the past fifteen years, following the fall of communism and the near-collapse of all state control over its northern borders, carefully homogenized Greece now finds itself with a highly diverse labour force, of which as many as 20 per cent may be of non-Greek origin. Albanians are the biggest category, with large contingents of Bulgarians, Poles, Filipinos, Nigerians, Indians and Chinese. The full effects of this have yet to be felt. Greece's electorate and citizenry remain more or less uniform because most immigrants are neither enfranchized nor integrated into the Greek body politic. Only as labour migrants gradually turn into voters, and their children emerge from the Greek school system, will it become obvious how unsustainable the Lausanne principle of 'Greece for the Greek Orthodox' will prove to be in the 21st century.

Turkey is at a somewhat earlier stage in the discovery of this painful truth. While 'modernization' in the 19th and 20th century obliged previously multi-ethnic societies to become mono-lingual, mono-cultural and mono-religious, things will be different in the 21st century. If Turkey is to pursue its ambition of qualifying for the European Union, it will no longer be able to impose a single, narrowly defined model of Turkishness on all its citizens. That is a terrifying prospect for a society and a political class which has always regarded that model as the only hope of national survival. EU membership will pose a challenge for the post-Lausanne order in very specific ways, too. It will no longer be possible to bar fellow citizens of the EU, including Greeks, from settling or buying property on any part of its territory. At that point, the Lausanne regime's stipulation that Greek Orthodox people may not live anywhere in Turkey except Istanbul and two small islands will be untenable – and the population exchange could, in theory, go into partial reverse.

But the hardest question for Turkey is whether it will be willing to call in question the *political legacy* of the population exchange, including the cherished principle that only a single language and ethnic consciousness should be allowed on Turkish soil, on pain of severe retribution by the state. Maintaining that principle is simply not compatible with membership of the European Union, although relatively few politically conscious Turks seem to have realized that. As of 2005, the tension between Turkey's desire to be part of Europe's most prestigious club, and its attachment to the founding principles of the Turkish republic, was palpable and it was entirely unclear how it would be resolved. After intense prodding from Europe, the Turkish parliament has passed a law which permits broadcasting in any language, including Kurdish. Thanks to a similar blast of pressure, the authorities released from prison the well-known Kurdish politician, Leyla Zana, who had been jailed for ten years for speaking her native language in the Turkish parliament. The bureaucrats in Brussels have also kept a watchful eye on Turkey's treatment of the Orthodox Patriarch and his tiny Christian flock. (And European bureaucrats, and judges have already had considerable influence in prodding Greece to behave with a minimum of decency towards the Muslim minority in western Thrace, as behoves an EU member.)

Among Turkey's smallish liberal intelligentsia, pressure from Brussels is seen as a benign influence, pushing the country in a direction which is in any case desirable. But for Turkey's nationalist establishment, both civilian and military, every concession to Brussels means surrendering a small part of the Lausanne principles on which the republic is based. And for many ordinary Turks, who have been taught all their lives that their nation's very existence depends on unity and uniformity, it is baffling and infuriating to be told by European organizations that they must dismantle the post-Lausanne republican order and go back to the older notion that more than one language, culture and religion can exist under the same political roof. It is bewildering because in this part of the world, the traditional order was multicultural, while the modern age has brought ruthlessly enforced uniformity of faith and ethnic consciousness.

So at the very moment when people on both sides of the Aegean have more or less absorbed their hard nationalist lessons – a process which has taken a couple of generations, and required a great deal of forced learning as well as forced amnesia – it suddenly turns out that an entirely different set of ideas about identity and territory have been mandated by the international institutions that have replaced the League of Nations as guardians of the European order.

That is a dangerous state of affairs. As Arnold Toynbee persuasively argued, the sudden arrival of western concepts about nationalism and statehood brought a tidal wave of misery, bloodshed and dislocation to an Ottoman world where such ideas were completely alien. It has taken most of the past eighty years for those ideas to be absorbed 'successfully' by the countries concerned. As globalization and liberal capitalism advance, they are bringing yet another set of principles about culture and citizenship to the partially modern, partially traditional societies of Turkey, Greece, and to many other places besides. Today's challenge is to ensure that these new understandings of identity and belonging do not exact such a high price in blood as the previous ones did.

Bibliography, sources and methodology

The aim of this book has been to describe in a straightforward, accessible way the extraordinary and fateful episode in European history known as the Turkish–Greek population exchange, and its effects on both countries. This event is a human story, and a landmark in diplomatic history. In the narrative I have switched backwards and forwards between high politics and the lives of ordinary people to bring home both the choices which politicians faced in 1923 and the impact of those choices on hundreds of thousands of Muslim and Christian families. The book is aimed at the general reader, not the university library – as a magazine reporter I have brought to bear my experience as a storyteller and setter of scenes, linking present day landscapes and townscapes with the changes that swept over the region in the 1920s.

One of the purposes of this section of the book is to identify and acknowledge the life-long specialists in this field who have in many cases shown me great personal kindness, and the scholars on whose shoulders I am gratefully standing. It is also to thank the patient people, in Turkish ports and Greek mountain villages who were willing to share with me their families' experience of crossing the Aegean under terrible duress.

In most books, Acknowledgements and Bibliography are treated as separate categories. The first is usually an expression of gratitude to all the individuals who have facilitated the author's task, and the second a list of all the books, academic papers and other written sources which have been used. In my case, it is difficult to distinguish the two headings, because so many of the authors who have studied the 1923 population exchange and its effects from various perspectives, were also personally helpful. Nor is it always possible to separate the help I received through their writings from the advice and encouragement which they offered in person.

Very broadly, the population exchange has been studied in two ways: from the viewpoint of those who decreed it – in other words, as a story of war, high politics and diplomacy; and from the perspective of those who endured it. In the final quarter of the 20th century, there has been a reaction against the first approach in favour of the second. In my presentation of this fateful episode in European history to readers who are newcomers to the subject and the region, I have drawn on both approaches.

The most detailed study of the Lausanne convention from a Hellenic perspective was written by a Greek diplomat in 1962, shortly before his early death. Dimitri Pentzopoulos' *The Balkan Exchange of Minorities and its Impact on Greece* (Paris, Mouton, republished London, Hurst, 2002) remains an indispensable reference point for any study of the population exchange, although many subsequent writers have legitimately queried his conclusions and his 'bureaucratic' bias. It is based on a remarkably diligent examination of Greek, American, British and League of Nations diplomatic archives as well as the Greek press, parliamentary proceedings and financial records. I managed to follow in the footsteps of Pentzopoulos as far as the Greek foreign ministry archives (*Archeion Ypourgeiou Exoterikon*), the Venizelos archives under the control of the Benaki museum in Athens, and the League of Nations archives at the Palais des Nations.

Some of the most important Turkish diplomatic records, forming as they do part of the 'sacred history' of the republic, are easily available: *Lozan Telgraflari* (Ankara, Turk Tarih Kurumu Basimevi, 1994) is a multivolume record of the cables exchanged between the delegation at the Lausanne conference, led by Ismet Pasha, and the Grand National Assembly in Ankara. The peppery reminiscences of Riza Nour, the second-ranking member of that delegation, are another important part of the diplomatic record: *Hayat ve Hatiratim* (Istanbul, Altindag Yayinevi, 1967).

The entire proceedings of the Lausanne meetings, from November 1922 until July 1923, were published in English as the *Lausanne Conference on Near Eastern Affairs* (HMSO). Another important source, easily accessible in the London Library as well as the British Library is provided by the *Official Journal of the League of Nations*, which includes reports from Fridtjof Nansen on his work as High Commissioner for Refugees, discussions on the creation of the Refugee Settlement Commission in Greece and regular accounts of its activities. A more detailed and franker account of the RSC's work is provided by the minutes of the regular meetings of the agency's four-person board which comprised an American, a Briton and two prominent Greeks. For an understanding of the background against which the Lausanne decisions were taken, especially but not exclusively from a Greek perspective, an indispensable work is that of Michael Llewellyn-Smith, *Ionian Vision: Greece in Asia Minor (1919–22)* (republished London, Hurst, 1998). This is a gripping and meticulous account by a scholar-diplomat of the Turkish–Greek war itself, and of the shifting role of the western powers, rooted in a very sophisticated understanding of Greek domestic politics. Mr Llewellyn-Smith gave me some very useful advice at the very start of my project when I was looking for a way into the subject of 'Near Eastern' affairs in the early 20th century.

Going further back, there is a sense in which every chronicler of this period walks in the giant footsteps of Arnold Toynbee and his brave and provocative work, *The Western Question in Greece and Turkey: A Study in the Contact of Civilizations* (Boston, Houghton Mifflin, 1922). A powerful mixture of on-the-ground reportage and historical reflection, the book was written in part as a denunciation of romantic philhellenism: the sort which assumed that because of the modern Greeks' connection with classical antiquity (or perhaps, a westernized version of classical antiquity), their political and military culture would be 'western' rather than 'eastern'. In his attacks on cultural determinism, Toynbee may himself have fallen into a degree of cultural determinism. But that is a quibble at most: because he denounced atrocities by Turks and Greeks alike, he is a courageous, and a troubling figure for anyone whose investigation of early 20th century European history is mainly inspired by nationalist passion, or by the desire to prove the unshakeable virtue of one nation and the irredeemable wickedness of another.

Unfortunately, such passions do inform most people who write about this period, and they are a pardonable sentiment among people who came from that region and consequently bear the scars, in their own or their families' history, of the wickedness of one side in particular. It is less understandable when outsiders become gripped by such passions, and yet most of them do succumb in some degree. Virtually all historians have shown bias by glossing over the misdeeds of one or more parties to the region's endless conflicts. Indeed, almost everyone falls into the trap of implying (if only by omission) that in certain circumstances, systematically terrorizing, killing or uprooting women, children and other non-combatants is at best justifiable, at worst an understandable excess. One of the few who stands firm against that principle is Toynbee. The fact that he has been denounced as a liar by Turks and Greeks is *prima facie* evidence that he was telling uncomfortable truths.

In our own times, an impressive example of fair-mindedness and courage has been shown by the Turkish economist and historian Dr Onur Yildirim in a doctoral thesis entitled, *Diplomats and Refugees: Mapping the Turco-Greek Population Exchange of 1922–1934* (unpublished PhD, Princeton University, 2002). One of the greatest merits of this work, which involved seven years of research into Greek, Turkish and English documents, is its critique of the existing bibliography; what Dr Yildirim calls the triumphalist tone of the official narratives in both Turkey and Greece, accounts which stress the 'heroic' nature of the population exchange as a necessary, if painful stage in bringing the nation together. Such accounts inevitably play down the consequences of the exchange for ordinary people, including the difficulties experienced by Orthodox Christians and Muslims alike in adapting to new countries which were their notional homelands. While my acquaintance with Dr Yildirim is only through correspondence, I feel his fair-mindedness should be an example to all scholars of the subject.

Among scholars of the social and cultural effects of the population exchange, Dr Renee Hirschon of St Peter's College, Oxford has been a trailblazer and a trendsetter in this field, as well as being a generous advisor and friend during the writing of this book. Her book, *Heirs of the Greek Catastrophe: The Social Life of Asia Minor Refugees in Piraeus* (Oxford, Clarendon Press, 1989; republished New York and Oxford, Berghahn, 1998), remains a seminal work in this field. Based on fieldwork in a district of Piraeus in the early 1970s, it shows how a community of Anatolian Greek origin continued, half a century after the population exchange, to differentiate itself sharply from the rest of Greek society by virtue of its religious practices, family values and relatively sophisticated urban culture.

In September 1998, Dr Hirschon organized a landmark conference of Turkish and Greek academics (and literary critics and musicians) on the consequences of the Lausanne convention. This gathering, hosted by the Refugee Studies Programme at Queen Elizabeth House, Oxford, led to the publication of her edited volume, *Crossing the Aegean: An Appraisal of the 1923 Compulsory Population Exchange Between Greece and Turkey* (Berghahn Books, 2003). Every one of the eighteen essays in this volume is of huge help to anyone who sets out to understand the Lausanne convention in its context. The perspectives include those of literary criticism (there are excellent essays by Dr Peter Mackridge and Dr Hercules Millas), architecture and popular musicology as well as political science and international relations. For a concise but highly intelligent discussion of the phenomenon of population swaps in the 20th century, there could be few better places to turn than the contribution by Dr Michael Barutciski of the University of Canterbury, New Zealand, *Population Exchanges in Law and International Policy* (pp 24–35). Other contributions which I found particularly valuable included those of Professor Baskin Oran, one of the most respected Turkish authorities on Turkish–Greek relations, and Dr Alexis Alexandris, a scholar who is also, at the time of writing, the Greek consul in his home city of Istanbul. Both these contributions focus on the story of those who stayed, in other words the people in Istanbul, Greek Thrace and two Turkish islands who were exempted from the population exchange.

As I quickly discovered, any enquiry into the nature of Ottoman Christian society at the time of the population transfer (and into the remembrance of that society after the exchange) must draw heavily on the work of Dr Paschalis Kitromilides, and in particular on his brilliant application of contemporary understandings of nationalism to the deconstruction of modern Greek national myths. Among his own writings, an excellent general treatment of the subject is provided by his essay, *Imagined Communities and the Origin of the National Question in the Balkans,* in *Modern Greece: Nationalism and Nationality* (ed. M Blinkhorn and T Veremis, published by the Greek think-tank ELIAMEP, 1989). But Dr Kitromilides has also contributed decisively to this field in other ways: above all through his directorship of the Centre for Asia Minor Studies (*Kentron Mikrasiatikon Spoudon)*in Athens (Kydathineon Street, 11, Plaka district) which serves as a unique repository for thousands of oral-history testimonies provided by Greek Orthodox people from Anatolia. These stories, untutored but often deeply moving, speak of life before, during and after the exchange. Some of the most striking, but also representative, accounts were published in a collection entitled *I Exodos* (*Volume I*, KMS, 1980; *Volume II*, 1982). As KMS director, Professor Kitromilides was responsible for the centre's annual journal, *Deltio Kentrou Mikrasiatikou Ellinismou*, which became an invaluable resource for research into any aspect of Ottoman Hellenism. Especially useful is *Volume 9* in the series, a special edition devoted to 'the Asia Minor catastrophe and Greek society', which was published in 1992. It includes essays by some distinguished historians of the region and the period, including one by Dr Mark Mazower, *The Refugees, the Economic Crisis and the Collapse of Venizelist Hegemony, 1929–32,* (pp 119–134) and one by Dr Vlasis Agtzidis on the nationalist movements launched by Pontic Greeks in the Turkish Black Sea region and later in the Soviet Union (pp 157–196). The volume is introduced by Professor George Mavrogordatos, whose work *Stillborn Republic: Social Coalitions and Party Strategies in Greece, 1922–36* is unmatched, and indispensable as an account of the interplay of politics and ethnicity in post-Lausanne Greece. As a believer in the 'success' of the population exchange, Professor Mavrogordatos is perhaps vulnerable to the critique of 'triumphalistic' narratives which was elaborated by Dr Yildirim. But as my final chapter suggests, it is possible to believe in, and be impressed by, the success of the population exchange in its own terms, while agreeing with Dr Yildirim that such triumphalism underestimates the huge human and psychological cost that it imposed on millions of people.

The KMS is outstanding, but not unique, as a repository of oral history, photographs, books and other records of Ottoman Greek life. Other important institutions include the *Kentron Meizonos Ellinismou* and the excellent *Istoriko Archeio Prosfygikou Ellinismou* in Kalamaria, a suburb of Salonika.

In Turkey, the gathering of oral history from people affected by the Lausanne convention has been a much more recent and less systematic business and there are reasons for this. In the early years of the Turkish republic, so powerful was the impetus to create a new way of life and a new national consciousness that the 'past lives' of its citizens were generally expunged from memory. Anything important in the formation of the new state is deemed to have happened within the borders of the republic and after its formation.

However, an admirable Turkish non-governmental organization has emerged in the nick of the time to fill that gap: the Foundation of Lausanne Treaty Emigrants. Its creators, Sefer Guvenc and Mufide Pekin have turned the organization into a focal point for elderly Turkish citizens who remember the population exchange and want to share their memories of early life in Greece, and of the transfer itself, before it is too late. The Foundation has sponsored an impressive series of group excursions to Greece, allowing elderly exchangees or their children to visit their home villages and share with their Greek counterparts some of the pain which the Lausanne convention engendered. By gathering in academics, exchangees and everybody else with an interest in the cultural, historical and aesthetic consequences of the Lausanne convention, the Foundation has managed to form a new kind of scholarly and humanitarian community, and I feel privileged to have been treated as a camp-follower, at least, of that community. Especially memorable was the Foundation's conference in Istanbul in November 2003, at which I was one of the very few participants who was neither Greek nor Turkish. Professor Halil Berktay, who has a well-deserved reputation as one of Turkey's bravest historians, gave an outstanding presentation, demonstrating with great rigour the process whereby ethnic and national communities nurse the memory of the pain they have suffered, and systematically deny the pain their members have inflicted. I am very grateful to Professor Berktay for two long talks, in November 2003 and October 2004, in which he discussed the changing fashions in Turkish historiography since the founding of the republic.

For insights into an area even closer to my own concerns, I am hugely appreciative of the help I was given by another speaker at the November 2003 conference, Professor Ayhan Aktar of Marmara University. Two of his essays were especially helpful: *Economic Nationalism in Turkey: The Formative Years 1912–25* (Bogazici Journal, *Review of Social and Administrative Studies*, 10, pp 263–290) and his contribution to Renee Hirschon's edited volume, *Homogenizing the Nation, Turkifying the Economy* (2003; pp 79–95). Some of the Foundation's recent gatherings have been co-organized with the Turkish and Greek branches of ICOMOS, an international movement

devoted to architectural conservation. These have included very fruit-
ful conferences in Cappadocia in September 2004 and in Rethymnon
in the spring of 2005. One of the leaders of Greek ICOMOS, the distinguished architect Dimitros Psarros, happens also to be an expert on
the history and physical environment of Ayvalik, from which his family
originates.

The proceedings of all the conferences organized or co-organized by
the Foundation have been painstakingly transcribed and edited. They are
a resource of immense value to anybody who is working in this field.
Equally valuable is the bibliographical booklet, *Mubadele Bibliografyasi
Adli Kitabi Yayinladi* prepared by the Foundation. This lists all books in
Turkish, Greek and English (including fiction) which bear directly or
indirectly on the population exchange.

The Foundation has also co-operated with my friend Dr Kostas
Tsitselikis, who has brought the rigorous thinking of a legal scholar to his
analysis of Greece's treatment of Muslim minorities since the foundation
of the Greek state. I am especially indebted to Kostas for showing me,
with documentary evidence, that Greek politicians did not always envis-
age their country as a mono-confessional state.

Among professors who approach history in a slightly more conven-
tional way, I owe a huge debt of gratitude to Professor Harry Psomiades,
who has written of matters dear to his heart with the rigour of a conscientious scholar. Among his most important works are *The Eastern
Question: The Last Phase: A Study in Greek–Turkish diplomacy* (Institute
of Balkan Studies, 1968). Equally helpful at a personal and professional
level were Professor Thanos Veremis and Professor Ted Couloumbis,
directors of the ELIAMEP think-tank, at a time when I was relying on
that institution for workspace and support.

Among the work of contemporary Turkish historians, perhaps the best
general account of the execution of the exchange is that of Professor
Kemal Ari, *Büyük Mübadele: Türkiye'ye Zorunlu Göc 1923–25* (The Great
Exchange: Forced Migration to Turkey). Based on intensive scrutiny of all
the available written sources in Turkish, it was first published by the Tarih
Vakfi (History Foundation) in 1995 and has gone into at least three edi-
tions. I benefited greatly from this book, especially the middle section (pp
71–158) which my friends Orhan and Murat patiently helped to read.

And the Turkish journalist and author Iskender Özsoy, to whom I refer in detail in Chapter 8, has been a wonderfully generous collaborator and professional friend. His book *Iki Vatan Yorgunlari* is a marvellously rich, and deceptively simple, presentation of oral history, in which the protagonists are mostly allowed to speak for themselves.

Any statement whatever about the destruction of Izmir/Smyrna, and in particular about the fire which destroyed most of the city, is intensely controversial. Among the most detailed accounts of these events is Marjorie Housepian Dobkin's book, *Smyrna 1922: The Destruction of a City* (First published as *The Smyrna Affair:* Harcourt Brace Jovanovich, 1971; Recently reprinted: Newmark Press, New York, 1998). The work is only marred, in my opinion, by its insistence (p 14) that the burning of cities by the retreating Greek army should be assessed much more leniently than the atrocities of the victorious Turks because the motives were different. To this I would counterargue that the pain suffered by victims of war crimes is not made any greater or less by the motives (whether 'understandable' or otherwise) of the perpetrators. She is right, however, to find fault with the view that one should give 'equal time' and 'equal emphasis' to the atrocities of every party. It is surely in the nature of crimes against humanity that each one stands alone; that is also true of acts of nobility and generosity.

I would also like to set on record the personal generosity of Professor Stanford J Shaw, who presented me with a copy of his five-volume work, *From Empire to Republic: The Turkish War of National Liberation 1918–1923*, (Ankara, Turk Tarih Kurumu Basimevi, 2000). This work is in the best sense encyclopedic, gathering together an enormous variety of diplomatic and other documents which are essential for an understanding of the period. Interestingly, many of the details of diplomatic and military history recounted by Professor Shaw are perfectly consistent with the narratives offered by historians with perspectives diametrically opposed to his own; it is only in their moral verdict that the two versions differ. I cannot share Professor Shaw's strong inclination to place the overwhelming blame on Christians, whether local or external, for virtually all the human pain suffered in Anatolia before and after the birth of the Turkish republic. Nor did I detect any such inclination in any of my Turkish interlocutors.

Like Professor Shaw, I applaud Arnold Toynbee's boldness in exposing the atrocities by Greek soldiers and irregulars, especially in the coastal region south of Istanbul in the spring and summer 1921. I agree with Toynbee's assertion that it is not in the ultimate interest of Greece that atrocities committed in its name should be denied or covered up. I agree too with Toynbee in arguing that powerful countries dishonour themselves when they collude in the denial of misdeeds of their allies. I also admire those very courageous Turks who are prepared, at considerable risk to themselves, to make a similar argument in relation to their own country, and who feel they are no less patriotic for doing so; in that respect I must part company with Professor Shaw.

General works of Ottoman, Turkish, Greek and Balkan history

Ahmad, Feroz, *The Making of Modern Turkey*, London, Routledge, 1993.

Campbell, John and Sherrard, Philip, *Modern Greece*, London, Ernest Benn, 1968.

Clogg, R, *A Short History of Modern Greece*, Cambridge University Press, 1979.

Keyder, Caglar, *State and Class in Turkey*, London, Verso Books, 1987.

Kinross, Lord, *Ataturk: The Rebirth of a Nation*, Nicosia, Rustem, first published 1964, reprinted 1981.

Lewis, Bernard, *The Emergence of Modern Turkey*, New York, Oxford University Press, 1968.

Macfie, A L, *The End of the Ottoman Empire, 1908–1923*, London and New York, Longman, 1998.

Mango, Andrew, *Ataturk*, Woodstock and New York, Overlook Press, 2002.

Mazower, Mark, *Salonica, City of Ghosts: Christians, Muslims and Jews 1430–1950*, London, Harper Collins, 2004.

Pamuk, Sevket, *The Ottoman Empire and European Capitalism, 1820–1913: Trade, Investment and Production*, Cambridge University Press, 1987.

Shankland, David, *Islam and Society in Turkey*, Huntingdon, Eothen Press, 1999.

Stavrianos L S, *The Balkans since 1453*, New York, Holt, Rinehart and Winston, 1961.

Tapper, Richard (ed), *Islam in Modern Turkey: Religion, Politics and Literature in a Secular State*, London, I B Tauris, 1991.

Wheatcroft, Andrew, *The Ottomans*, London, Viking, 1993.

Zurcher, Erik, *Turkey: A Modern History*, New York, I B Tauris, 1993; London, 1998.

Military, political and diplomatic events

Andrew, Prince of Greece, *Towards Disaster*, London, John Murray, 1930.

Eddy, Charles B, *Greece and the Greek Refugees*, London, George Allen and Unwin, 1931.

Huntford, Roland Nansen, *The Explorer as Hero*, London, Duckworth, 1997.

Ladas, Stephen, *The Exchanges of Minorities – Bulgaria, Greece and Turkey*, New York, Macmillan, 1932.

Llewellyn-Smith, Michael, *Ionian Vision: Greece in Asia Minor 1919–1922*, Hurst, 1998.

MacMillan, Margaret, *Peacemakers: Six Months That Changed the World*, John Murray, London, 2001.

Mears, E G, *Greece Today – The Aftermath of the Refugee Impact*, Stanford, Stanford University Press, 1929.

Morgenthau, Henry, *I Was Sent to Athens*, Garden City, New York, 1929.

Noel-Baker, Barbro, *An Isle of Greece: the Noels in Euboea*, privately published Procopi, 2002.

Pallis, A A, *Greece's Anatolian Adventure – and After*, London, Methuen, 1937.

Pentzopoulos, Dimitri, *The Balkan Exchange of Minorities and its Impact on Greece*, London, Hurst, 2002.

Toynbee, Arnold, *The Western Question in Greece and Turkey*, London, 1922.

Anatolian Greek society before and after the exchange

Anagnostopoulou, Sia, *Mikra Asia, 19os Aionas–1919, Oi Ellinorthodoxes Koinotites*, Athens, Ellinika Grammata, 1997.

Augoustinos, G, *The Greeks of Asia Minor: Confession, Community, and Ethnicity in the Nineteenth Century*, Ohio University Press, 1992.

Gondicas, D, and Issawi, C (eds), *Ottoman Greeks in the Age of Nationalism: Politics, Economy, and Society in the Nineteenth Century*, Princeton, New Jersey, The Darwin Press, c 1999. (This volume includes the following especially useful contributions: *The Greek Census of Anatolia and Thrace (1910–1912), A Contribution to Ottoman Historical Demography*, Alexis Alexandris; *The Greek Millet in Turkish Politics: Greeks in the Ottoman Parliament 1908–1918*, Catherina Boura; A *Millet Within a Millet, the Karamanlides*, Richard Clogg; *The Hellenic Kingdom and the Ottoman Greeks: The Experiment of the Society of Constantinople*, Thanos Veremis.

Noutsos, P, *The Role of the Greek Community in the Genesis and Development of the Socialist Movement in the Ottoman Empire: 1876–1925*, in Zurcher, E, and Tuncay, M (eds), *Socialism and Nationalism in the Ottoman Empire, 1876–1923*, British Academic Press, 1994.

Pelagidis, Stathis, *O Ellinismos tis Mikras Asia kai tou Pontou*, Thessaloniki, Malliaris, 2001.

Salamone, Stephen, *The Genesis of a Rural Greek Community and its Refugee Heritage*, New York, Boulder, East European Monographs, (distributed by Columbia University Press), 1987.

Essays and academic papers

Balta, Evangelia, *Oi Prologoi ton Karamanlidikon Vivlion, Pigi yia tin Meleti tis Ethnikis Syneidisis ton Tourkofonon Orthodoxon Plithysmon tis Mikras Asias*, Mnimon, number 11, 1987.

Mackridge, Peter, *Turco-Greek Inscription at Urgup in Cappadocia*, in *Byzantine and Modern Greek Studies* 13, 1989; pp 286–289.

Jacquith, H C, *America's aid to 1,000,000 Near Eastern Refugees*, in *Current History*, Vol XXI, No 3.

Kitromilides, P, *Greek Irredentism in Asia Minor and Cyprus*, in *Middle Eastern Studies*, Vol 6, No 1, 1990; pp 3–17.

Kritikos, George, *State Policy and Urban Employment of Refugees: The Greek Case (1923–30)*, in *European Review of History* Vol 7, No 2, 2000; pp 189–206.

Markham, Violet, *Greece and the Refugees from Asia Minor*, in *The Fortnightly Review*, Vol CXVII, February 1925; pp 176–184.

Petropoulos, John A, *The Compulsory Exchange of Populations: Greek–Turkish Peacemaking, 1922–1930*, in *Byzantine and Modern Greek Studies*, Vol 2, 1976; pp 135–160.

Polyzoides, Adamantios, *Greece in the Agonies of Revolutionary Conflict*, in *Current History*, Vol XXI, No 3, December 1924.

Serif, M, *Ideology and Religion in the Turkish Revolution*, in *International Journal of Middle Eastern Studies*, Vol 2, 1971; pp 197–211.

Voutira, Effie, *Pontic Greeks today: migrants or refugees?* in *Journal of Refugee Studies*, 4, 1991; pp 400–420

Yiannouli, D, *Greeks or 'Strangers at Home': The Experiences of Ottoman Greek Refugees during their Exodus to Greece, 1922–1923*, in *Journal of Modern Greek Studies*, Vol 13, No 2, 1995; pp 271–287.

Yiannouli/Giannuli, Dimitra, *American Philanthropy in Action: The American Red Cross in Action, 1918–1923*, in *East European Politics and Societies*, Vol 10, No 1, 1996; pp 108–132.

Chapter-by-chapter notes

Chapter 1

I visited Ayvalik in May 2003 and again in December 2003. The second visit in particular enabled me to carry out some detailed interviews with leading local characters, including Ali Onay from Crete, Ferhat Eris from Mytilene and the local politician, Mujdat Soylu. For details of the town's architectural heritage, I am indebted to Dimitros Psarros and his article, *Kydonies-Aivali* (in *Tekhnika Khronika*, the journal of Greece's Technical Chamber of Commerce, March/April issue, 1977). Also very helpful as a source on the Greek history of the town, was *Istoria ton Kydonion*, by Georgios Sakkaris (first published Athens, 1920; republished with an addendum on the extinction of the town's Greek presence by Ioannis Karamblias). *I Exodos* includes a set of arresting and internally consistent reminiscences from Greeks who fled Ayvali or nearby places (see in particular pp 94–104).

From my May 2003 visit to the region, I have especially fond memories of a long and memorable conversation with Mrs Filio Katsarou, born around 1912, who has lived most of her life in Mytilene after being spirited away from Ayvali in the nick of time after her father received a warning from a Turkish friend. The true story of the flight from Ayvali by Agape Molyviati – whose son Petros is the Greek foreign minister – is told by her brother, the writer Ilias Venezis, in *Mikrasia, Chaire* (Athens, Vivliopoleion tis Estias, 1974; pp 50–67).

I am grateful for the help and advice of a Greek social anthropologist,

Sophia Koufopoulou, who has done extensive fieldwork among the people (especially the women) who live now in Cunda/Moschonisi but trace their origins to Crete. Her contribution to Renee Hirschon's edited volume is entitled 'Muslim Cretans in Turkey' (pp 209–219) and includes a memorable reflection on the sub-text of Greco-Turkish expressions like 'oturmak myrodia-si', which literally means 'sitting smell' and refers to laundry which has been left to soak for too long. Another scholar who has drawn very interesting conclusions from fieldwork in Ayvalik is Chris Williams, a musicologist and leader of Troa Nova, a London-based company of Turkish and Greek musicians.

The feelings of Mustafa Kemal Ataturk about the Izmir conflagration are recorded on page 346 of Andrew Mango's biography.

The Cretan reminiscences of Robert Pashley were first published as *Travels in Crete* (London, 1837). They are quoted in *Across Crete*, an anthology compiled by Johan de Baker (London, World Discovery Guide Books, 2001). For interreligious political alliances in 19th century Crete, the best authority is Professor Theocharis Detorakis of University of Crete, whose *History of Crete* has been translated into English and published locally.

Chapter 2

Some of the material in this chapter derives from research I was able to do in the Greek foreign ministry archives in late 2003, thanks to a scholarship from the Alexander S Onassis Foundation and the much-appreciated help from the director of the archives, Mrs Photini Thomai and her colleague Yannis Bengos. Some of the most interesting documents in the correspondence which led up to the Lausanne conference are to be found in file number 173 of the year 1922. The most crucial of these documents include: a letter dated 10 October from Nansen (in Istanbul) to Venizelos in London; a letter from Venizelos to Lord Curzon dated 13 October, complaining bitterly about the terms of the Moudania armistice; a letter from Venizelos (in London) to the Greek government, dated 17 October, suggesting a unilateral expulsion of Muslims from Greece; a letter dated 30 October from the Greek embassy in London to Lord Curzon, drawing his attention to a secret Turkish–Bulgarian compact; a letter sent by Nikolaos Politis, the Greek foreign minister, to Nansen in late October, protesting bitterly over the proposed inclusion of the Istanbul region in the population exchange; and a letter from Nansen to the Greek foreign ministry, dated 22 October, which seeks clarification of the Greek position on a population exchange.

A more unusual source, perhaps, is the delightful, privately produced book by the late Mrs Barbro Noel-Baker about the colourful English family of landowners into which she married. I was very grateful for her help and hospitality in late 2003. In particular she allowed me to study the diaries of Philip Noel-Baker, quite large sections of which are reproduced verbatim in her book.

For the role played by Nansen, and his personality, see Chapter 71 of Roland Huntford's biography. A Norwegian writer, Berit Tolleshaug, has recently made a more detailed moral assessment of her compatriot's activities in this period, *En Norsk Helt i En Gresk Tragedie?* (A Norwegian Hero or a Greek Tragedy?).

Professor Harry Psomiades, who turned the City University of New York into a distinguished centre for the study of Byzantine and modern Greek history, is a recognized authority on international diplomacy before and during the Lausanne conference, as it affected Greece. Among his many helpful papers is *Eastern Thrace and the Armistice of Mudanya* (in *Journal of Modern Hellenism*, Winter 2000–2001; pp 1–67). The flight of Greek civilians from eastern Thrace was vividly described by Ernest Hemingway in a dispatch in the *Toronto Daily Star*, published on 22 October 1922. This and other dispatches from the region are to be found in *By-Line* (ed William White, London, 1967).

Chapter 3

I visited Samsun in July 2003, and Drama in August 2004 and again in October 2004. In addition to the people I name, there were many ordinary *Draminoi* who offered a great deal of practical help and hospitality, especially a promising young journalist, Isaac Karipides, and his extended family. The assertion that almost every Pontic Greek family has a story of miraculous survival is based on many conversations with people in and around Drama, and also on fieldwork in the Grevena region in January 2005. Perhaps the best-known survival story of a Black Sea Greek family is the one told by Thea Halo in *Not Even My Name* (New York, Picador, 2000). This is a powerful and moving narrative which deserves to be read widely, even by those who cannot agree with

Ms Halo's contention that the Greeks were merely 'taking back their own' when their army marched into the heart of Anatolia, with such tragic consequences for her family.

One of the most objective summaries of the irregular warfare which raged around the Samsun area in the early 20th century, and of the brutal methods used by both sides, is offered by Nikos Marantzidis, a political scientist, in an excellent and fascinating book about the political behaviour of Turkish-speaking Christians from the Black Sea region, before and after their transfer to Greece. The book has the Greco-Turkish title *Yasasin Millet, Zito To Ethnos* (Iraklion, Panepistemiakes Ekdoseis Kritis, 2001). It covers the period immediately prior to the Christians' expulsion on pp 39–83.

During my travels in the Drama region, the most useful work in the impressive oeuvre of schoolmaster Vassilis Hadzitheodorides was *I Drama tou 20ou Aiona, Anadromi sto Choro, sto Chrono kai stous Anthropous* (Drama in the 20th Century, a Look Back at Places, Times and People); published Drama, 2001. His brother Theofylaktos produced *To Perasma* (Athens, 1997). This is a remarkable labour of love which devotes nearly 300 pages to the village north of Drama where the Hadzitheodorides family and twenty-four other households established themselves in the 1920s after a tortuous journey from their native Black Sea region.

Another scholar/schoolmaster, Savvas Papadopoulos, has produced no less than three detailed volumes about the ethnography and folklore of the town of Karakurt from which his ancestors came. These works (Thessaloniki, Maiandros, 1982 and 1984) range over burial and marriage customs, folk tales, herbal medicine and many other aspects of life in a community with a remarkable gift of collective memory. He has written a shorter booklet, simply entitled *Mavrovatos*, on the village south of Drama which the Karakurt people founded.

Chapter 4
The consequences of the Cappadocian Christians' unexpected inclusion in the population exchange are all too visible in places like Mustafapasha, formerly Sinasos, which was one of the most prosperous outposts of Orthodox Christian life in that eerily beautiful part of Anatolia. The Foundation of Lausanne Treaty Emigrants held an exceptionally useful and informative gathering in the town in October 2004, in co-operation

with the Association of 'Sinasites' in Greece, headed by Spyros Isopoulos, and the local mayor Mustafa Ozer.

The writings of Dr Evangelia Balta from the National Research Institute (*Ethniko Idryma Erevnon*) in Athens are indispensable for anybody who is trying to understand the culture of the Cappadocian Christians before and after the exchange. So too a lovingly produced volume of photographs, *I Sinasos*, which the people of that town published in Athens shortly after their well-organized but painful exodus.

On the finer details of the negotiations in Lausanne which permitted the Patriarch to remain in his ancient see, there are few better authorities than Professor Harry Psomiades.

Both the official records of Turkish diplomatic cables (*Lozan Telgraflari*) and the memoirs of Riza Nour throw light on official Turkish thinking about the future, if any of the Orthodox church in the Turkish republic.

Dr Anthony O'Mahoney of Heythrop College, London has written and lectured quite extensively on the phenomenon of Papa Eftim and the 'Turkish Orthodox church' as well as its significance for relations between religion and the state in secular Turkey.

Chapter 5

The Post-Byzantine Monuments of the Pontos, by Anthony Bryer and others, Aldershot, England, Ashgate, 2002) is a mine of information about people and cultures as well as buildings. The same can be said of Professor Bryer himself, and of all his works on the Pontos.

I spent a week in Trabzon, to use the modern Turkish name, in July 2003, and also visited places in the hinterland where traces of Christian and crypto-Christian life continue to abound: Gumushane, Imera, Kurum (Kromni). For rich and unsentimental insights into the economic vigour, cultural riches and educational accomplishments of the Greek Orthodox community from that region, I owe much to Father Alexander Fostiropoulos and his extended family. Indeed, my debts to Father Alexander are much bigger than that. His uncle George Siamanides, a humorous, bright-eyed and witty interlocutor at the age of ninety-two, was an invaluable informant as well as a delightful friend.

I am very grateful indeed to Maria Koukou of the *Istoriko Archeio Prosfygikou Ellinismou* in Kalamaria, for her help transcribing four of the most interesting oral history testimonies from Imera: those of George Chrysopoulos, Anna Chrysopoulou, Yannis Yakoustides and Spiros Yakoustides.

For a robustly Greek point of view on the cultural and political history of the Black Sea Greeks, including the final phase of their community's existence, one can turn to lavishly and lovingly produced volumes such as *Istoria tou Pontiakou Ellinismou* by Christos Samouilides (Athens, Livanis, 2002). An important reference point on the Kromni valley, once the heartland of crypto-Christianity, is a book entitled simply *Kromni* by George Firtinidis (published by the fraternity of Kromniots of Kalamaria [*Adelphotis Kromnaion Kalamarias*] 1994).

I Imera tou Pontou by Agathangelos Fostiropoulos (republished Olympos, 2002) is a precious labour of love, as are *I Imera* by Panayiotis Tanimanidis and *Oi Teleftaies Meres tis Trapezoundas* (The Last Days of Trebizond) by Dimitris Fillizis (both published Thessaloniki, Kyriakidis Brothers).

Merimna Pontion Kyrion is an account of charitable work by Trapezountine ladies before and after their expulsion (Thessaloniki, Kyriakidis Brothers). For the latter I am grateful to Mrs Anna Theofylaktou, a deservedly respected fount of Pontic knowledge.

George Andreades is a prolific and passionate writer of popular books on the Black Sea Greeks, including the crypto-Christians, from whom he descends. Some of his works are non-fiction, others take the form of novels which are heavily influenced by true stories. His books include *Tamama*, a novel based on siblings divided between Greece and Turkey by the Black Sea upheaval, and then reunited (Salonika, Gordios); and *Oi Klostoi* (Thessaloniki, Kyriakidis Brothers, 1995) which has been translated into English as *The Crypto-Christians*. The novel *Tamama* was one of the inspirations for the Turkish film *Journey to the Sun*, by writer–director Yesim Ustaoglu.

The most comprehensive work on the crypto-Christians has been published in German by Professor Costas Fotiadis.

Chapter 6

An essay by Dr Alexis Alexandris in *Archeion Pontou* (1982) has provided one of the best accounts of a particularly tragic episode in the history of the population exchange: the arrival in early 1923 of ships carrying infectiously ill refugees from Black Sea ports to the shores of the Bosphorus, where the Allied occupiers of Constantinople were unable to cope with the spreading epidemic. For the efforts by American and other charities to cope with the resulting humanitarian crisis in Greece, I turned in particular to works by the late Dr Dimitra Yiannouli of Ohio State University. The reminiscences of Anna Karabetsou and Saroula Skyfti are from the Archives of the Centre for Asia Minor Studies and quoted in *I Exodos*.

American Influence in Greece, 1917–1929 by Louis Cassimatis (Kent, Ohio and London, Kent State University Press, 1988) is an outstanding study of the diplomatic background to the humanitarian aid and refugee settlement missions that were mounted in Greece. Particularly helpful are Chapters 6–8, which throw light on the tensions between the American government on the one hand, and the British-dominated League of Nations on the other.

The British charity, Save the Children (formerly the Save the Children Fund) was for a time one of the main voluntary agencies engaged in helping the Greek refugees. Miss Pippa Ranger at STC's London headquarters showed great kindness in making available to me the records of the agency's Greek operations in 1923 and 1924. These included a series of 'situation reports' on the needs of displaced persons to Greece, circulated among all the main charities in the field. The files also include increasingly desperate cables from SCF fieldworkers to the London headquarters who reported, in late 1924, that Greek ports were becoming saturated with new arrivals, while for a third winter running, the onset of bad weather was making further transfers of migrants to inland towns impossible.

Another useful account of the international effort to aid victims of the Turkish–Greek war is Robert Daniel's *American Philanthropy in the Near East, 1920–1960* (Ohio University Press, 1970). *Certain Samaritans* by Esther Pohl Lovejoy (New York, MacMillan, 1933) is a delightful, honest, human and vulnerable account by the author of her work for American Women's Hospitals, on which I have drawn extensively.

Chapter 7
Henry Morgenthau describes his arrival in Salonika, and his subsequent role as a pro-consul and power broker in Greece, in Chapter 6 of *I Was Sent to Athens*. The remainder of this book is a breezy, self-confident

memoir which provides a highly readable but also illuminating account of the politics, both international and local, which underpinned the population exchange and made the deportation of the Muslims of Greece a virtual precondition for obtaining a refugee settlement loan.

Mark Mazower's dazzling 2004 history of Salonika, *City of Ghosts* has already become indispensable reading for anyone who is trying to imagine the city at the time when Muslim exchangees were sailing away and Christian refugees were arriving. Chapter 17 (pp 332–355) and Chapter 18 (pp 356–370) focus on the Muslim exodus and the absorption of the Christian arrivals respectively, but the entire book is invaluable as a way of understanding the place which the Ottoman Muslims left and the Anatolian Christians made their own. Among Professor Mazower's best sources for Muslim life in Salonika was a memoir by Resat Tesal, *Selanik'ten Istanbul'a* (Istanbul, 1998).

All the material based on reminiscences from 'ordinary' Muslim exchangees, both in this chapter and the next, I owe directly or indirectly to Iskender Ozsoy, a deeply conscientious journalist and indefatigable chronicler of the exchange. With an introduction from Iskender I was able to meet two grand Greek-born ladies, Vedia Elgun and Raziye Ogus, in their Istanbul homes in June 2004; also Ramazan Ezer, who described the bizarre co-existence between arriving Christians and soon-to-depart Muslims; and the highly articulate Isa Erol, who settled in Silivri but still dreams occasionally of his northern Greek village.

Chapter 8

I interviewed Fatma Gültekin and Hüseyin Çetin, Turkish citizens of Cretan origin, in their native Darica in June 2004, with the help of Iskender Özsoy. For insights into Bektashi practices in Anatolia and the southern Balkans, and into Christian–Muslim syncretism in popular religious practice, there is still no better starting point than F W Hasluck's 1929 work, *Christianity and Islam Under the Sultans* (reprinted in two vols, Istanbul, Isis Press, 2000). For the Bektashi shrines in present-day northern Greece, described by Iskender Ozsoy's interlocutors, see *Vol II*, pp 424–6.

Professor Ayhan Aktar of Marmara University read this chapter and (with the usual disclaimers) made some very helpful corrections.

Chapter 9

The terms of the Greek–Turkish reconciliation of 1930, and the spectacular hospitality offered to Eleftherios Venizelos in Istanbul and Ankara, are vividly described in Alexandris' work, *The Greek Minority in Istanbul*, especially Chapter 6. Alexandris also describes the twists and turns of Greek–Turkish relations which led up to the reconciliation, and the reaction in Greece.

For the work of the Refugee Settlement Commission, a basic source is the RSC's quarterly reports to the League of Nations, published in the League's official journal. A more detailed and franker account of the RSC's work is provided by the minutes of the regular meetings of the agency's four-person board, which convened over 400 times between 1923 and 1930. I am very grateful to Mme Bernhardine Pejovic, a librarian at the League of Nations archive who made this material (from dossier number c.130) available to me.

Dr Elizabeth Kontogeorgi wrote her Oxford D. Phil thesis on the agricultural achievements of the RSC. Her conclusions are summarized in a contribution to Renee Hirschon's edited volume *Crossing the Aegean*.

For insights into politics and above all the psychology of intercommunal relations in western Thrace I owe much to Dr Thalia Dragona and her paper, *Ekpaidevontas to Anoikeio Allo* in *Psychologia* (2004); and to Dimo Yagcioglou, who wrote an excellent PhD on the subject at George Mason University.

Other informants on this sensitive matter must remain anonymous.

Chapter 10

For the way in which Orthodox Christian beliefs and rituals help to bind an otherwise antagonistic Greek society together, I am hugely indebted to the observations of Dr Juliet du Boulay in her classic *Portrait of a Greek Mountain Village* (republished Limni, Evvia, Denise Harvey, 1994).

And finally, a trip to the Grevena region, assisted by Panos Papoulias, a promising young political scientist, yielded some important insights, as did a meeting with the wise and generous local historian, V K Anastasiades.

Index

Numbers in italics refer to illustrations.